GEORGE LODGE

artist naturalist

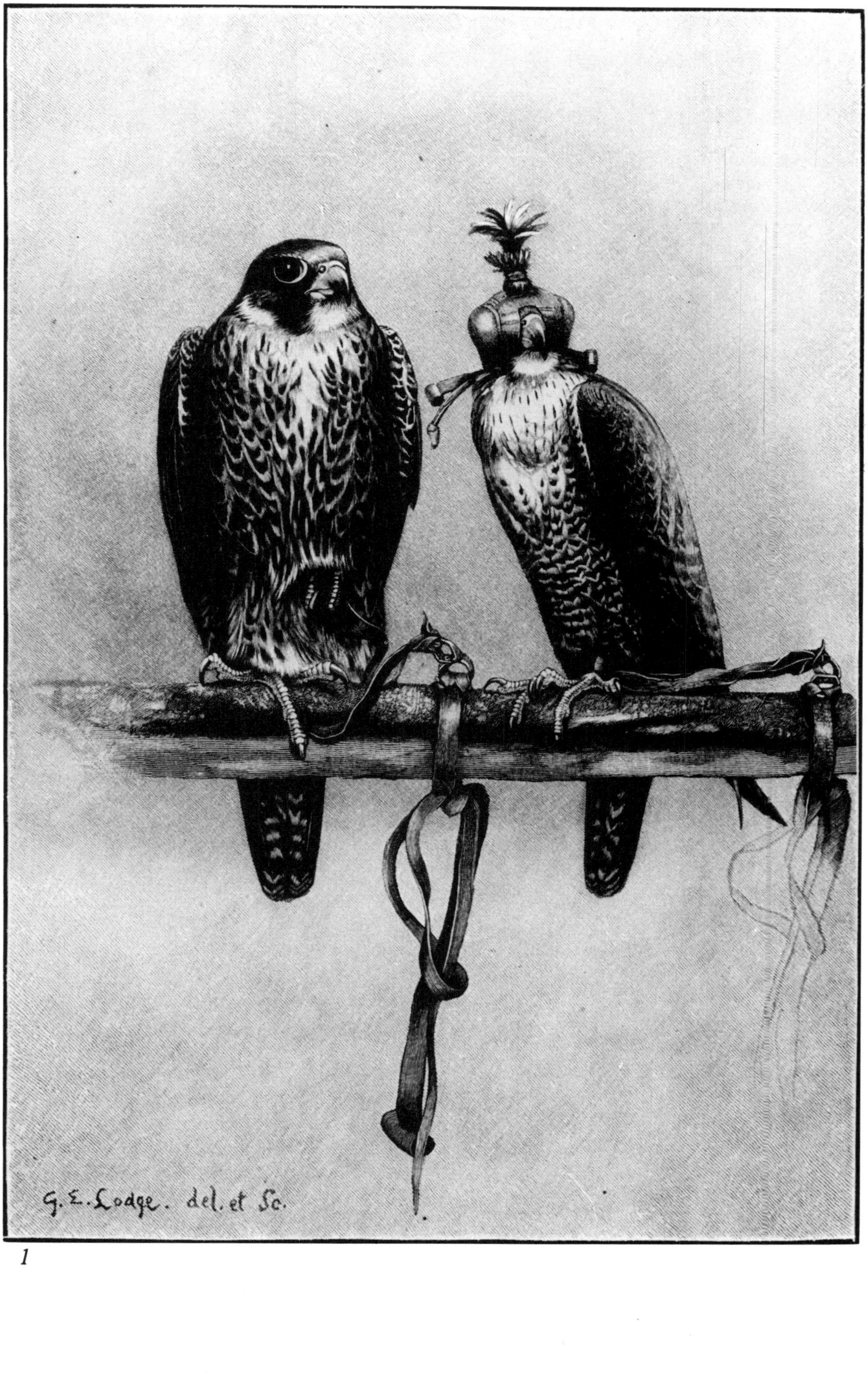

1

GEORGE LODGE

artist naturalist

Edited by John Savory

TANAGER
BOOKS

Dover, New Hampshire

First published 1986 by Tanager Books (a division of Longwood Publishing Group, Inc.)
51 Washington Street, Dover, NH 03820

Library of Congress Cataloging in Publication Data

Lodge, George Edward.
George Lodge, Artist Naturalist.
Pictures exhibited at the Royal Academy by George Lodge: p.
Bibliography: p.
1. Lodge, George Edward—Exhibitions. 2. Falcons in Art—Exhibitions. 3. Wildlife Art—England—Exhibitions.
I. Savory, John. II. Title.
N6797.L63A4 1986 760′.092′4 85-27716
ISBN 0-88072-074-3

1. A cast of peregrines — red (immature) falcon and blue (adult) tiercel

2. Falconer with hawks (self portrait?)

Typeset in ITC Cheltenham by Leaper & Gard Ltd, Bristol, England
Printed and bound in Great Britain

CONTENTS

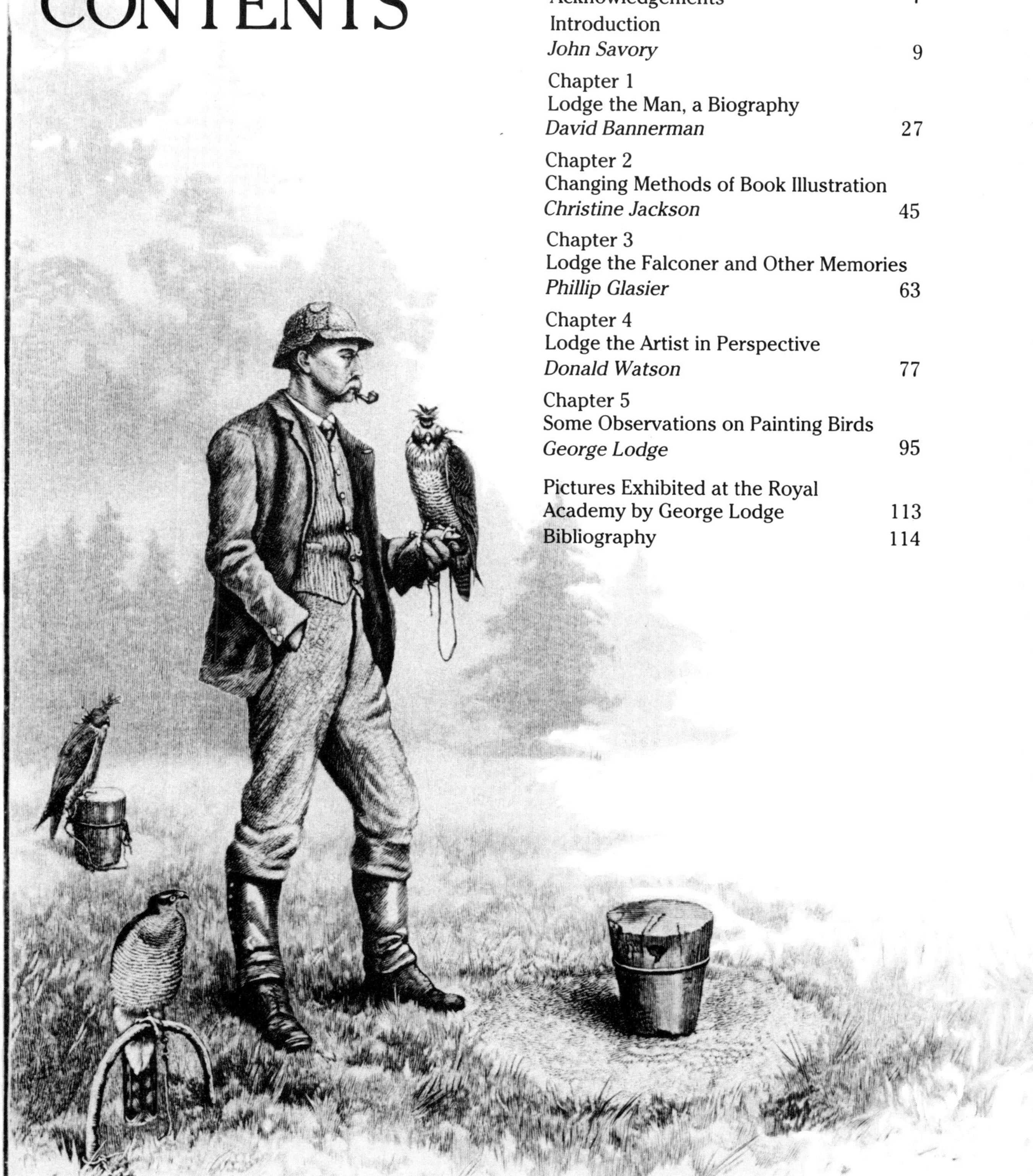

What a lesson to all of us, what a life to have led. To have made a living out of the thing you liked best in the world. To have known that your work sends those who see it back delightedly in thought to the salmon river, the forest, the crags and the hills, and the deer and the birds they have watched there.

from J.K. Stanford's obituary of
George Lodge in *The Field*, 25 February 1954

ACKNOWLEDGEMENTS

I am grateful to the following for the help they gave at various stages in the preparation of this book: Allan Allison, Mary Bannerman, Dr H.M.S. Blair, Bristol Museum (Anne Hollowell), British Museum (Natural History) departments at South Kensington (Zoology Library and Administrative Services) and Tring (Ornithology), Keith Brockie, John Busby, Dr Theresa Clay, Sir Charles Connell, R.A.H. Coombes (whose book *Mountain Birds* was the last one illustrated by Lodge), J.T. Fisher, Douglas Grant, Richard Green Gallery, Bruce Henry, Ray Hill, Malcolm Innes Gallery, Robin Lloyd Antiques, Douglas Mann, William Marler Gallery, Mick Marquiss, National Library of Scotland, Royal Scottish Museum (Ian Lyster), Royal Society for the Protection of Birds (Ian Dawson), John Savidge, Chas. J. Sawyer (Booksellers), Scottish Ornithologists' Club (Bill Harper), Sotheby's, Spink and Son Gallery, Thorburn Museum and Gallery (John Southern), Roger Upton, Wheldon and Wesley Ltd (H.K. Swann), Zoological Society of London (Michael Lyster), and owners of Lodge paintings who prefer to remain anonymous.

Special thanks are due to Peter Keyser (Keyser Gallery) for arranging much of the photography, Tryon and Moorland Gallery (Major Brian Booth) for permission to reproduce Lodge's work, George Lodge Trust for financial assistance towards payment of copyright fees, my three collaborators, Phillip Glasier, Christine Jackson and Donald Watson for their written contributions, Jo Hemmings (Croom Helm Ltd) for her faith in my ability, Kath Tracey for typing manuscripts, and my wife, Eileen, and family for their help and encouragement throughout the project.

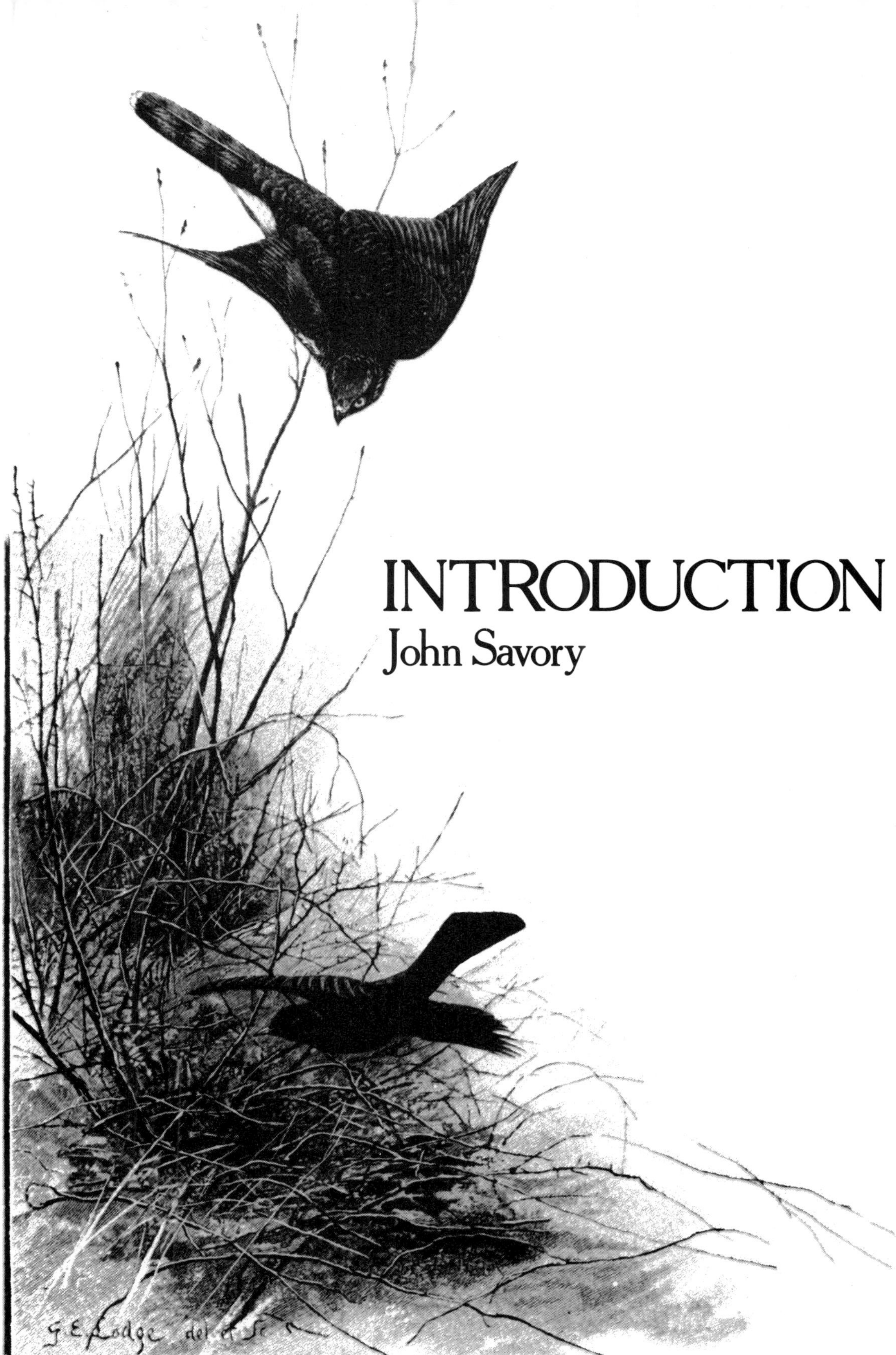

3

INTRODUCTION

John Savory

I was too young to know much about George Lodge when he died in 1954, but not too young to realise that my late father, Harry Savory, had the highest opinion of him as a friend and wildlife artist. I never had the opportunity to meet him personally, but I have a short note he sent in 1951 when I was eight, thanking me for some complimentary remarks I had made about his *Memoirs of an Artist Naturalist*, published five years previously.

My father first met Lodge in 1930 at Avebury, where both had been invited to take part in a hawking holiday at the Red Lion Inn together with the brothers Charles and Hugh Knight, their families and a few other falconers. Thus began my father's interest in falconry, which lasted for most of the 1930s, and his friendship with Lodge, which lasted

4

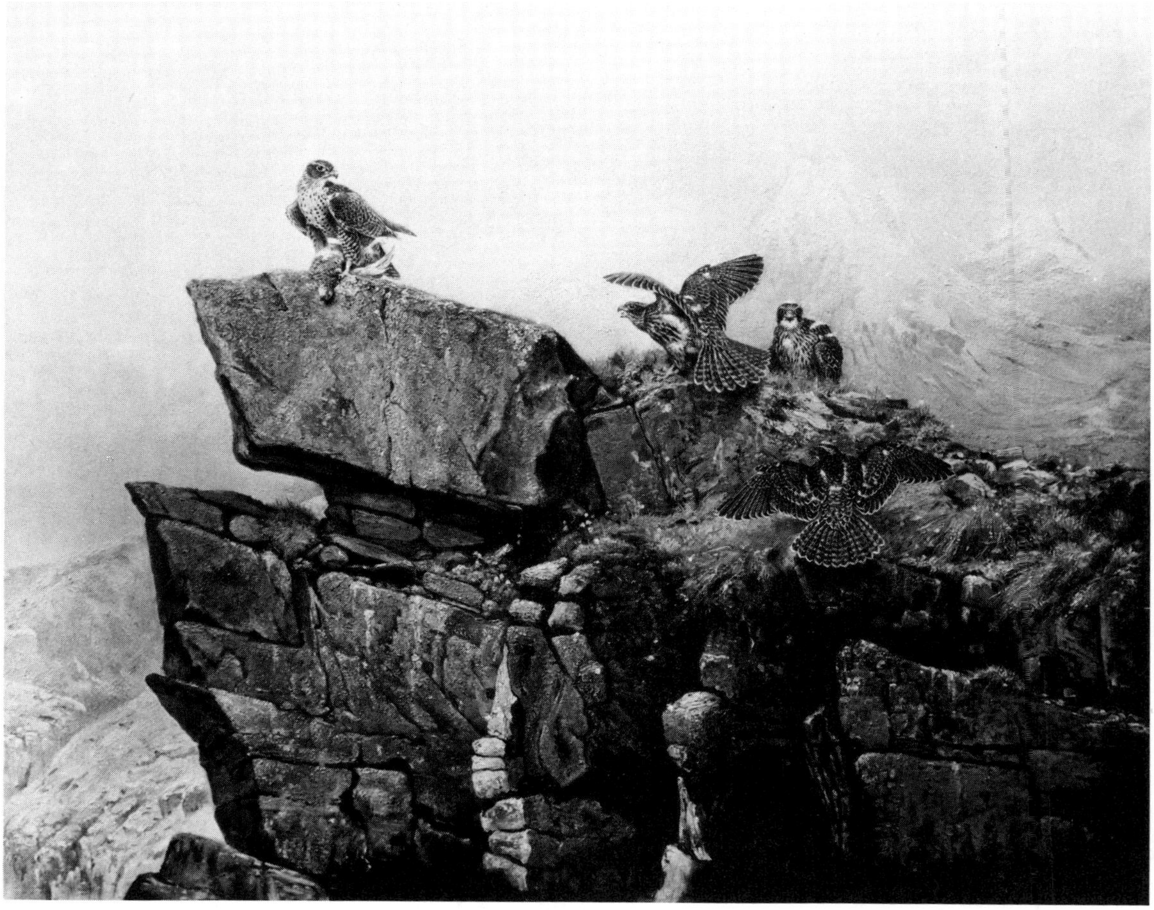

till Lodge's death. The summer hawking holidays of the British Falconers' Club had started at Avebury in 1928 and were annual affairs. However, they gradually got larger and began to attract over-enthusiastic attention from the press, so in 1936 they moved to Bodmin Moor and my father ceased to attend. He remained a member of the British Falconers' Club for the rest of his life, went to their annual dinners at Fleet Street hostelries, and continued to see Lodge regularly at his home in Camberley or at exhibitions of his pictures at Rowland Ward's in Piccadilly. He and Lodge had much in common because, apart from falconry, my father was acquainted with other wildlife artists in connection with his profession as a printer of greetings cards, and was a keen ornithologist. There would have been much to talk about in Lodge's studio, where the walls were covered with his paintings and where there were hundreds of mounted specimens and study skins.

At Camberley, Lodge had lived with an elder sister and a niece, Brenda, and after his death Brenda asked my father to assist in winding up the estate. She very kindly arranged for my father to receive from the publishers Oliver and Boyd all 12 volumes of Lodge's joint work with David Bannerman entitled *The Birds of the British Isles*, which had reached volume II when Lodge died, and I well remember his eager inspection as each one arrived. A photograph of Lodge that my father had taken at Avebury in 1933 appeared with Bannerman's tribute to his partner in volume V. My father died in 1962, before the series was complete, but thankfully the publishers agreed to provide my mother with the last two volumes. Brenda Lodge had moved to Shepton Beauchamp in Somerset, where I visited her once or twice with my parents.

As a result of my father's great interest in Lodge's art, and his books containing the artist's work, I had learned to recognise Lodge's unique style and his influence on younger artists, such as Jack Harrison and Philip Rickman, whom he had encouraged at an early stage in their careers. I was also aware that my father had felt that Lodge never really received the

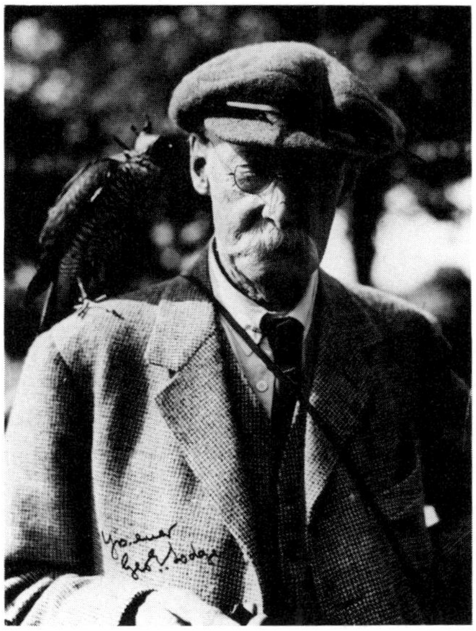

5

3. Sparrow-hawk and blackbird
4. A family of gyr falcons
5. George Lodge at Avebury in 1933

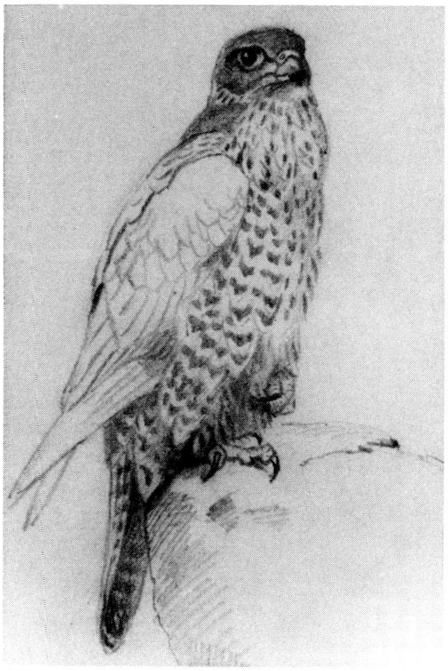

6

6. Immature gyr falcon
7. Peregrine sketches

recognition he was due, either before or after his death. This may have been because much of his best work was either never published, was poorly presented or was long out of print. He had a habit of hanging on to his favourite pictures, and these were the ones which filled his studio. I was therefore most interested to hear from the artist Donald Watson in 1977 that the George Lodge Trust intended to publish a book on his work, because here, I thought, was an opportunity to set the record straight. Lodge at his best must surely rank together with the greatest names in wildlife art.

The George Lodge Trust was formed in 1944, at the suggestion of Robert Grant of Oliver and Boyd, in order to subsidise the cost of production of the *Birds of the British Isles* series and similar original works in natural history. Lodge himself contributed the 384 original paintings used for the series and £5,000 to the formation of the Trust. The Trust receives royalties from sales of *The Birds of the British Isles*, and today consists of a committee of seven, including Donald Watson and chaired by General Sir Philip Christison, a cousin of David Bannerman. In the mid-1970s it was proposed to boost the Trust's assets by producing a book, either of the best plates in *The Birds of the British Isles*, to be entitled *The Best of Lodge*, or of previously unpublished work.

I heard nothing more of this proposed book, and was told subsequently that publishers had felt that the financial situation at the time was not conducive for such a venture. My imagination had been stirred, however, and eventually I started thinking in terms of possibly taking on the project myself. It is amazing what publication of a few scientific papers will do to raise confidence in one's own literary ability! I thought it was important that all aspects of Lodge's work should be covered — wood-engravings, lithographs, sketches and paintings — and that there should be short chapters on his biography, changing methods of book illustration (to account for his varied forms of art), falconry (which formed an important part of his life) and a critical appraisal of his work. I had no intention of

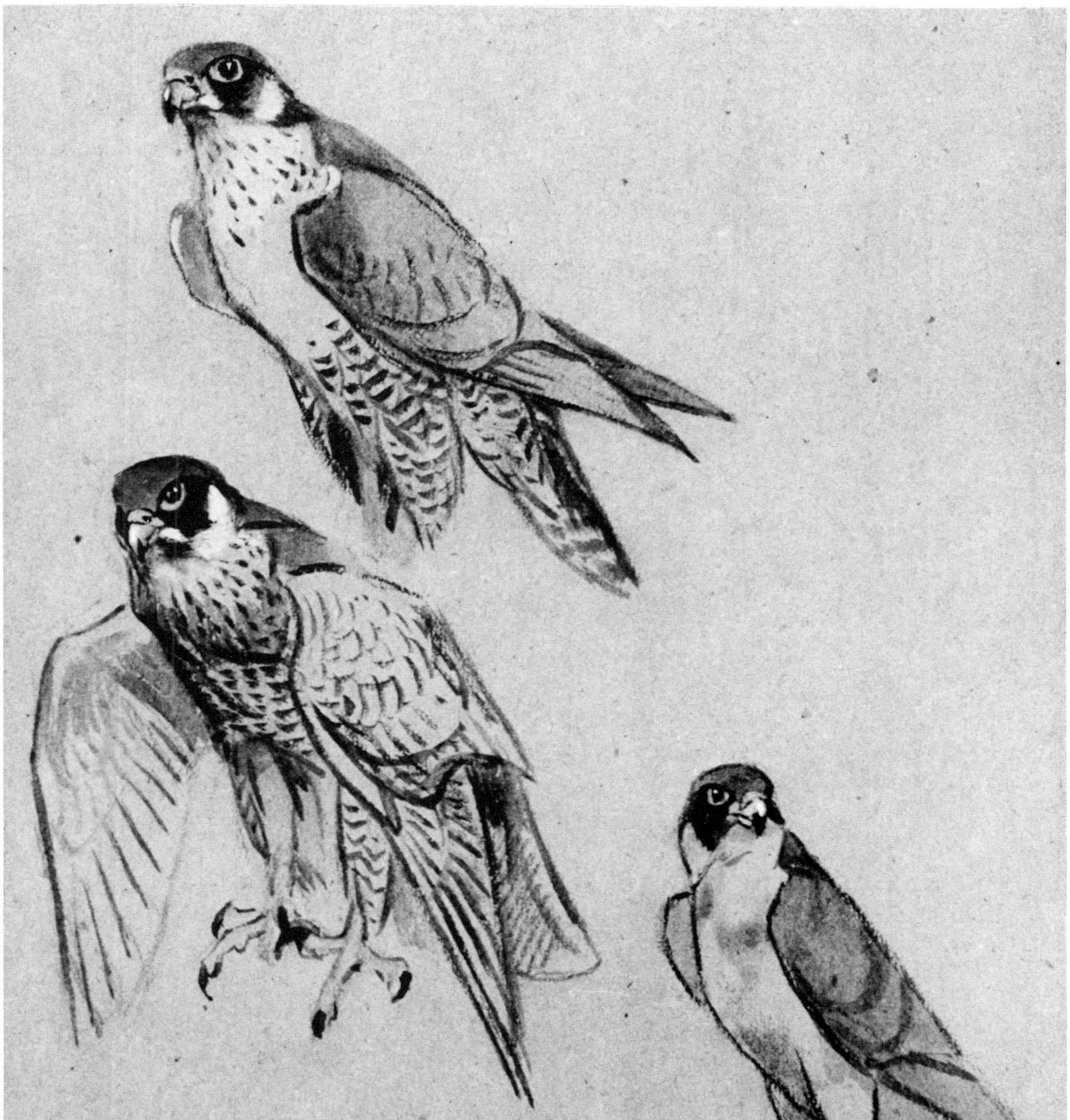

7

writing the whole book myself, owing to lack of both time and detailed knowledge, so thought of some names of appropriate people who might be approached to undertake these chapters.

I wrote to General Christison in 1980 to explain my interest in Lodge, to enquire about the Trust's plans, and to offer my own proposed scheme for a book. I also accepted that since the original aim of such a book was to help the Trust's funds, they should naturally receive a proportion of any royalties. The Trust's reply expressed their warmest support for my proposal and gave me much encouragement. One of the first questions to settle was that of copyright, and it was eventually established that the Trust hold this for the pictures in *The Birds of the British Isles*, but that the Tryon and Moorland Gallery hold it for nearly all the rest of Lodge's art and written material, having purchased it from the Westminster Bank, a trustee of Lodge's estate. The Gallery approved of my project in principle, and once I had found authors for the various chapters, I started approaching prospective publishers. I did this in rather a half-hearted manner for a year or so, without much success, but at the end of 1983 I produced a detailed outline/ prospectus for the book and sent it to a number of publishers, and Croom Helm agreed to take it on. I was now committed.

8

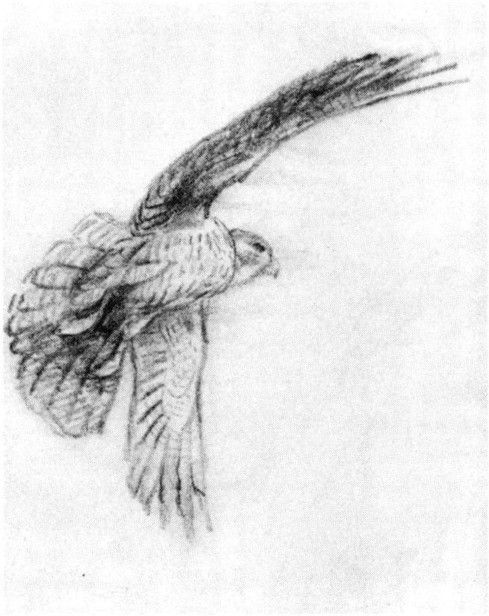

Soon after the Lodge Trust's original decision to produce a book on Lodge's work, David Bannerman, then a member of the Trust, had written a short biography of the artist. This was given to me in 1981 and seemed well suited for my book especially since there was probably nobody still alive who had known Lodge better. Bannerman died in 1979, but his widow, Mary Bannerman, and the Trust kindly gave their permission for me to use the biography. It probably tells us almost as much about Bannerman as it does about Lodge, but is no less interesting for that. As Donald Watson wrote in his obituary of Bannerman in *British Birds*: 'His contributions to knowledge, especially on distribution and taxonomy of birds, were massive, but he will be remembered most of all for his monumental books, the like of which will not be seen again.'

For the sake of completeness I have taken the liberty of adding a few details to the biography from certain obituaries of Lodge. The problem is that little is known about his early life. From talking to people who knew him, it is clear that he was a very modest man, and it is difficult to gain much information about him from his Memoirs, which consist mainly of a wealth of detailed notes on various groups of birds. It is not certain when he left his childhood home in Lincolnshire or where he did his apprenticeship as a wood-engraver, but he had an address in London by the age of 21. He moved to Camberley in 1920. At some stage he was in the army voluntary reserve (City of London), and his friend Dr Hugh Blair has told me that 'at lunchtime he always drank his ale from the mug that Rifleman Lodge had won for marksmanship while a volunteer'! His shrewdness and humour are

8. Peregrine in flight (colour plate 6)
9. Peregrine preening
10. Peregrine on a Sussex cliff

9

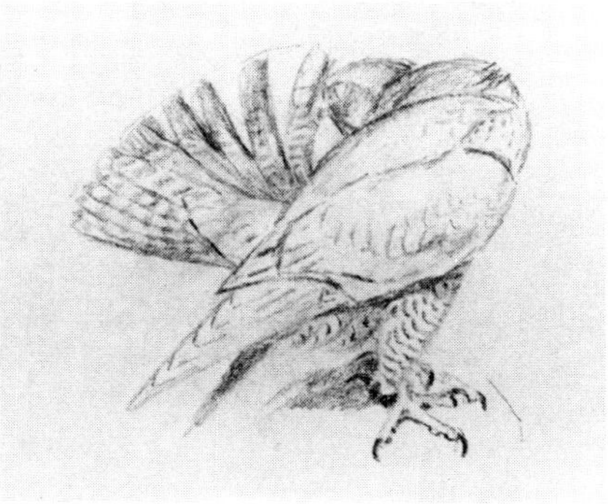

10

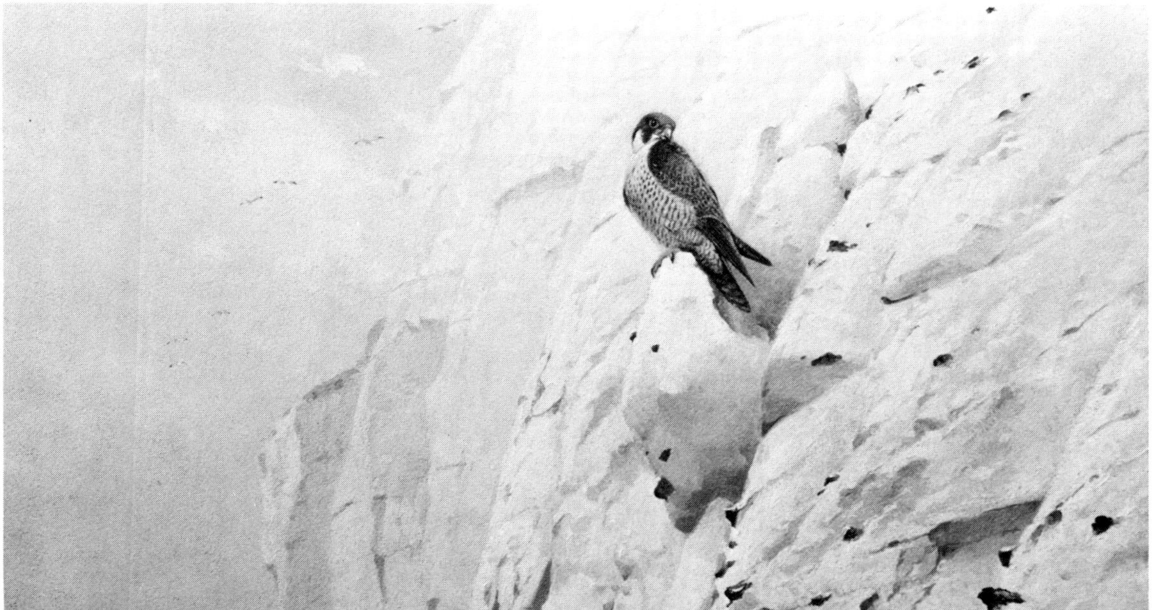

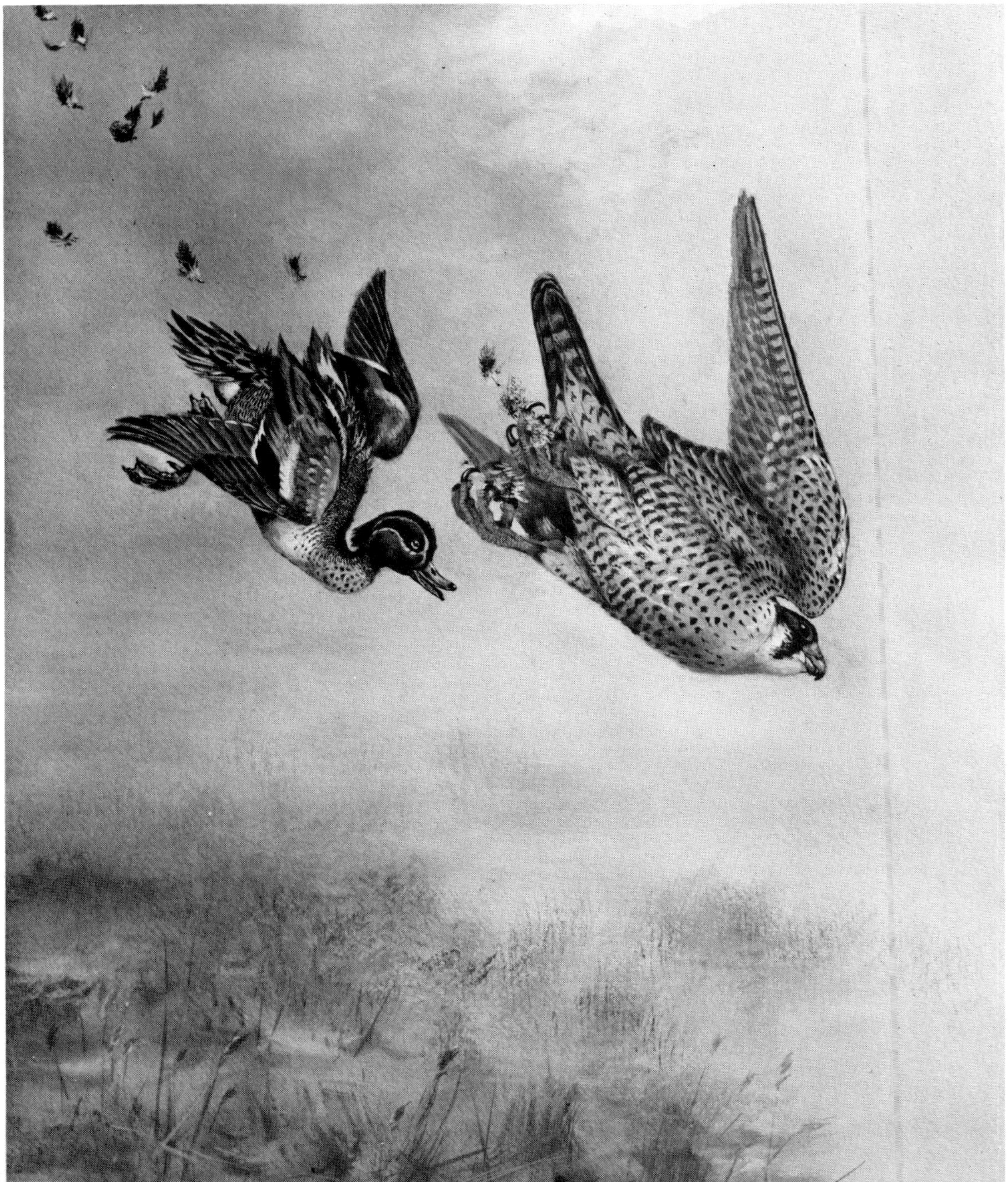

11

illustrated by another anecdote from Dr Blair, who arrived with his wife at Camberley one day to be greeted by Brenda Lodge, 'who hurriedly told us "I have got a cat, but he does not know". When I reached the studio, the old gentleman winked and said "She's got a cat; she *thinks* I don't know"! Then it would be on to tales of Lord Lilford or the Meinertzhagens.'

Lodge's great friends were the Mann family, who introduced him to falconry, and with whom he shot for 40 years. To them he was 'Uncle Dick' (dicky bird!), a great attraction on their Scottish shooting holidays, who taught them much about birds. During breaks in stalking he sometimes became so absorbed in sketching rocks and lichens that he had to be reminded of the business in hand, and on one occasion he skinned a ptarmigan with unusual plumage on the billiard table at a Glenlyon shooting lodge to add to his reference collection. Such abnormal specimens were of great interest to him,

11. The strike — peregrine striking a teal

12. The one that got away — peregrine and red grouse

12

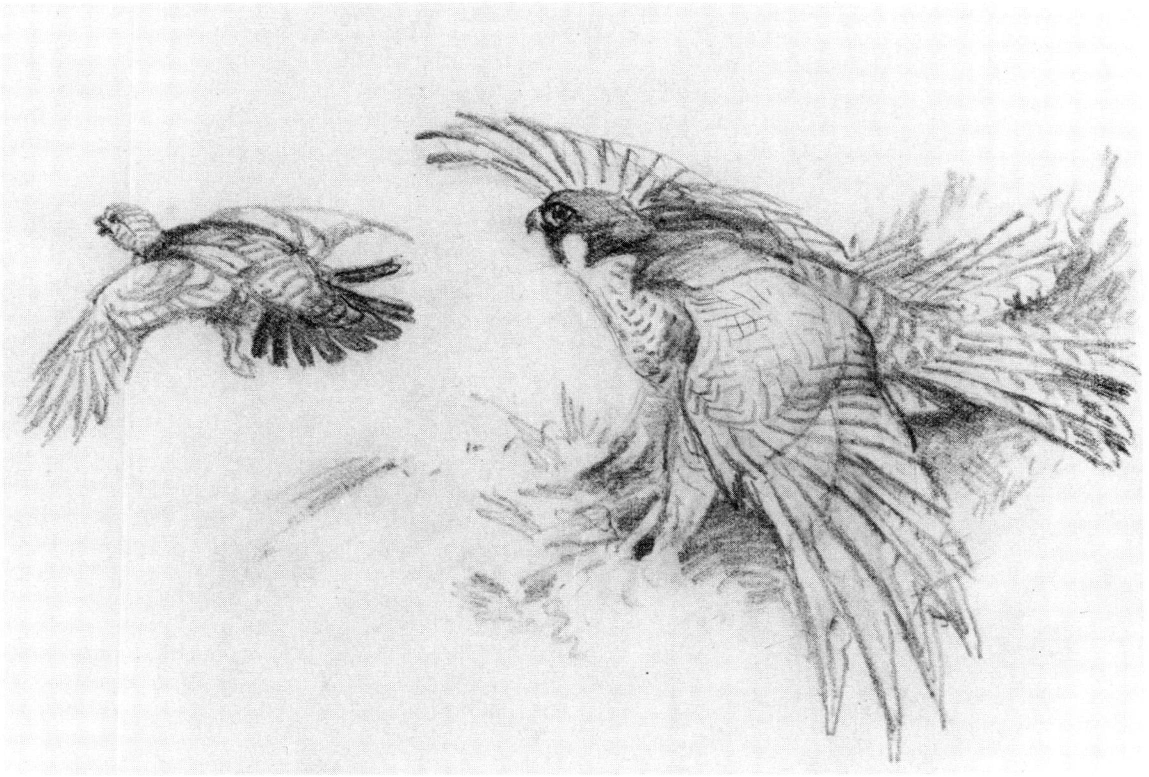

and some were recorded in his Memoirs as well as in his art. Long after most men would have given up walking for exercise, he was found crawling round his studio, rifle in hand, to decide for himself if he was really too old to stalk again.

Illustrations by Lodge have featured in at least 90 published works to date, the earliest appearing when he was 25 and quite a few since his death. A list of these (which I cannot guarantee to be complete) is given in the Bibliography at the end of this book. The different methods of printing employed during his lifetime often imposed limitations on his commissioned work, and I thought that an explanatory chapter on these methods might be of interest to many. Christine Jackson, who kindly agreed to write the chapter, is ideally suited since she is a recognised expert in this field, and is authoress of four books on birds and bird illustration. She was already familiar with Lodge's work, having covered it in her book *Bird Illustrators: Some Artists in Early Lithography* (1975), and she has produced a comprehensive survey with references to many of the titles that included his work. Both Christine Jackson and David Bannerman mention the poor quality colour plates in Lodge's own book, *Memoirs of an Artist Naturalist*, which undoubtedly disappointed him as well as his readers. Douglas Grant, a member of the Lodge Trust who was with Oliver and Boyd, has told me that the main reason why many of these were out of register (blurred) was that the machine used was unsuited for printing all 16 on one sheet of paper. Later Oliver and Boyd did reprint one or two of these plates, as Bannerman states, in order to reassure Lodge of their ability to produce good quality illustrations for *The Birds of the British Isles*.

I had originally hoped that Jack Mavrogordato, the doyen of modern British falconry, might write the chapter on Lodge the falconer. Mavrogordato was a regular attender with Lodge at the British Falconers' Club's hawking holidays in the 1930s, and used Lodge's paintings and sketches to illustrate his two classic books *A Hawk for the Bush* (1960) and *A Falcon in the Field* (1966). He felt unable to

13. Hobby stooping at a skylark

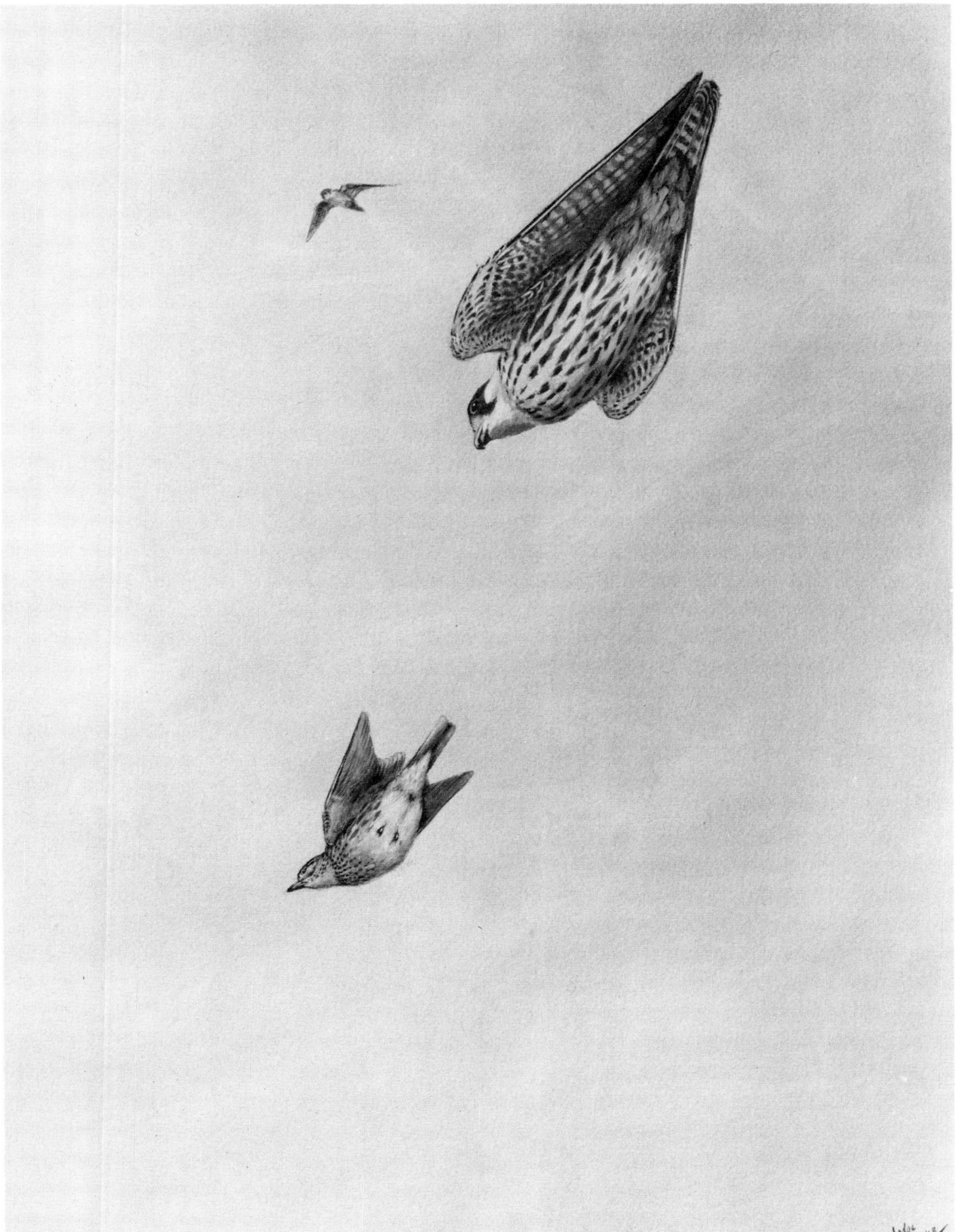

13

contribute more than a page or two of his reminiscences, however, so instead I asked Phillip Glasier, who also went to Avebury in the early 1930s with his uncle, Charles Knight. Glasier has been a professional falconer for much of his life, has written books on the subject, and during the last war, while stationed at Sandhurst, he visited Lodge frequently at his home in Camberley. The Avebury days are described vividly in his book *As the Falcon Her Bells* (1963), and here he describes them again, briefly, together with his other memories of Lodge. To this chapter I have added Lodge's own description of his introduction to falconry, from his notes, the first and last entries in his hawking diary, with 53 years between them, and a small sample of other entries. Extracts from this diary featured in early numbers of *The Falconer* (journal of the British Falconers' Club, first issued in 1937), and describe days spent flying various short- and long-winged hawks at a wide variety of quarry. It should be remembered that when Lodge went to Avebury and Bodmin in the 1930s, he was there mainly as observer and artist, and that most of his active hawking had been done years before, in the days of the Old Hawking Club, with the Mann family (mainly in Norfolk) and later with Gilbert Blaine (mainly in Scotland). Indeed, his travels and sporting activities in his earlier years must have taken up so much time that his artistic output then appears even more remarkable. A good idea of the atmosphere of these early hawking expeditions can be obtained from Roger Upton's book *A Bird in the Hand: Celebrated Falconers of the Past* (1980).

I asked Donald Watson to appraise Lodge's art because I felt that he had more in common with Lodge that most modern wildlife portrait painters, in that he is also a fine landscape artist who pays as much attention to habitat as to his animal subjects. His illustrations have featured in several books on natural history, the richest selection appearing in his own *Birds of Moor and Mountain* (1972). His position on the Lodge Trust is as artistic adviser, and does not imply any favourable bias towards Lodge's work. Here he discusses Lodge in relation

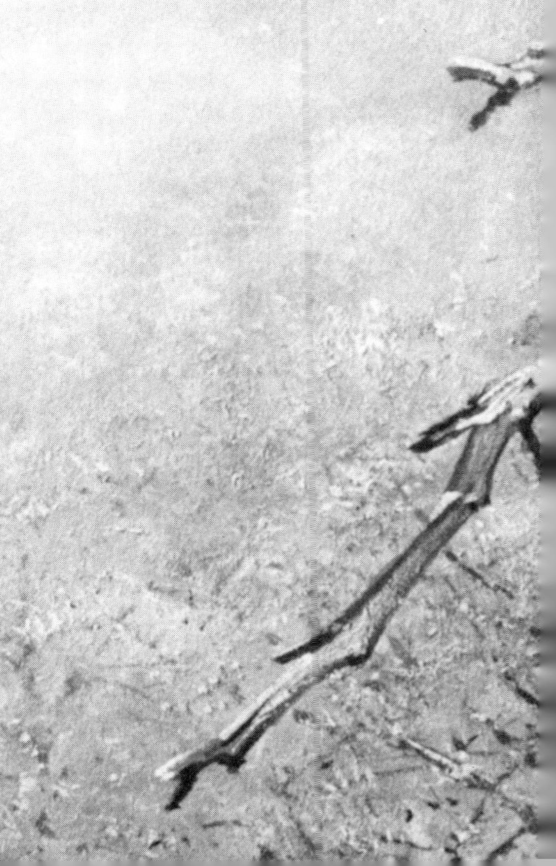

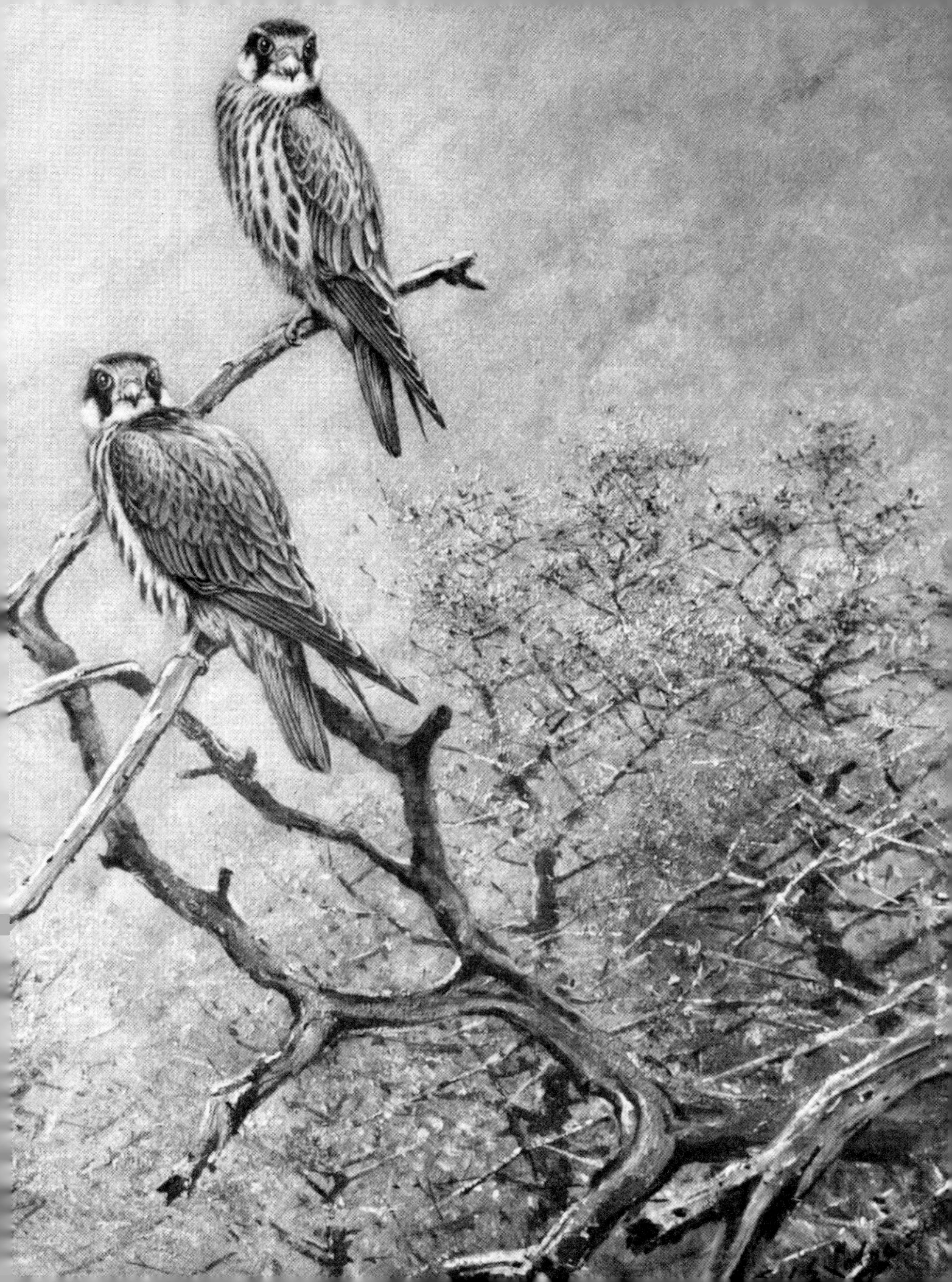

to other contemporary artists, and comments specifically on many of the illustrations selected for this book.

Lodge was born in 1860, the same year as Archibald Thorburn (as was also the Swedish wildlife artist Bruno Liljefors, regarded by some as the greatest of them all), and both were greatly influenced by Joseph Wolf (1820-99), who was the first major artist to study and draw animals in their natural surroundings, rather than from museum specimens. In turn, both Lodge and Thorburn instructed and influenced Jack Harrison and Philip Rickman, and later David Reid-Henry, and the Wolf tradition can be seen in all their work. Lodge was always rather overshadowed by Thorburn, probably because Thorburn was more prolific and had better sales promotion, but they were firm friends. John Southern, of the Thorburn Gallery near Liskeard, has told me that Thorburn could produce paintings in half the time that Lodge took (the large ones by Thorburn taking about a week), and that their total outputs would have been in the order of 3,000-4,000 and 1,500-2,000 finished paintings respectively. Both had their strengths and weaknesses and, in their own way, each was probably as good as the other. Unlike Lodge, of course, Thorburn did not produce hundreds of time-consuming wood-engravings, and he probably also devoted less time to outside interests. Lodge appears to have had greater mastery over oil paints, although his preferred medium was tempera and that of Thorburn was watercolour. Both artists received patronage from Lord Lilford and illustrated books by him.

While researching for this book several people remarked to me on the helpful and instructive comments made by Lodge in the last chapter of his Memoirs, entitled ‘Some observations on painting birds’. Since *Memoirs of an Artist Naturalist* is long out of print and will not have been seen by many, and since most of Lodge’s remarks are just as relevant now as they were in 1946, the publishers agreed that they should reappear here. Owing to lack of space, however, they have had to be abbreviated, and I have picked out what I hope to be

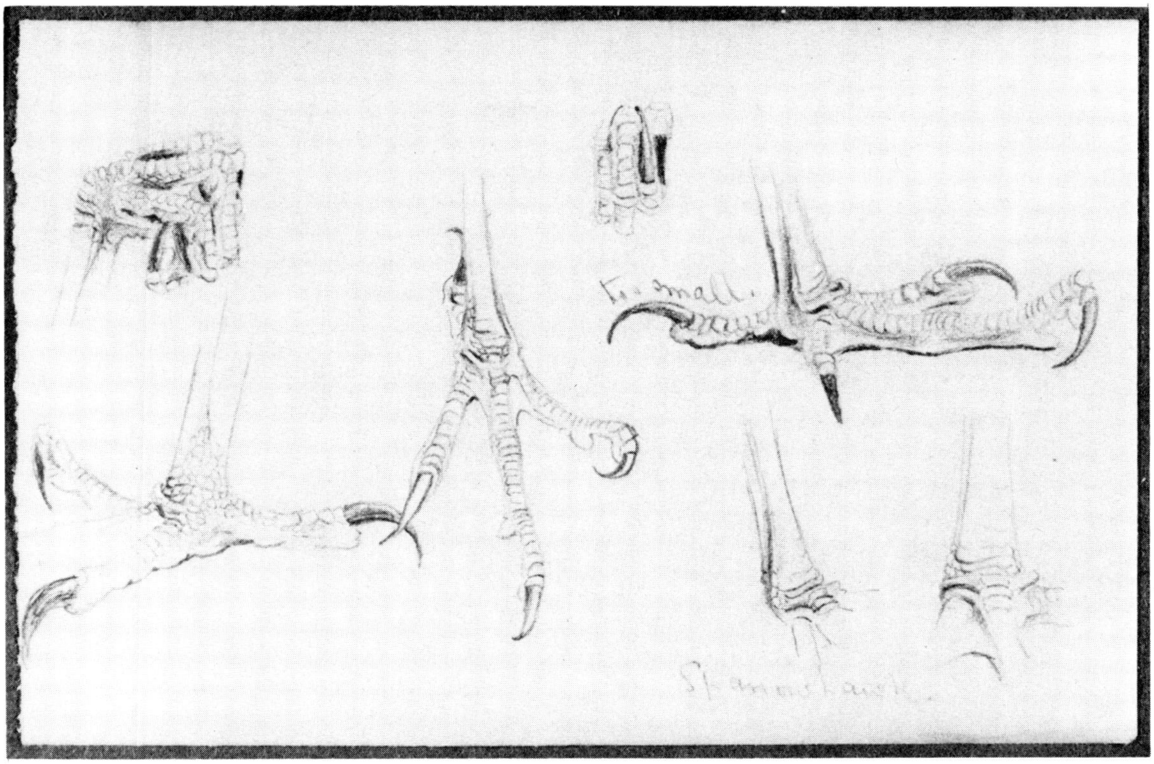

15

the most useful tips. Also included at the end of this book is a list of 12 paintings that Lodge exhibited at the Royal Academy between the ages of 21 and 57. In the Royal Academy's catalogue they appear next to five paintings exhibited by his brother, Reginald B. Lodge, artist, bird photographer and author. The two brothers had been close companions in their youth, both dedicated naturalists, and in 1895 Reginald was awarded the Royal Photographic Society's first medal for natural history.

During the summer of 1984 I made an extensive search for suitable art material for the book. I corresponded with many people who had known Lodge personally or who owned pictures by him, and visited the homes of several of them in various parts of the country. All expressed great interest in the project and allowed me to make use of their pictures if required. I also visited galleries and auctioneers that I thought might have dealt with Lodge paintings, and some of these proved to be

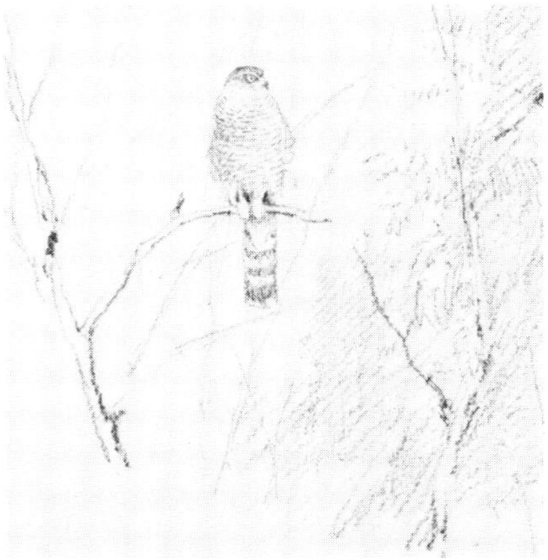

16

14. Hobbys above a misty valley
15. Studies of sparrow-hawk feet
16. Sparrow-hawk taking stand

important sources of material. With my family I made a pilgrimage to Avebury, and found the Red Lion little changed outwardly from its appearance in my father's photographs taken 50 years before. I even visited Lodge's old home in Camberley, where I was kindly shown round and given tea by the wife of the present owner.

I obtained a copy of Lodge's will from Somerset House, and in it discovered that he had bequeathed his wood-engraving proofs and two pictures to the Victoria and Albert Museum, and his natural history specimens, data books and sketch books to the Natural History Department of the British Museum. It was his desire 'that the same should be utilised in such a way as may render them of value to the nation as a means of art or natural history education'. At the Victoria and Albert Museum I found a volume containing proofs of the engravings in Lord Lilford's *Birds of Northamptonshire* (1895), two preliminary paintings for engravings in Howard Saunders' *Illustrated Manual of British Birds* (1889), and a very untypical Normandy landscape, presented in 1922. At the Natural History Museum I found five paintings for plates in Lord Rothschild's *Extinct Birds* (1907) (Rothschild bequest), 19 files of hand-written and typed notes on various subjects from raptors and game-birds to 'fowls of the air' and lepidoptera, and 35 files of sketches covering all types of subject matter that he used for his pictures. I recognised that the notes had obviously formed the basis of his Memoirs, and they and the sketches provided additional information on his movements and activities. I discovered, for example, that he had sketched the big cats (which he greatly admired) and other exotica at the Whipsnade and Regent's Park zoos, and it seems unlikely that he ever saw them in the wild state, as David Bannerman suggests. Most of his illustrations of foreign birds (and many of indigenous species) were done from skins in various collections. Lodge's own collection of 430 study skins, together with numerous wings and tails, is now housed at the British Museum's Natural History Department at Tring. His collection of lepidoptera, and some eggs and mounted specimens, were given by Brenda Lodge to Bristol Museum.

Between about 1930 and 1951, Lodge's photographer in Camberley photographed some 130 of his paintings as a permanent record for the artist. In more than half of these the main subjects were birds of prey. Game-birds, waterfowl and mammals made up most of the rest, and passerines were in a minority. Roughly 20 per cent of them were done in oils and all the rest in tempera. This sample is probably fairly representative of Lodge's output, and of his preferences for subject matter and painting medium. In the choice of art material for this book, therefore, I have stuck to similar proportions, with a definite bias towards birds of prey, for which Lodge was most famous. The falcons were clearly his favourites, especially the gyr which he painted many times. It is therefore rather surprising to note from his Memoirs that he saw only three wild gyr falcons in his life, in Sweden and Norway, a fact that he greatly regretted. His passion for falconry and other forms of sport often gave him opportunities to

17. Osprey sketches

17

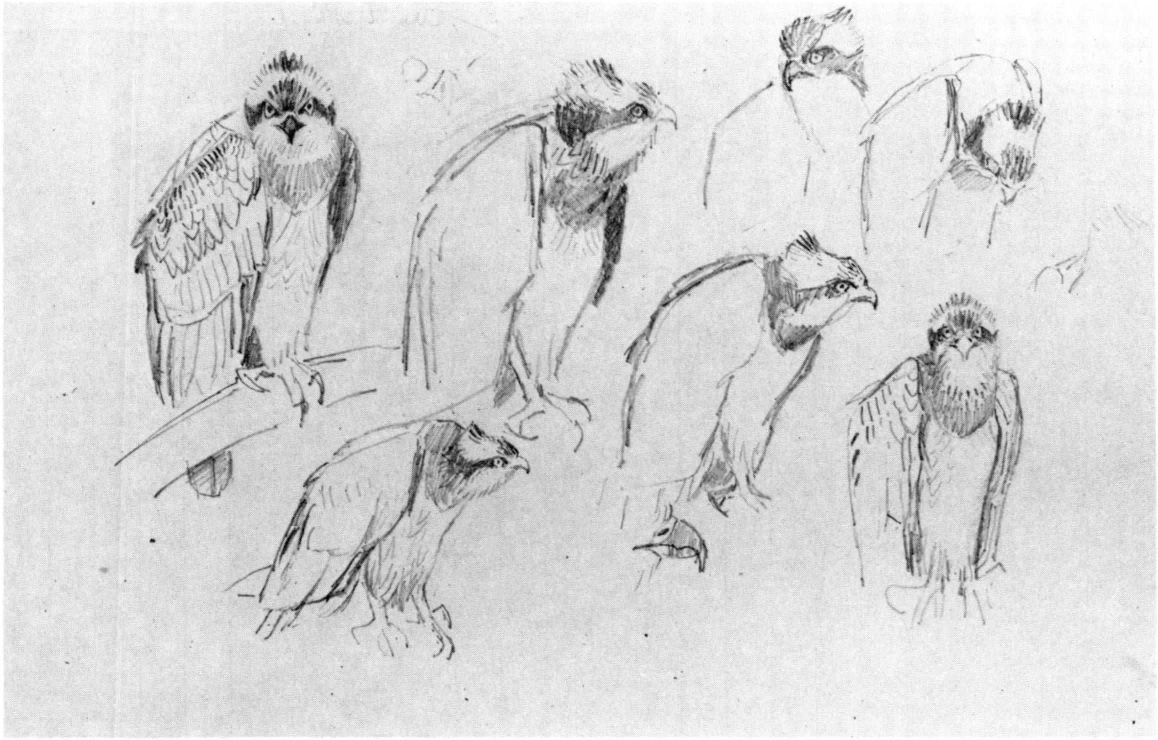

observe dramatic scenes involving predator and prey, and many of these he later painted most successfully. With the help of a few advisers, I have chosen a selection of wood-engravings, one hand-coloured lithograph, pencil and coloured sketches, and finished paintings, and these are grouped broadly into birds of prey, game-birds, other birds, mammals and landscapes (at which Lodge was particularly good). The wood-engravings and lithograph are all from published works long out of print, but few of the others will have been seen before. No attempt has been made to present them in chronological order, mainly because the dates of many of his pictures are unknown. It was not until late in his life that he started dating them regularly.

Since plans for this book were set in motion, two others illustrated entirely by Lodge have appeared. These are *A Season of Birds (A Norfolk Diary): 1911* (1980) and *Unpublished (New Zealand) Bird Paintings* (1983). Both are delightful books, but can hardly be claimed to represent the artist at his best. In particular they lack the harmony of subject and surroundings and sense of atmosphere that were Lodge's greatest strengths.

I was interested to see in the catalogue for a George Lodge exhibition at the Moorland Gallery in 1977 that David Bannerman had written in his introduction: '. . . when writing a few words about my partner in the fifth volume of our joint work I expressed the hope that one of his contemporaries (Captain Gilbert Blaine, for example, or Harry Savory) would publish an account of his life, his art, his travels, his knowledge and love of falconry and his devotion to birds, but the challenge was never taken up. It would have made fascinating reading.' On my father's behalf then, better late than never, this book is an attempt to fill the gap.

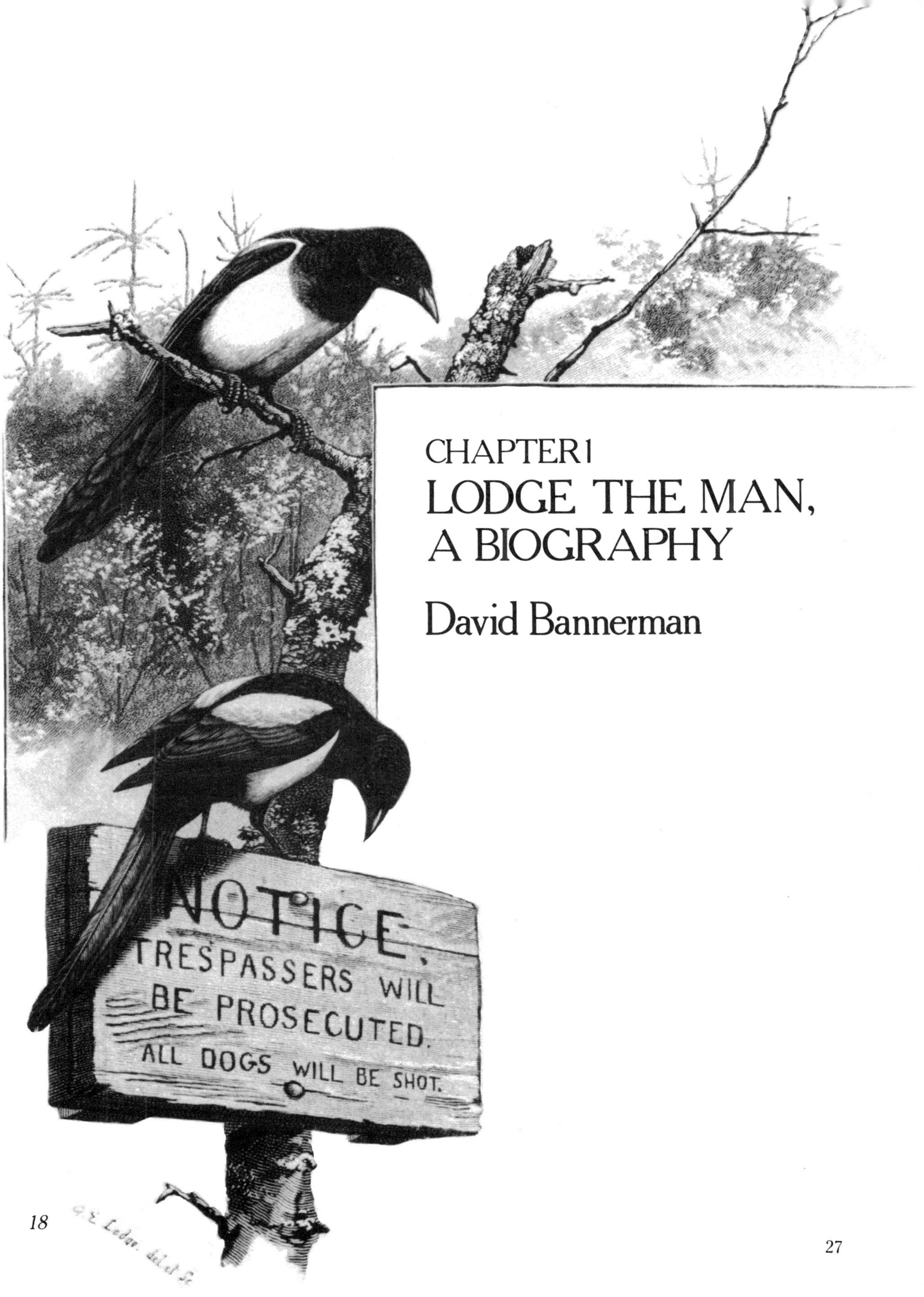

18

CHAPTER 1

LODGE THE MAN, A BIOGRAPHY

David Bannerman

I well remember my first meeting with George Lodge and the impression it made upon me, but I am less clear of the year in which it took place. I was then undergoing preliminary training in the Natural History Museum, London, with a view eventually to appointment on the established staff. I had been taken under the wing of W.R. Ogilvie-Grant who, at the time of which I am writing, was second in charge of the 'Bird Room' under his celebrated chief Dr R. Bowdler-Sharpe. The Bird Room of the British Museum was in those distant days, and for many years afterwards, a rendezvous for the leading ornithologists of the world and, with a view to my future role in the establishment, Bill Grant (as he was known to his friends) made a point of summoning me to his room to make their acquaintance. It was thus I met for the first time the man with whom, many years later, I was to collaborate in *The Birds of the British Isles* (1953-63). My recollection is of a tall, kindly man with a warm hand-clasp who immediately put one at ease. I doubt if I had reached the age of 20 and 'Mr Lodge' (as I respectfully called him) was 26 years my senior, but I am sure I was already aware he was a great bird painter, for my interest in such things stemmed from the age of eight.

For many years George Lodge and I had no close contact; the 1914-18 World War saw to that. Four years' active service in France had also put other ideas into my head, and the choice of becoming a civil servant with less than a month's holiday a year and a salary starting at £150 per annum held less attraction for me than formerly. When I returned from France both Bowdler-Sharpe and Ogilvie-Grant had left the scene of my earlier ambitions. The former died before the war and Ogilvie-Grant held the senior appointment for a very short time, succumbing to a stroke brought on by combining too-strenuous war work with his other duties. The Bird Room appointment was literally going begging, and while I know now that I could have had it for the asking, I had tasted too much freedom to tie myself to the conventional and restricted life of a London civil servant. Instead I chose to be a member of the

18. Magpies
19. Goshawk sketches

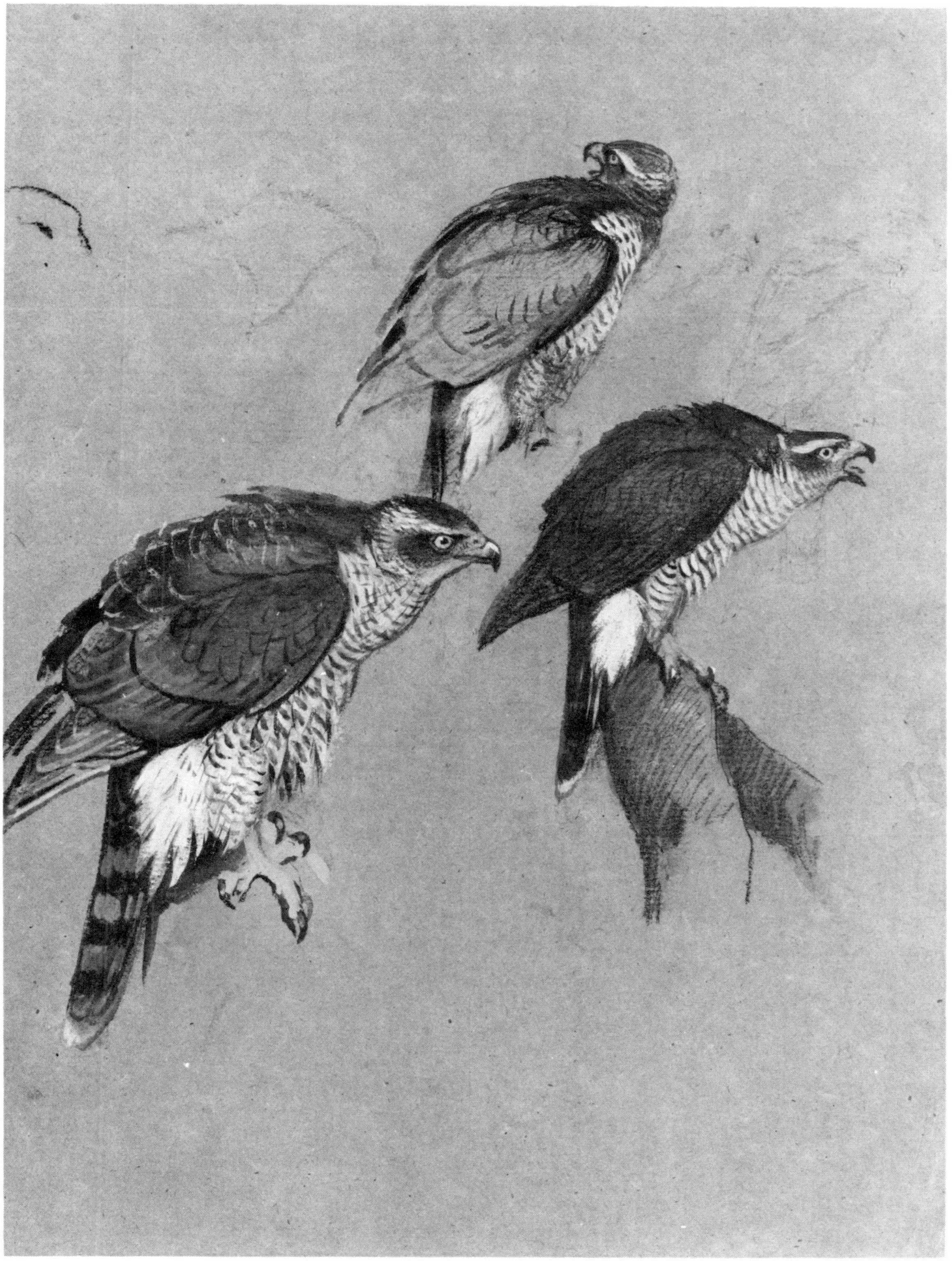

19

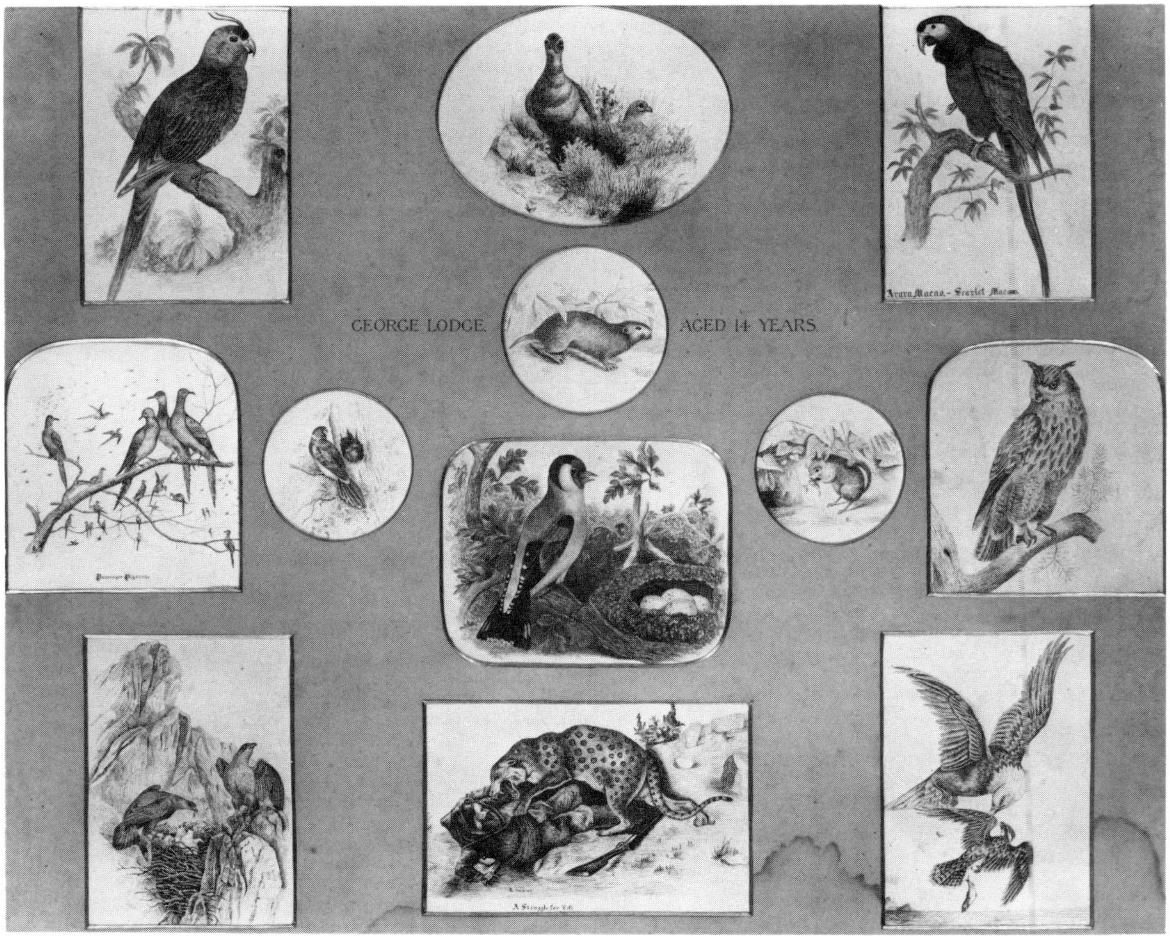

20

20. Lodge's artwork at 14 years Old, when at Lincoln School of Art

supernumerary museum staff at the princely salary of £200 per annum, to be worked off at 2/6d per hour. It gave me an official standing in the British Museum, my own study in the Bird Room, keys to all the cabinets, and many other favoured treatments of which I took full advantage. I was directly under the Keeper of Zoology and devoted myself to the study of West African birds. The West African Colonial Governments had commissioned me to write in five volumes, which increased to eight, *The Birds of Tropical West Africa* and generously gave me a free choice of bird artists with which to illustrate the text. When it came to the brilliantly coloured species such as glossy starlings and sunbirds my choice was George Lodge, and so it was that we met again. His many paintings in volumes 2 to 7 of that series are there for all to see and the original pictures adorn the walls of the Librarian's private sanctum at the Commonwealth Office in Whitehall.

Born on 3 December 1860 at Scrivelsby in Lincolnshire, George Edward was the seventh son of a seventh son, and was one of a family of eleven, of whom eight lived to over 80 and three, including himself, to over 90. His mother, from whose family he inherited his artistic tastes, had herself attained the age of 91. She was descended from Francis Wheatley and Clara Pope, both celebrated painters who exhibited at the Royal Academy. His father, Samuel Lodge, was a Canon of Lincoln and for many years Rector of Scrivelsby; he wrote a history of the Champions of England, of whom Scrivelsby is the home. So George grew up in the heart of English tradition. He was educated at home and from an early age he and his brother Reginald, the pioneer bird photographer, were keen naturalists and roamed the local countryside in search of subjects. At the age of 12 he stuffed his first bird, an owl, at 14 he won prizes for drawing at the Lincoln School of Art, and at 16 he was apprenticed to a wood-engraver.

I knew little of Lodge's early life and high achievements until after his death, and learned much about my distinguished friend from the numerous obituary notices which filled our press, especially those devoted to sporting or artistic subjects such as *The Field, Country Life* and *Country Fair*. Lodge started his artistic career as a wood-engraver, at which he became expert, and one can find fine examples of his engraving in books by Evans, Lilford, Millais, Saunders, Seebohm and others. Falconry was one of his favourite pursuits for most of his life, and many pages are devoted to describing the art of the falconer in the only book he ever wrote and illustrated himself, *Memoirs of an Artist Naturalist*. He also illustrated books on falconry for hawking friends such as E.B. Michell, J.E. Harting and Gerald Lascelles. Around the turn of the century several of his paintings were exhibited in the Royal Academy, but neither he nor his friend

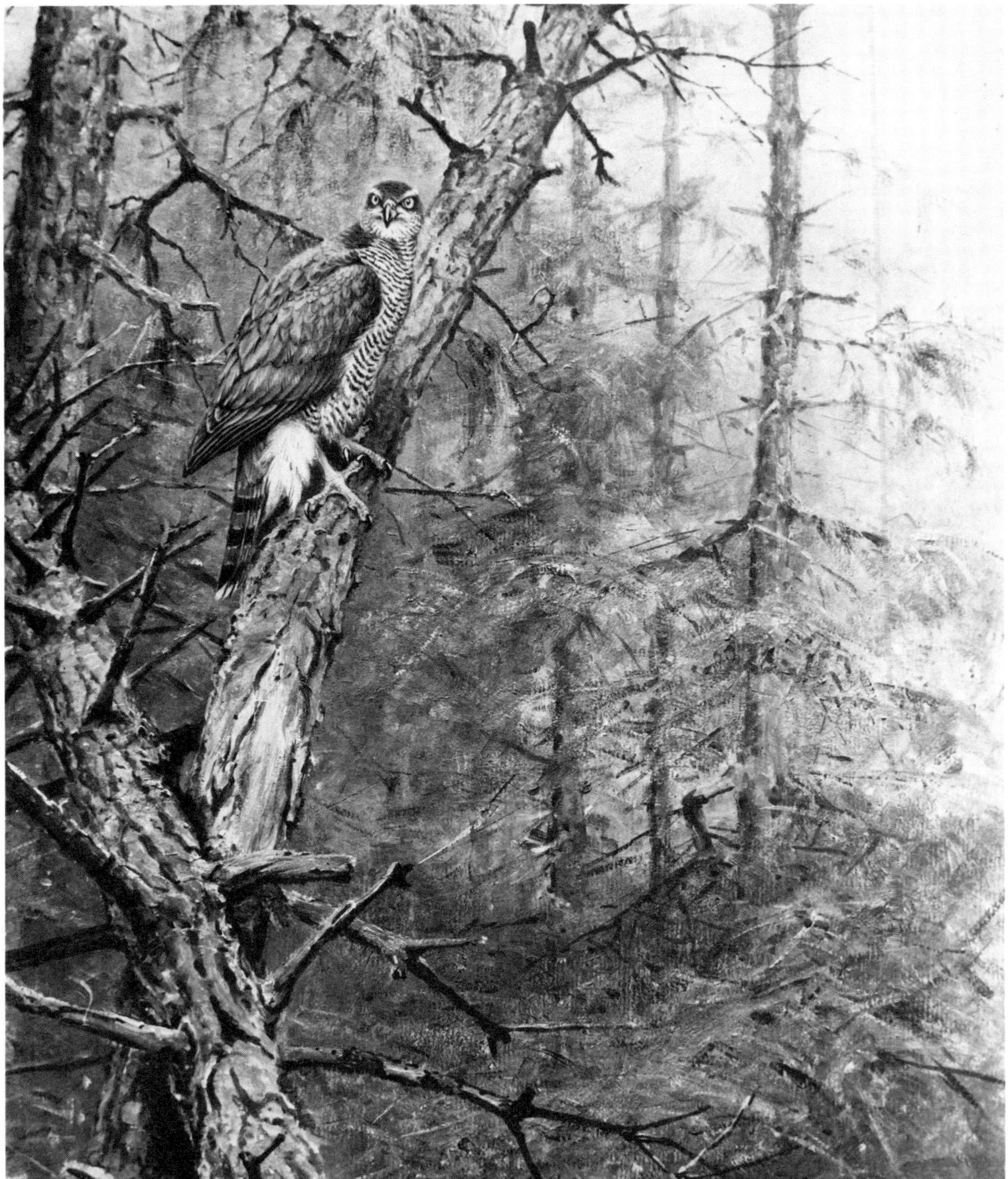

21

Archibald Thorburn were elected Royal Academicians as they surely should have been, for no two men have excelled in bird portraiture more than they. Both admired the other's work although they used different techniques. Of the great bird painters I have known personally Charles Tunnicliffe is the only one who can put R.A. after his name.

The days when fine wood-engraving was the fashion were soon to pass and Lodge took to painting in oils and in tempera, the latter medium he preferred for illustrating bird books. His pictures of game-birds ran those of his birds of prey very close in perfection, and many country houses in Scotland and England have splendid examples of his art hanging on their walls. He was a first-rate sportsman, a fine shot at driven game and equally distinguished as a deer-stalker, and was a welcome guest on numerous estates. His pictures of stags in typical Scottish scenery are as delightfully pleasing as those of grouse and ptarmigan in their natural setting. In *Memoirs of an Artist Naturalist* is reproduced a picture of a Scottish deer forest entitled 'Stags separating from hinds, Eilanreach', which gives a good idea of Lodge's skill at painting such a difficult subject. In all his pictures, whether of birds, beasts or simply landscape, Lodge had a wonderful eye for detail, and the backgrounds of his pictures needed just as much care and attention by blockmakers when they were reproduced as did the main subject. Phillip Glasier was correct when he wrote in *Country Fair* that 'Much of the charm of his pictures lies in the great pains he took, not only in painting the birds themselves, at which he was second to none, but in the other details; flowers, trees and backgrounds, and their correctness in relation to the birds' particular habitat.' That indeed was the secret of his pictures, which immediately distinguishes them from those of his contemporary artists. 'That's a Lodge' I have often heard remarked, even though no bird was in sight.

Strange as it seems to look back on, with the exception of those whose particular fancy was birds of prey, or the owners of grouse moors and deer forests who commissioned his pictures, Lodge never

21. Adult goshawk
22. Golden eagle

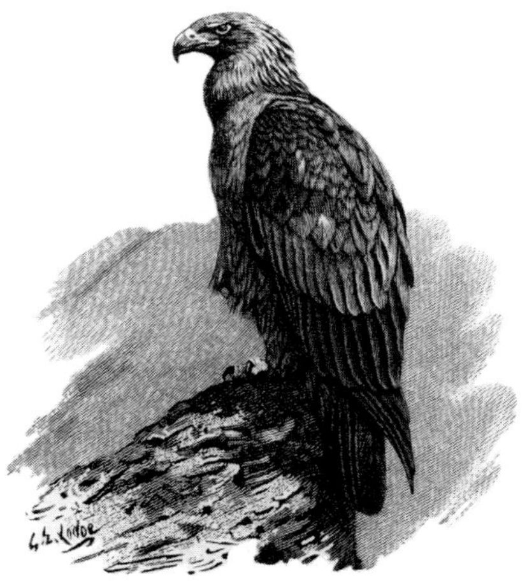

22

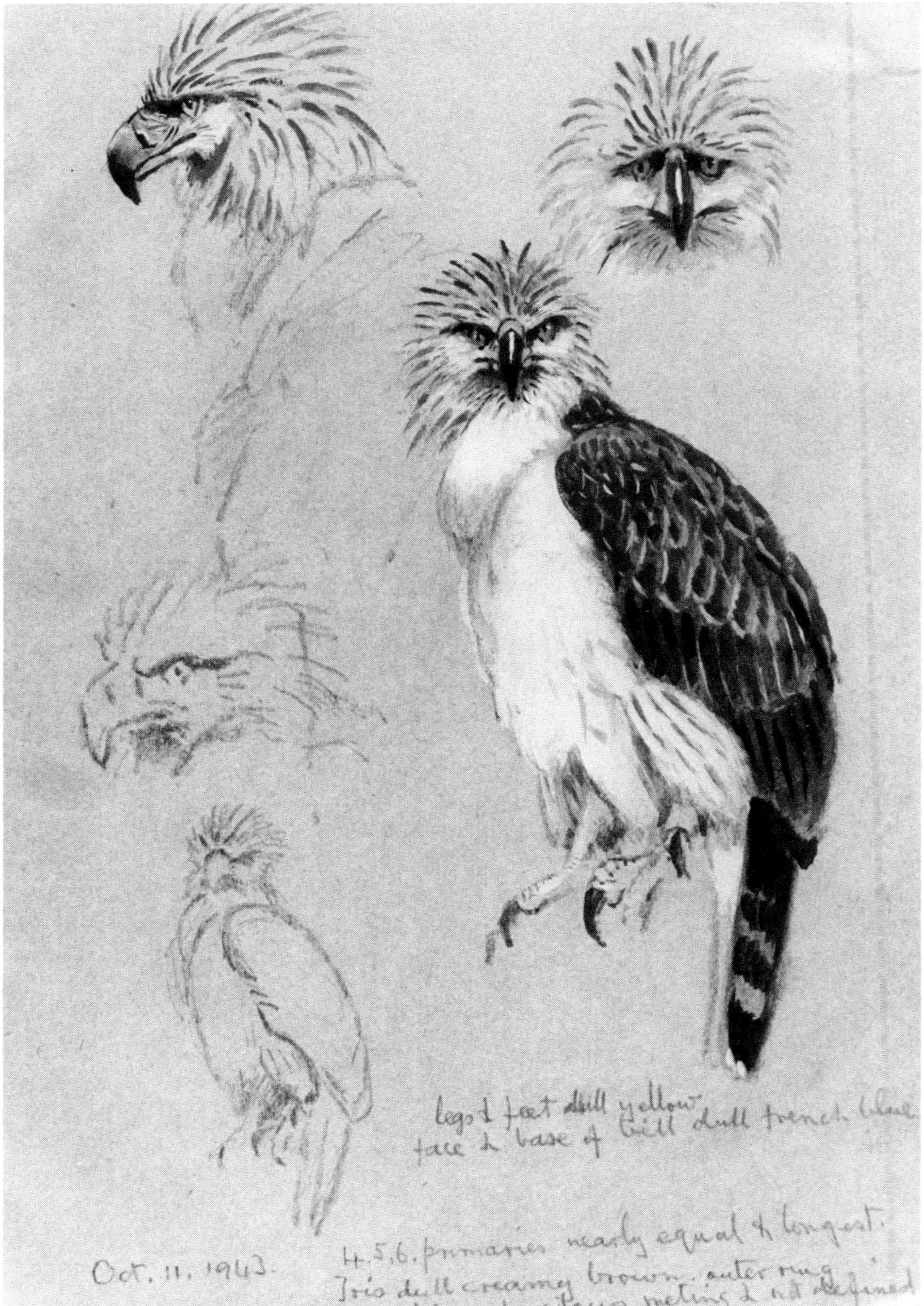
legs & feet dull yellow
face & base of bill dull french blue
Oct. 11. 1943.
4.5.6. primaries nearly equal & longest.
Iris dull creamy brown. outer ring
brownish red. colours meeting & not defined

23

really received full recognition until after his death at the advanced age of 94. When, as often happened, I visited his studio, he complained to me that his pictures did not *sell* as did those of his friend Thorburn, whose works were snapped up as quickly as he could turn them out. To spend an afternoon in his studio at Camberley was always tantalising, for I wanted to possess every picture I saw. His studio walls were crammed and folios of his earlier work were piled one upon another. Oh! that in those days I had had the spare cash to purchase a tenth of what I longed to possess. Visitors whom I took to see him were invariably captivated by what they saw, and I have vivid recollections of a visit during the last war with the Chief of the Imperial General Staff, Field Marshal Lord Alanbrooke as he later became, who took an afternoon off to refresh his mind in Lodge's studio, both of us revelling in what he had to show us. We arrived from London in time for luncheon and that simple meal with our charming host has remained a happy memory ever since. We were waited upon by his favourite sister, who must have been well over 90 at the time, and his niece Brenda, both of whom cared for him in his old age (he had never married). On another occasion I took my wife with me, and after admiring the contents of his studio we sat with Lodge in his garden. He produced a packet of mealworms and introduced us to his feathered friends: sparrows, blue tits, chaffinches, and a robin perched fearlessly on his knees which peeped through the much-worn, tweed plus-fours in which he was invariably garbed. The birds of his little shut-in garden knew they would come to no harm from the man who offered them mealworms, his gentleness and love for them being in some way communicated to them. Kindness exuded from him, and many a young artist, to whom he was always ready to give advice or assistance, must have had cause to be grateful for the warmth of his welcome and the wise counsel they received. Two at least of his pupils acquired eminence in the same branch of art as himself.

Lodge was an active member of the Executive Council of the Society for the Promotion of Nature

23. Philippine monkey-eating eagle, sketched at Regent's Park Zoo in 1943 (colour plate 19)
24. Tawny owl

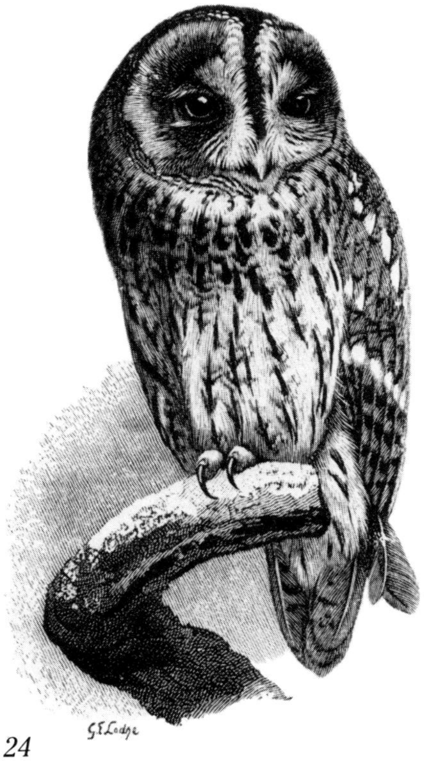

24

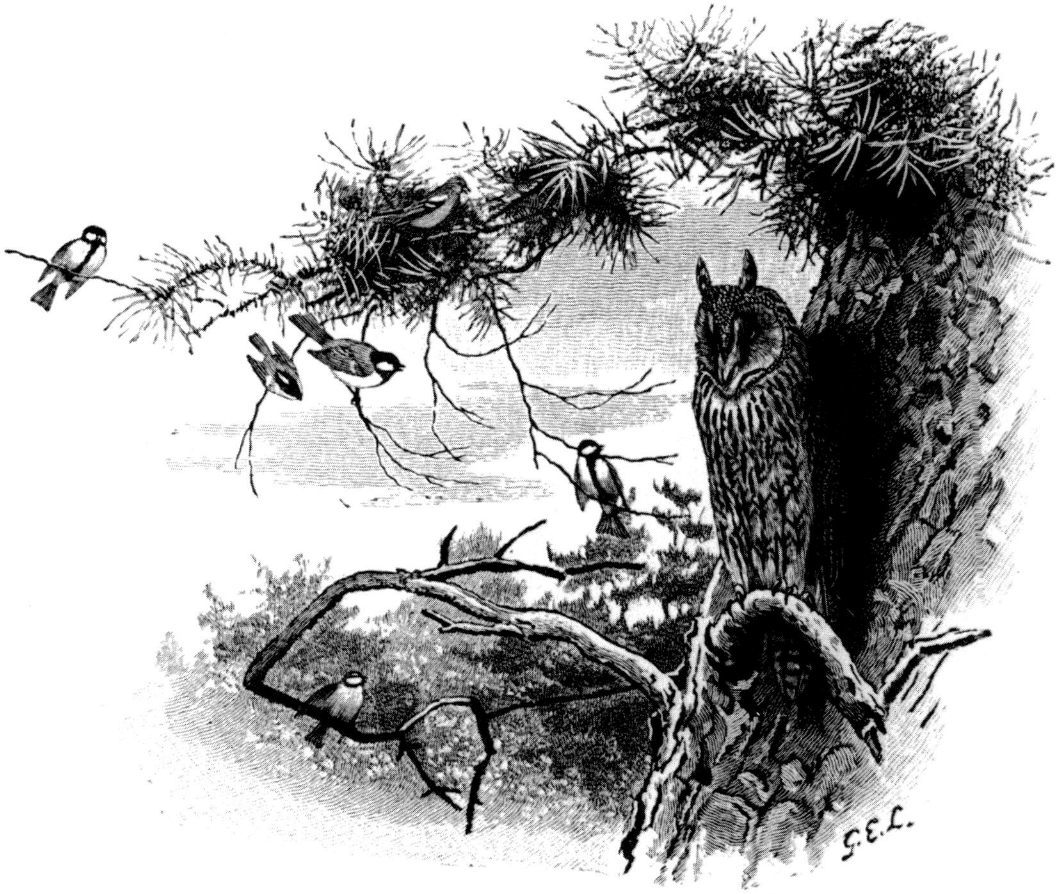

25

25. Long-eared owl mobbed by tits and a chaffinch

26. Partridge

Reserves and of the International Committee for Bird Protection, a distinguished Fellow of the Zoological Society of London and Vice-President for eight years of the Camberley Natural History Society, in all of which he took the greatest interest. Elected a member of the B.O.U. (British Ornithologists' Union) in 1897, he was made a Vice-President in 1945, the only artist naturalist to be so honoured. He knew many leading ornithologists personally, having met them in connection with his work and at meetings such as the International Ornithological Congress at Oxford in 1934. During the last war, anxious to help the war effort, he learned to knit and became so proficient that he completed 320 scarves for the Royal Air Force. When it came to my turn to pay him tribute in the fifth volume of our joint work, *The Birds of the British Isles*, I wrote these words: 'George Lodge was a wonderful example of the best which Britain can produce, a sportsman, a naturalist and a very fine gentleman. No-one could meet him without feeling the kindliness of his nature and his great integrity, and all who came in contact with him learned to love and admire him. The B.O.U. has lost a great bird artist and his many admirers a wonderful friend.' These words were penned at the time of his death and I do not think I can better them today. They have been echoed by his countless friends the world over.

But I have anticipated and must go back to 1942 when the idea that Lodge and I might collaborate in a book, for which he should paint every British bird, began to take root. In a letter which he wrote to me he asked me to correct the impression I had given in my Preface to volume I, that he had been the instigator of our combined work, and with that I complied in volume V in the notice I wrote about my friend, quoting his letter to me. My error was forgivable, for on more than one occasion when we were discussing bird illustrating in books, he had stressed his desire to identify himself with a book on the subject in which he was the sole artist. I must have daringly followed that up and remember his coming to London to stay with me when we discussed the plan of such a work. The letter he wrote to me from Hawkhouse, dated 23 February 1942, did in fact clinch the matter. I marvel today that he ever had the faith in my writing to undertake such an immense task, much less to complete it, for at that date he had already turned 81. 'Though I do not think that my work is deteriorating yet', as he put it, adding 'If such a book could be completed, with your name as writer and mine as illustrator, I feel sure that it would at once become a best seller.' His prophecy was realised thanks in no small measure to the collaboration of our publishers, Oliver and Boyd of Edinburgh, and the splendid workmanship which went into every volume, worthy indeed of that old established firm, but, alas functioning no more so far as bird books are concerned.

Before saying more of our proposed

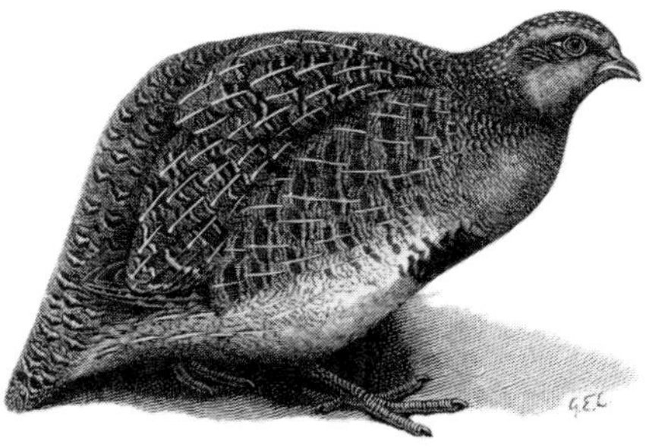

26

collaboration, I must mention once more Lodge's own book, *Memoirs of an Artist Naturalist*, which had appeared in 1946, an unfortunate time for the launching of any book. Reviewers were quick to point out the 'woolly' appearance of the 16 full-page colour plates, which in many instances were but muzzy reflections of the originals, doing scant justice to the artist's known talents. The cause of this unfortunate occurrence was the wartime quality of the art paper upon which the plates were printed, some being much worse than others in the way indicated. Many owners of this book never knew the reason for the pictures falling so far short of the usual high standard, and it is only fair to Lodge to put the record straight. When good paper was again obtainable one of the same plates was reprinted at my request by Robert Grant of Oliver and Boyd, when the woolly appearance was entirely lost and the artist's brush-work as clearly depicted as ever. The fault in this book did not lie with the artist, but it did him no good. The text was divided into five sections and was in the nature of the author's reminiscences, an important section being devoted to hawks and hawking, for as already noted Lodge was a skilled devotee of that sport.

His falconry was done mainly in Lincolnshire, Norfolk and Cambridgeshire with his friend T.J. Mann, and later at Avebury near Marlborough with a circle of hawking friends. He also flew his hawks on Islay with Gilbert Blaine, whose home in Caithness I once visited to discover it was filled with Lodge's paintings. Grouse were then the quarry and ideal game for the peregrine; the gyr falcon, as he tells us, is wasted on grouse and needs to be flown at larger game such as blackcock, geese or pheasants. In contrast, the merlin, for which Lodge had a special affection, is seen to perfection when after skylarks on Salisbury Plain.

Scanning the pages of his book we realise how far afield Lodge's travels took him and how diverse were his interests as a naturalist. In 1881, 1882 and 1883 he was in Sweden where he studied the flight of the European kite, for which he had a high admiration, and made acquaintance with the black woodpecker, a fine portrait of which, painted by Lodge at the time, hangs in the hall of my home. It is reproduced in our book volume IV plate 13, where the colour of the background is at fault; it should have been blue. The year 1896 found him touring the West Indies and examining a pelican roosting place in Granada. In 1899 he joined his friend Johnny Millais on a shooting and fishing trip to Norway, when Lodge went after ptarmigan and willow grouse and Millais went after elk. There were no houses or people within miles and the wildness of that mountainous country appealed to him greatly. He met many interesting birds in the vast pine forests, and one, the hawk-owl, intrigued him greatly with its inquisitive and confiding nature. It was possible to walk right up to them and Lodge sketched them at his leisure. Further trips to Norway followed in 1900, 1901, 1902, 1904 and 1916.

In 1903 he went round the world with two of his old friends, John and Percy Mann. They stayed in

27. Ptarmigan on a rock slab

27

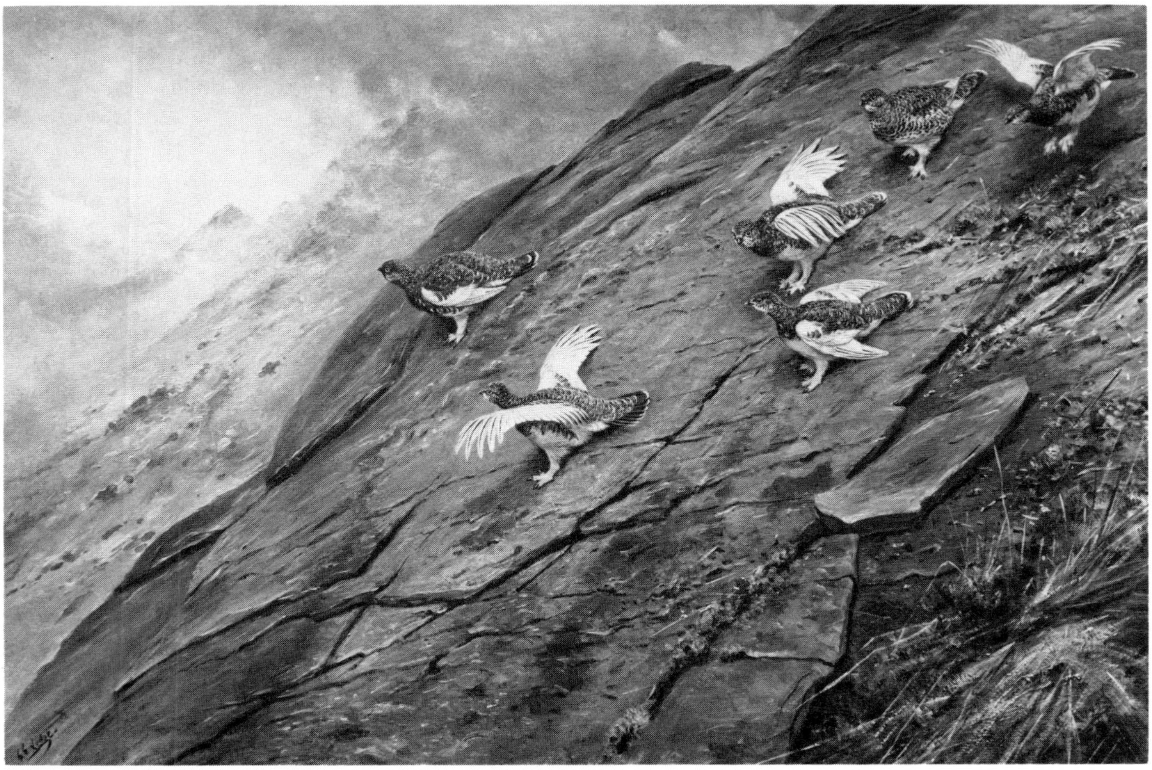

Ceylon, Singapore, Hong Kong and Japan on the way, where he made collections of local butterflies and moths, and returned home through Canada. Did he perhaps also visit India and stay with some rajah? For a plate in *Memoirs of an Artist Naturalist* depicts 'a pair of tigers', the only occasion on which I have seen a Lodge portrait of big game. There is no allusion to this picture in the text or explanation as to why it was included. In 1907-8 he was in America, and while there spent three days with Frank Chapman of the American Museum of Natural History as guests of the owner of Gardiner's Island (north of Long Island), where there was the largest breeding colony of ospreys in the world. There they encountered a vast congregation of 'crows' settling on the fields before going to roost, whose numbers were estimated by Chapman at about 100,000. Elsewhere on the same trip Lodge also spent several days observing bald eagles. Most of the dates and places mentioned here are culled from his book and are unlikely to exhaust his travels. Wherever he went he carried his sketch book, even when stalking, and when shooting grouse on Scottish or Pennine moors he made sketches of the scenery from every butt he occupied.

Visitors to Camberley will soon have realised Lodge's skill as a taxidermist, and though in his final chapter entitled 'Some observations on painting birds' he deprecates drawing from 'stuffed' examples, it would have been possible to paint from his beautifully mounted specimens of falcons and other birds of prey as if they had been alive. A sound knowledge of avian anatomy and pterylosis (feather arrangement) he considered essential before attempting to place birds on canvas.

The amount of knowledge he acquired from close observation fills every page of his book, but it is not an easy book to read and the lack of any index, admittedly almost an impossible task, does not help, for once a statement has been read it is difficult to find again! It was with such a background to his life that at the age of 82 he settled down in his studio to paint every British bird, a tremendous feat which he accomplished years before I had completed the text

28

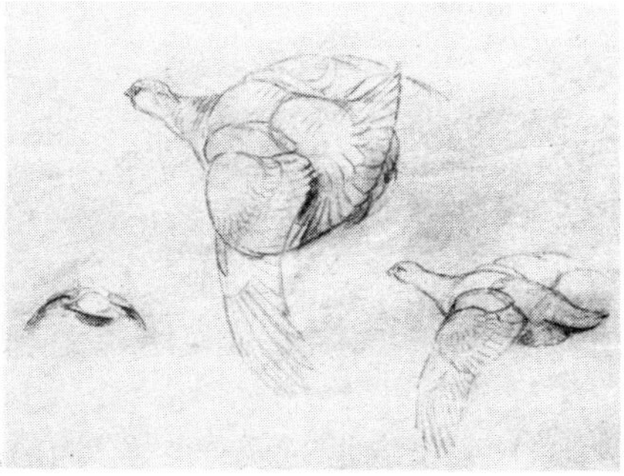

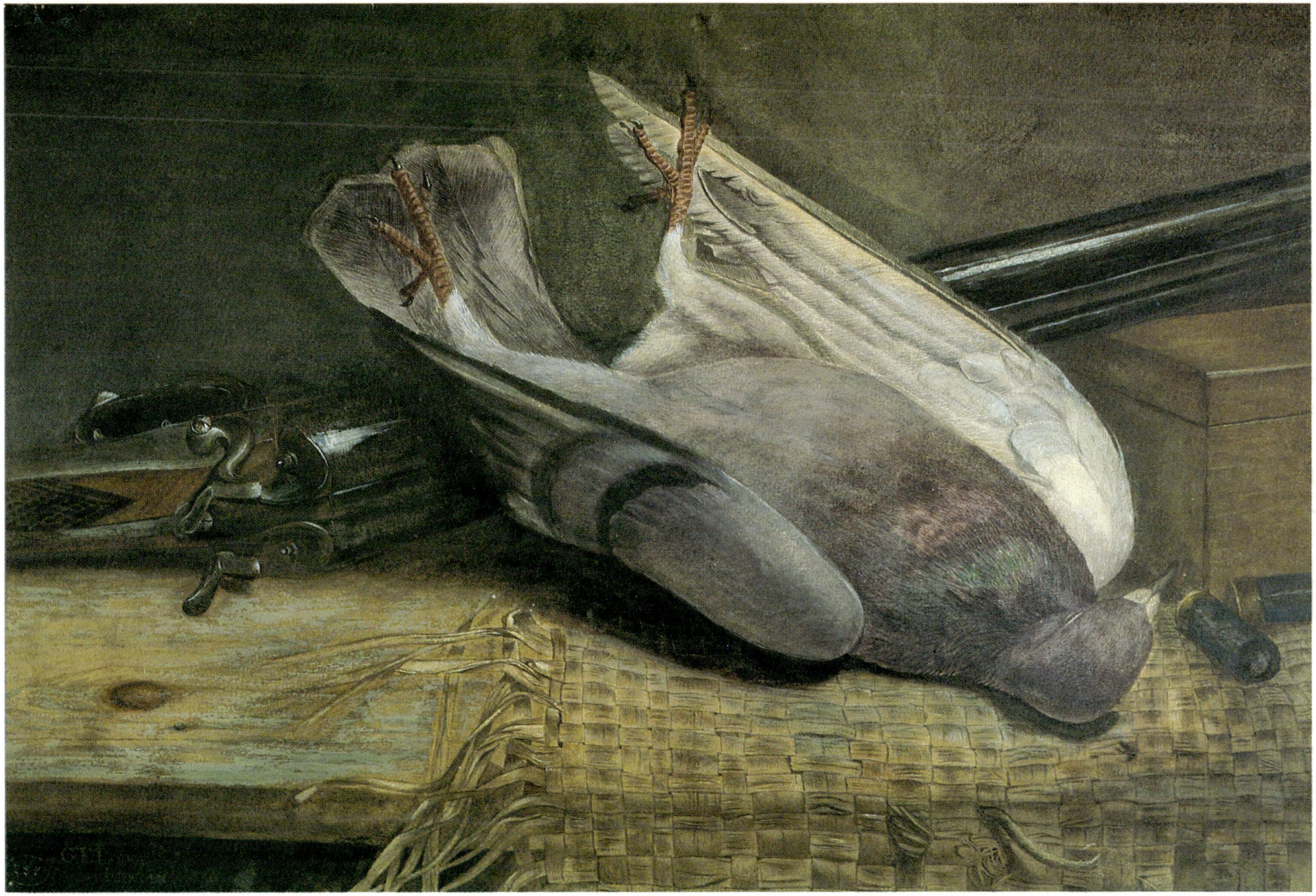

1 Still life, signed 'G.E. Lodge Lincoln', probably painted while at Lincoln School of Art, aged 14 to 16.

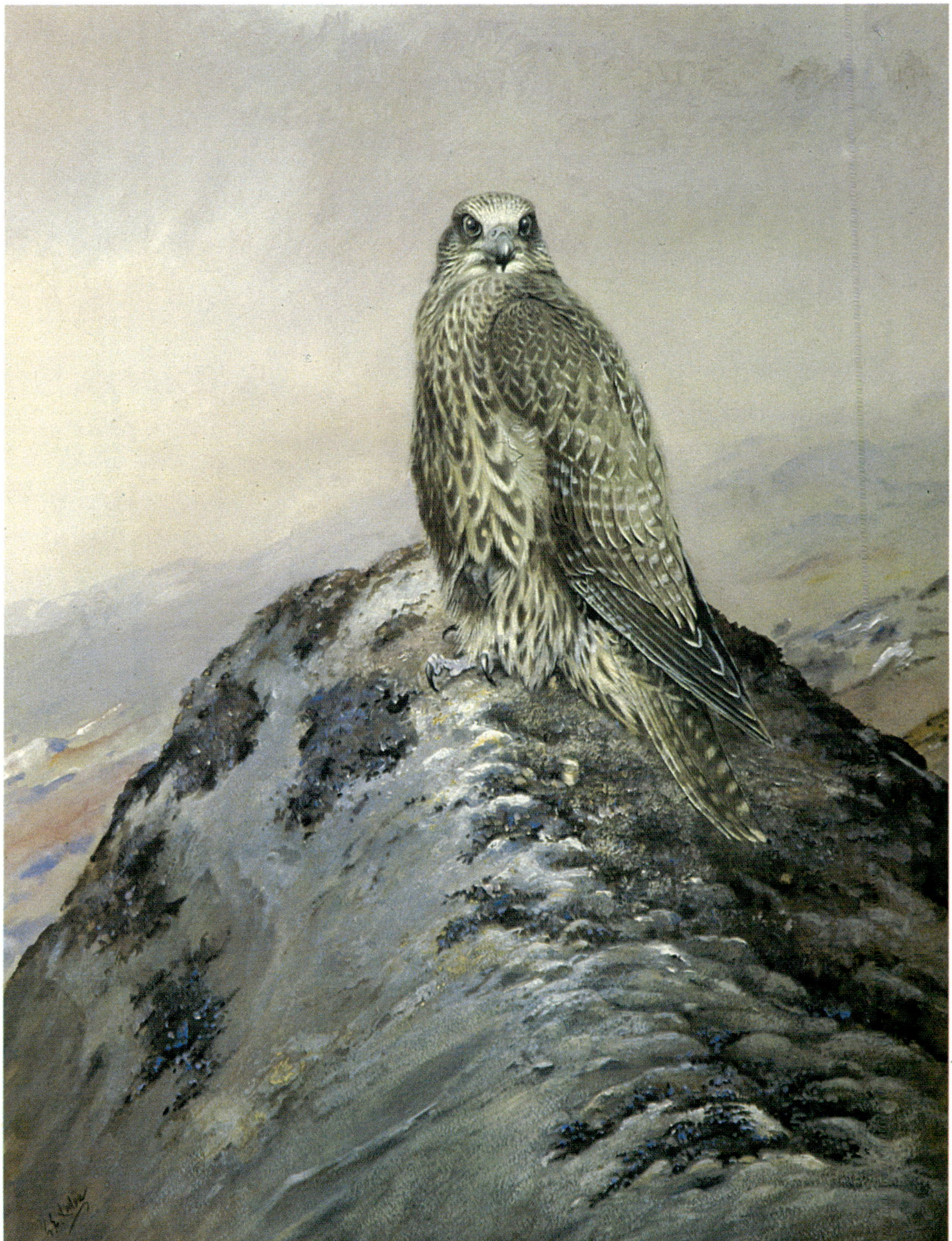

2 *Immature Iceland gyr falcon*

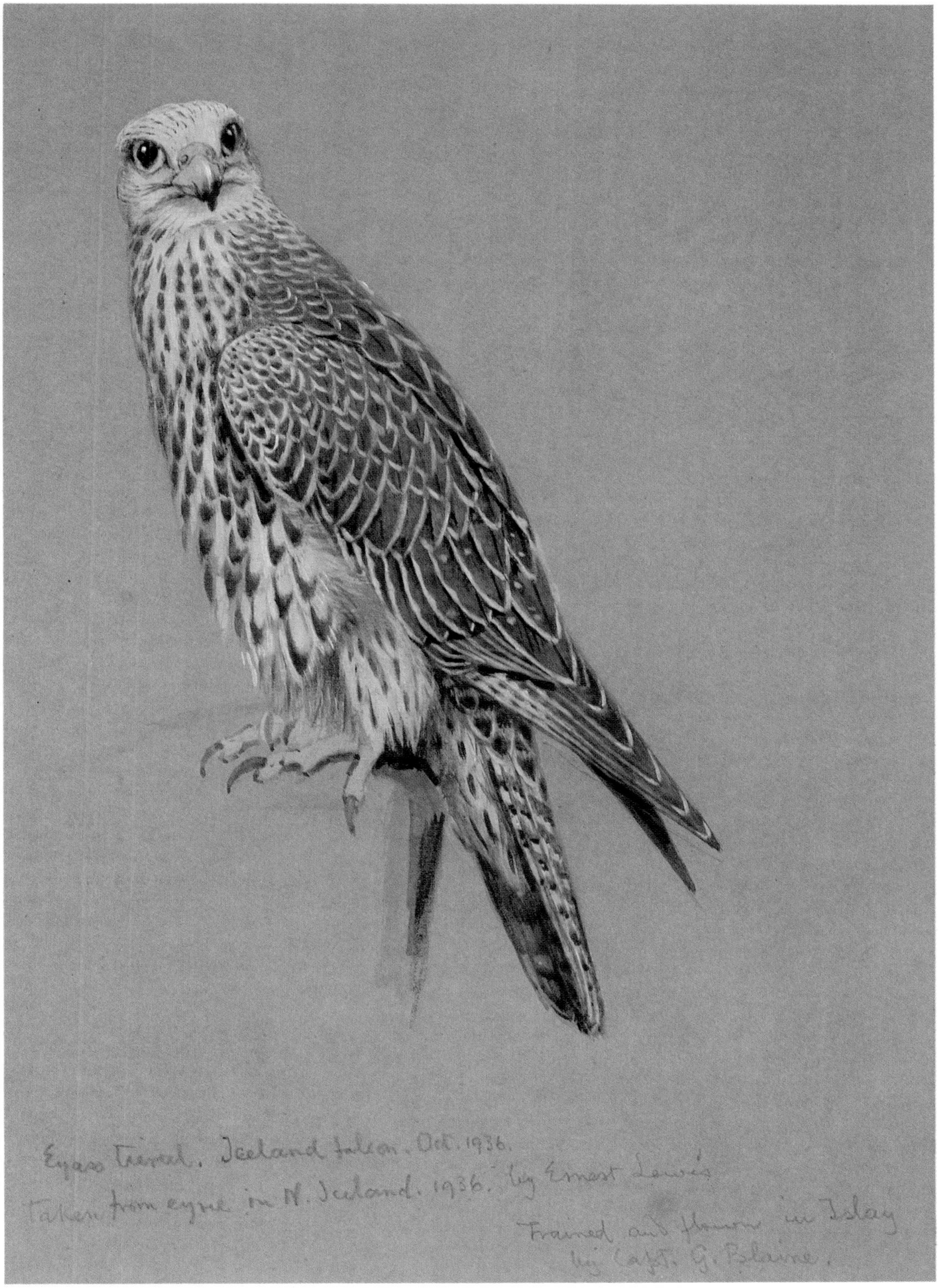

3 Eyass tiercel Iceland gyr falcon flown at grouse by Gilbert Blaine

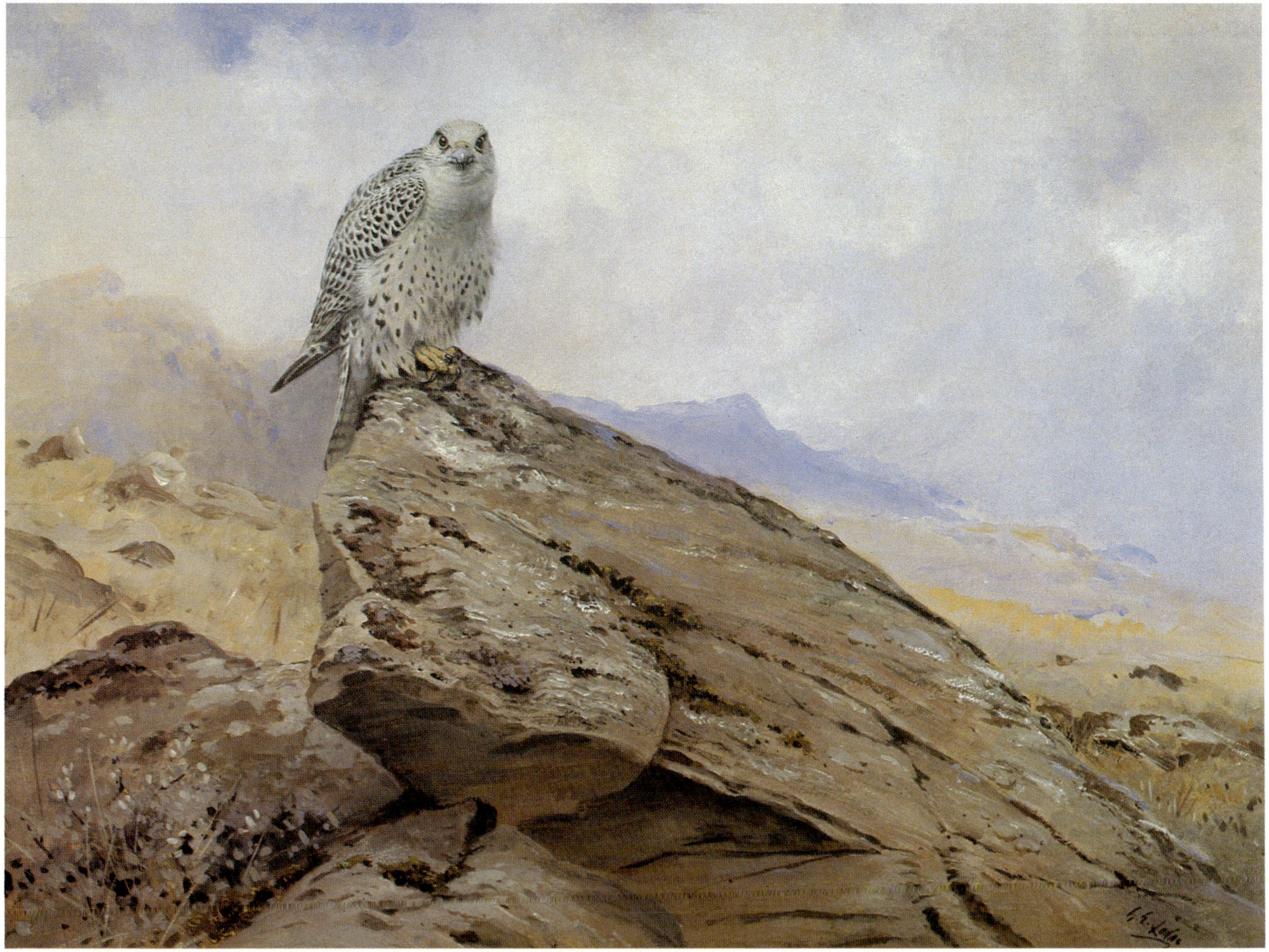

4 Adult Iceland gyr falcon

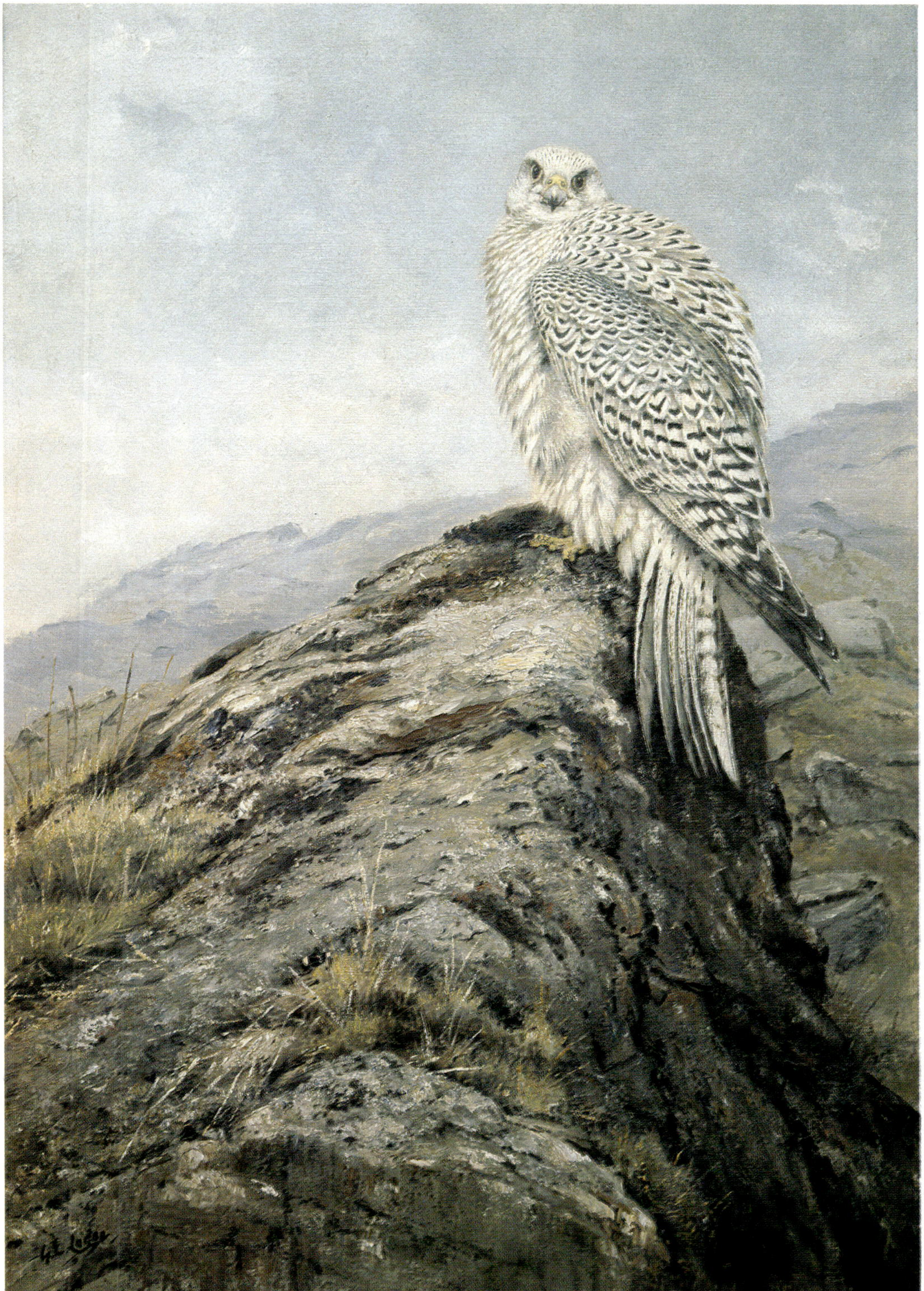

5 *Adult Greenland gyr falcon*

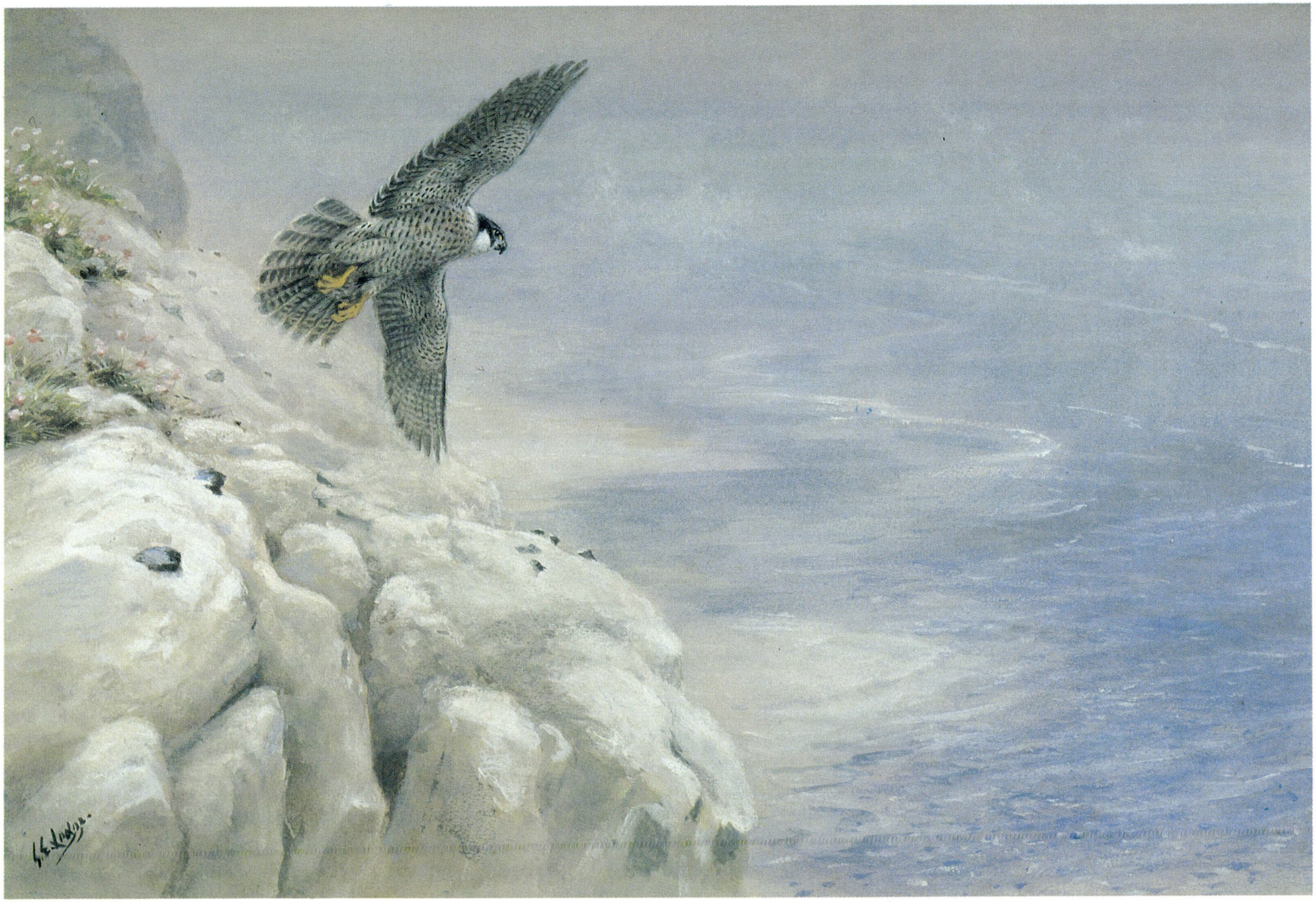

6 Peregrine falcon on the Sussex coast

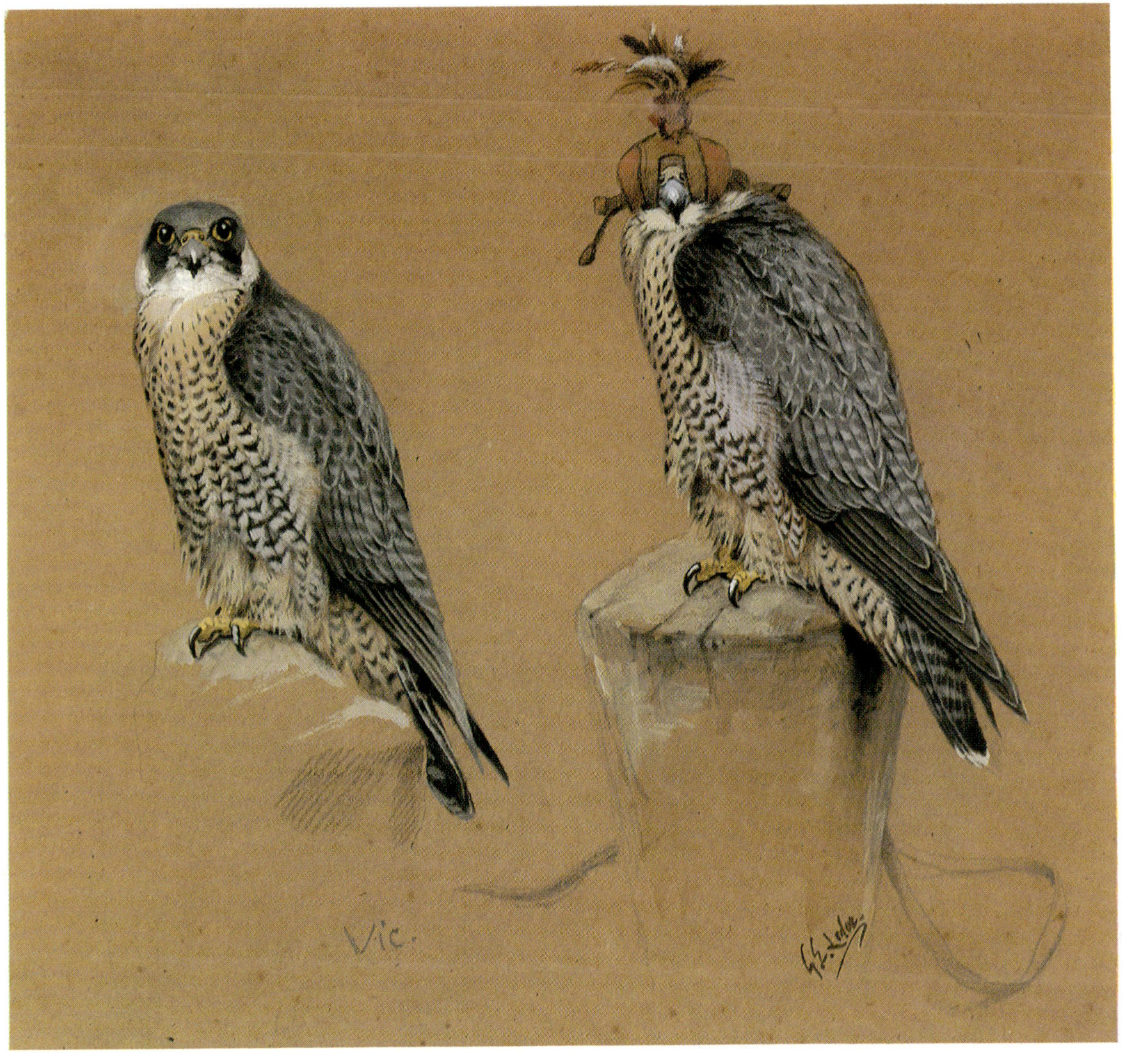

7 'Vic', a peregrine falcon belonging to Thomas Mann *(see p. 66)*

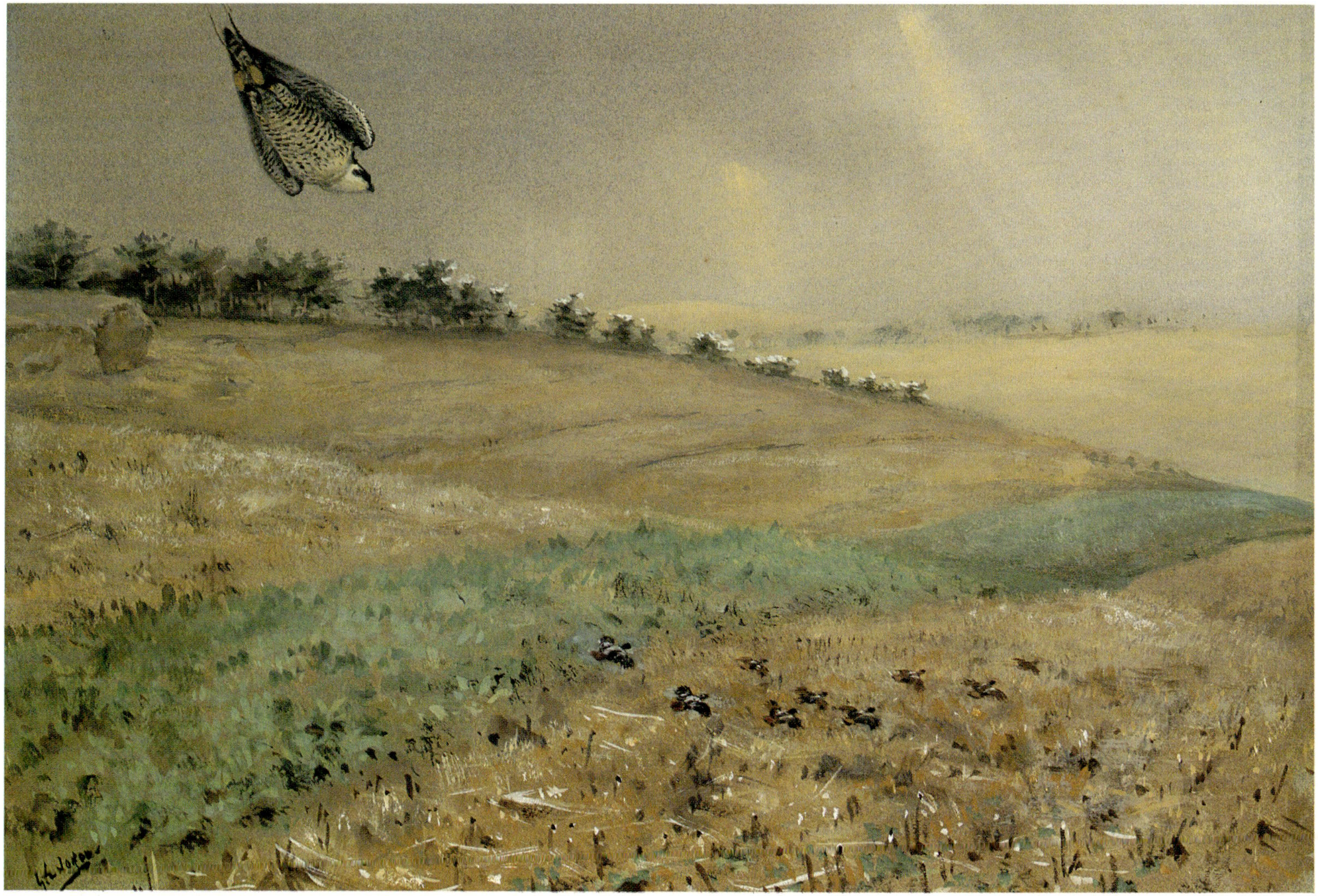

8 The stoop — partridge hawking with a peregrine

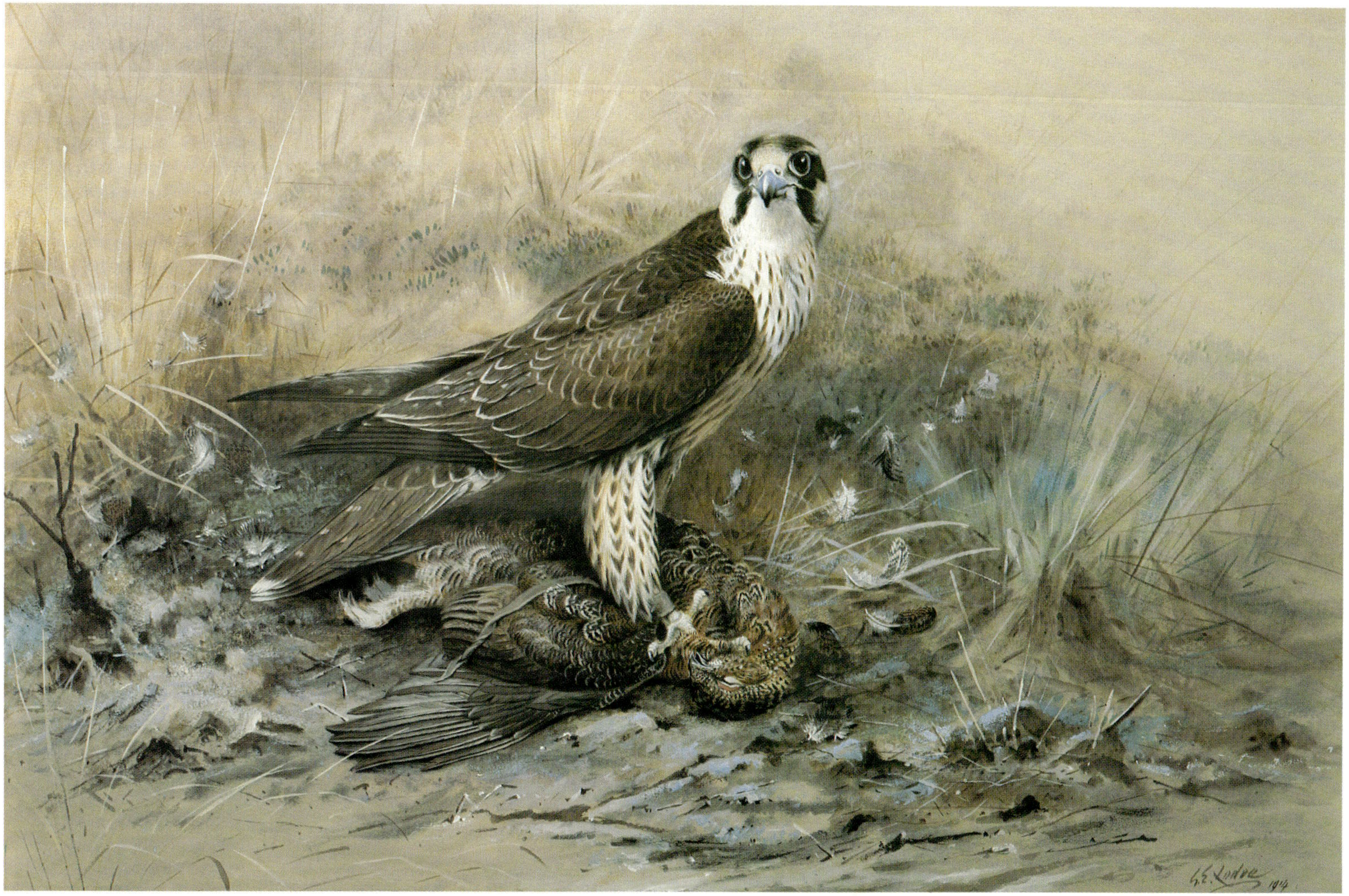

9 *The kill — 'Sylvia', an eyass peregrine falcon from Lundy, belonging to Gilbert Blaine, that scored 90 grouse and 3 sundries out of 96 flights in 1913* (see p. 67)

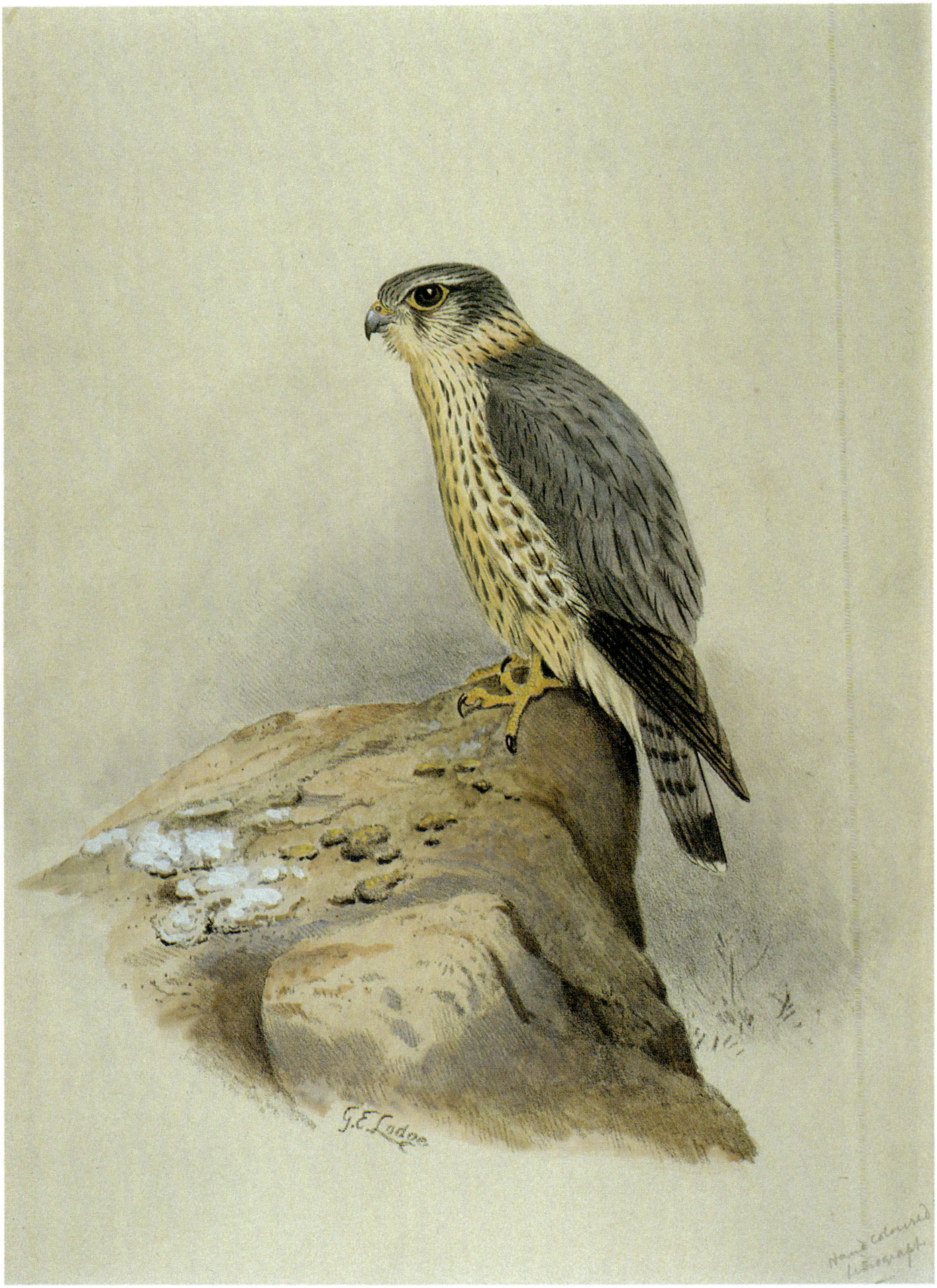

10 Male merlin (the jack), hand-coloured lithograph

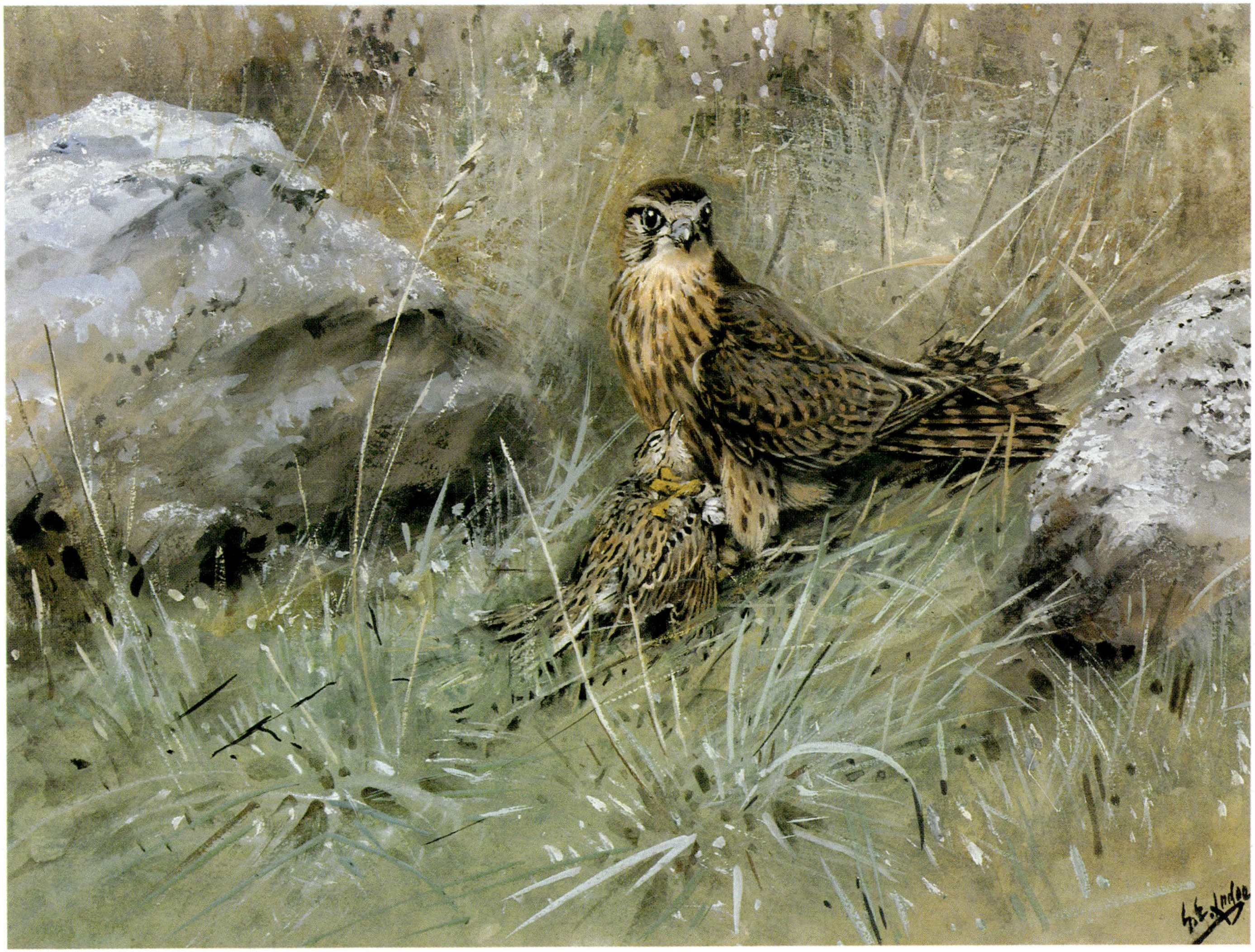

11 *Female merlin with a skylark*

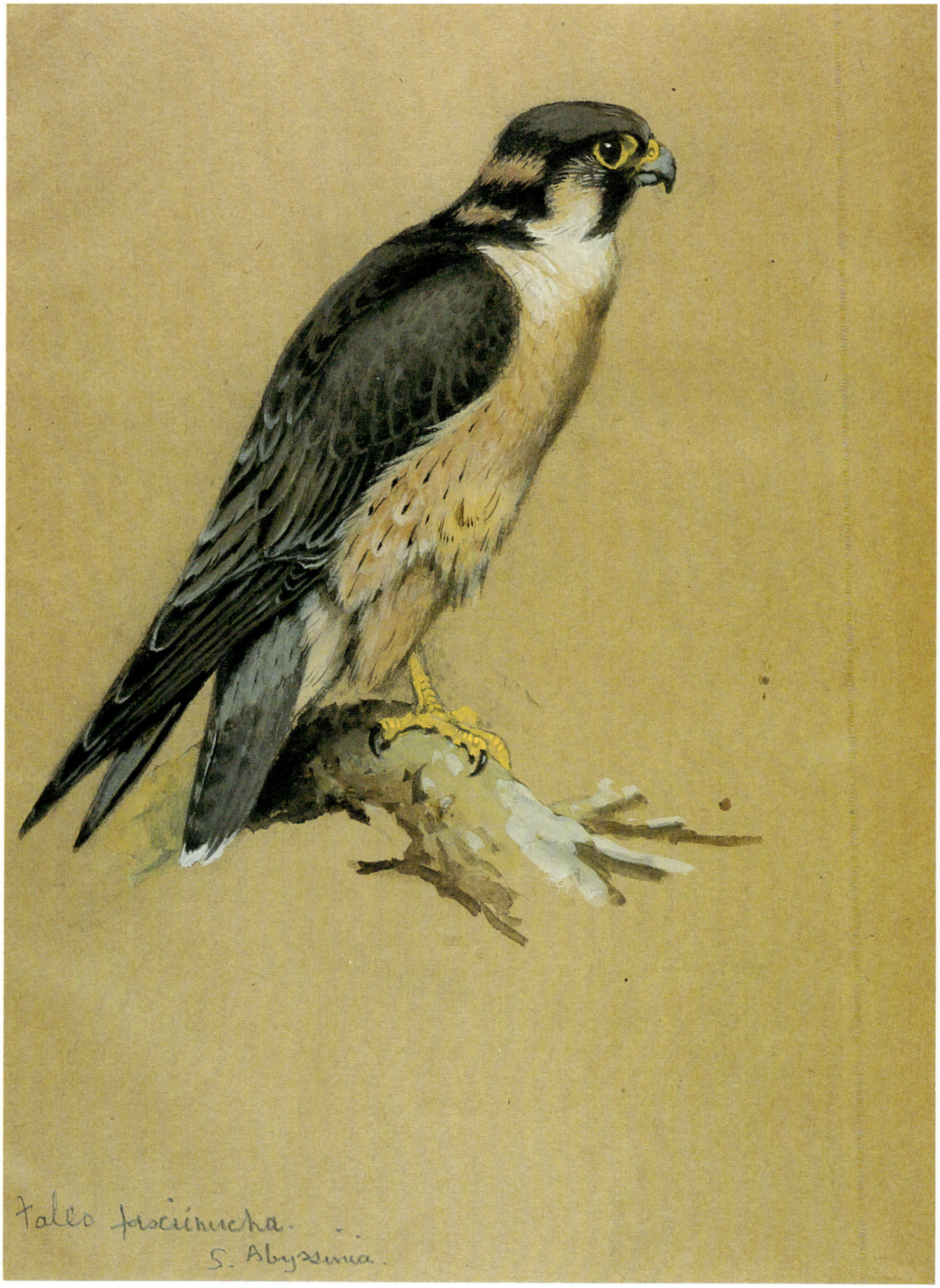

12 *Taita falcon*

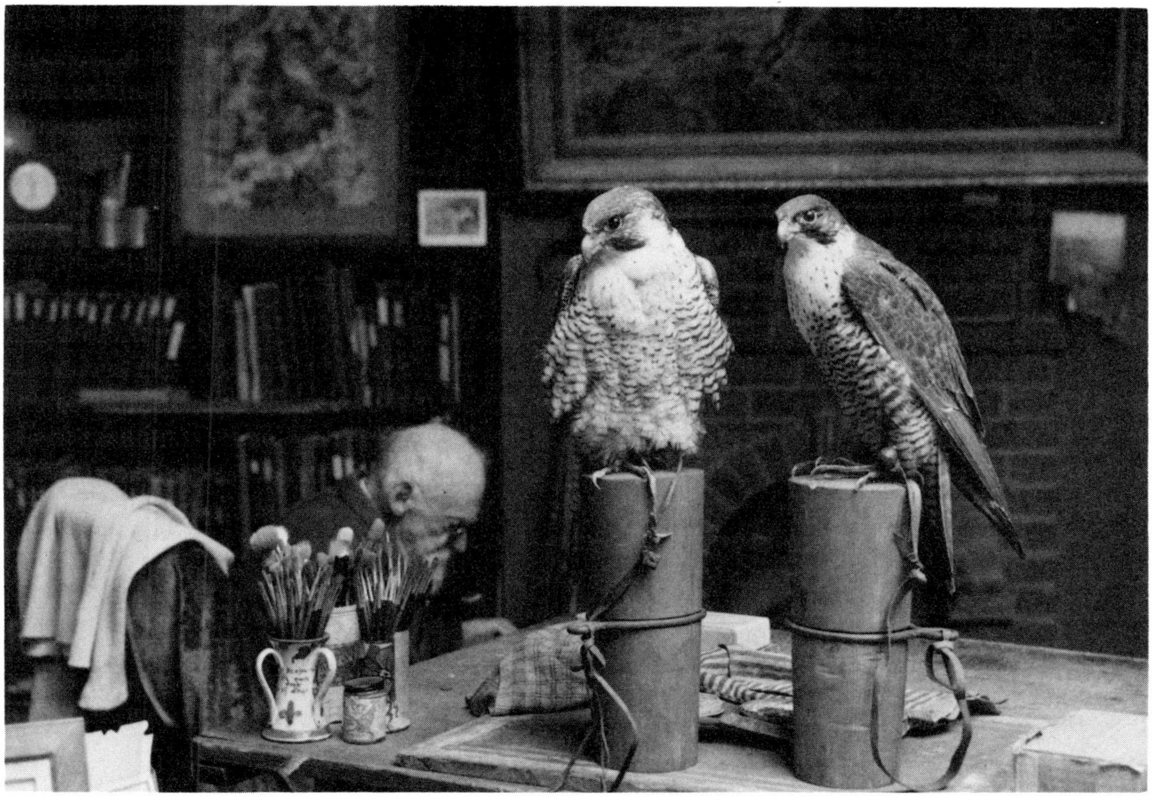

29

of what finally ran to 12 volumes. He gave me full permission to make use of any picture already in his studio and many which I selected from his folios had been painted in earlier years, thus reducing the number still required.

As this is probably the last occasion I shall write of my old friend, I cannot refrain from once more drawing attention to the letter he wrote to our publishers long after they had received what they thought were all the illustrations required for reproduction in our book. In it Lodge asked permission to include five additional paintings, which he had not even begun, to illustrate the immature plumages of the peregrine, goshawk and three other falcons whose portraits he had already depicted in adult dress. Our publishers were very perturbed by his request for they knew he had practically lost the sight of one eye. Tentative permission was given by Douglas Grant, then

28. Red grouse in flight
29. Mounted peregrines in Lodge's studio

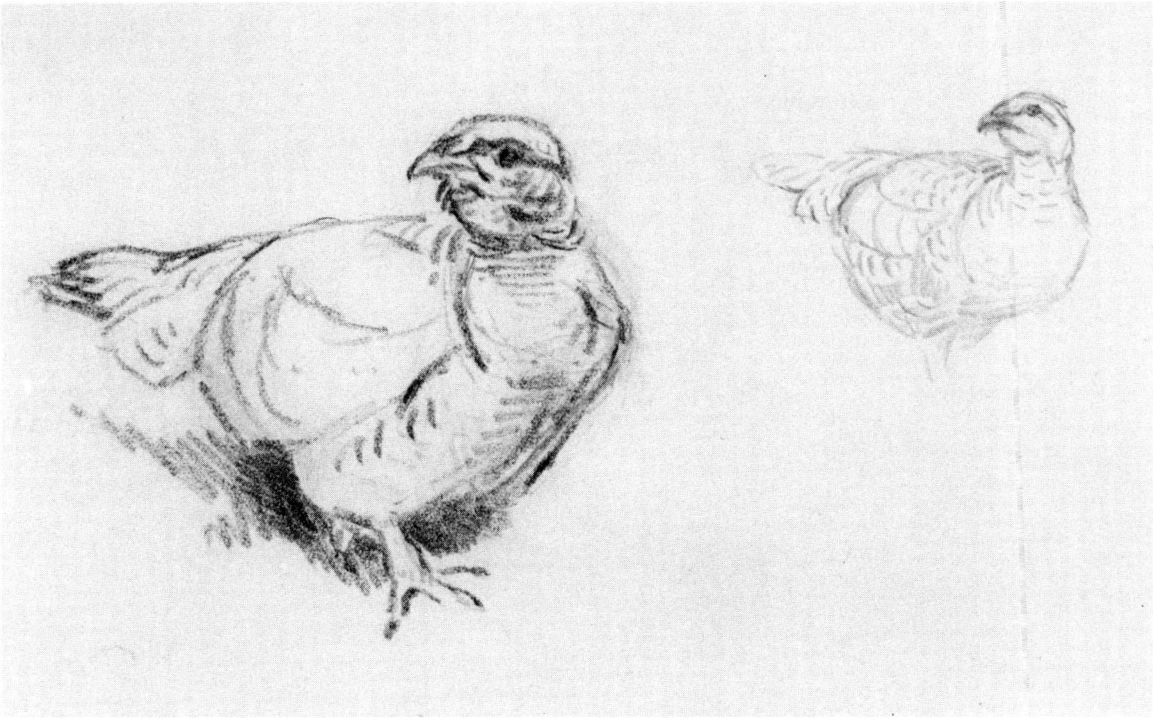

30

Managing Director of Oliver and Boyd, subject to approval of the paintings. They were all remarkable in execution and appear in volume V as plates 3, 5, 7, 9 and 26. They were handed over in Lodge's 92nd year and all are reproduced for the world to judge. When checking the 384 pictures which George Lodge and I had chosen to illustrate every British bird, I noticed shortly after my partner's death that there was one important picture missing: a ptarmigan in its white winter plumage, an *essential* to complete our book. He had already painted the bird (plate 24 in volume XII) in its summer garb and surroundings with a peregrine overhead, but had overlooked the equally important winter dress. An advertisement which I inserted in *The Scotsman*, appealing to anyone who had such a picture in his possession painted by Lodge to get in touch with me, brought several responses; one from Sir John Stirling K.T., a member of my own Club (the New Club) in Edinburgh. His picture had been painted while Lodge had been his guest at Muir of Ord, when

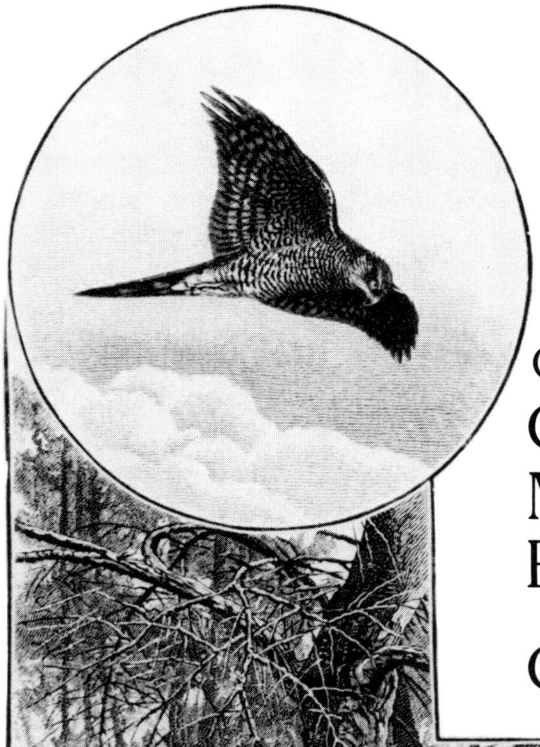

CHAPTER 2

CHANGING METHODS OF BOOK ILLUSTRATION

Christine Jackson

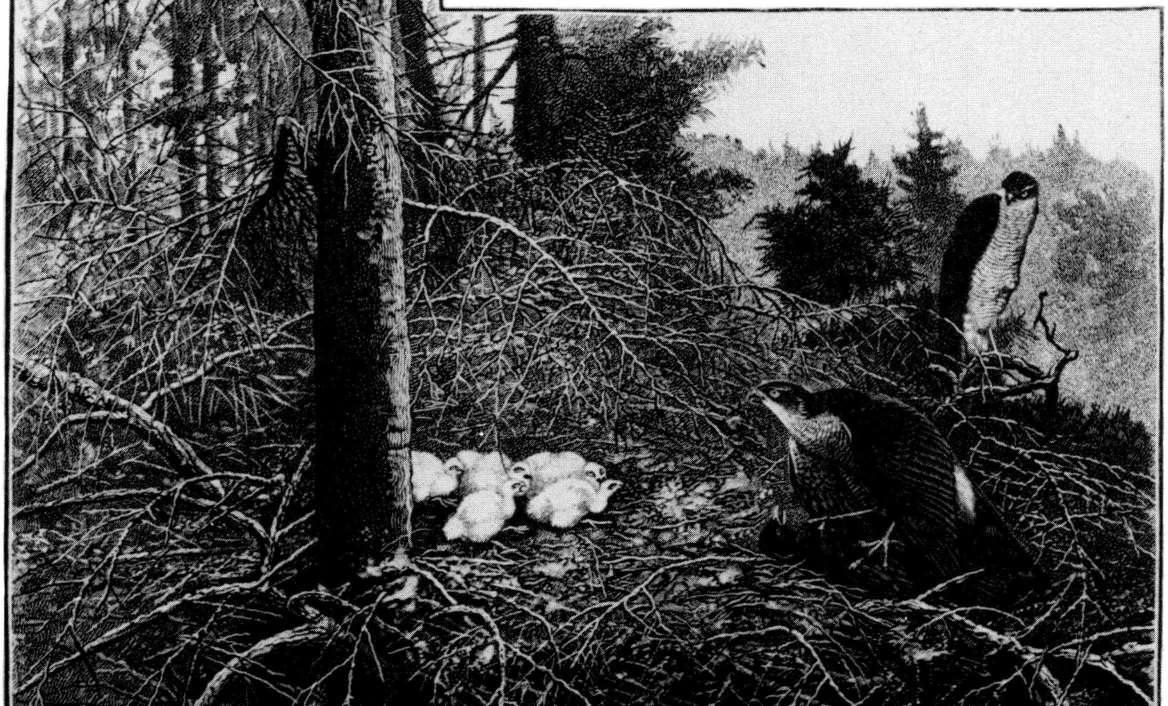

32

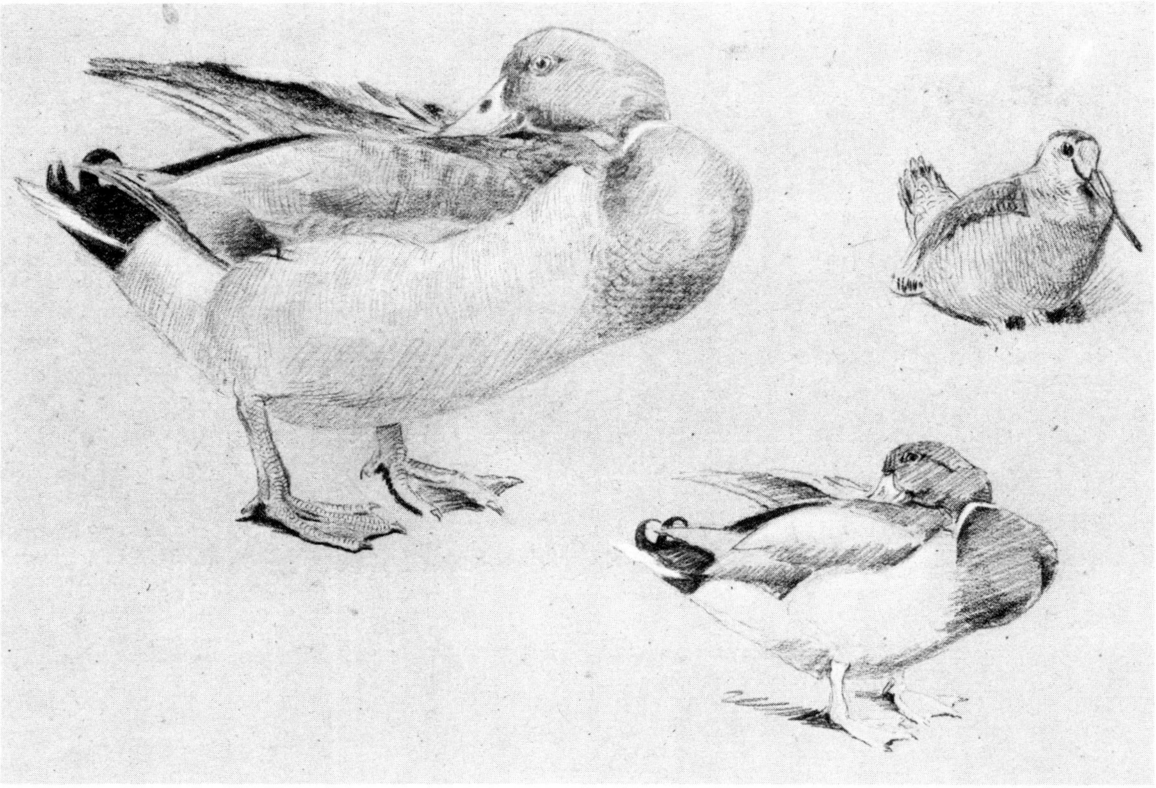

33

George Lodge's life spanned nearly a century whose dates coincided with a period of rapid and radical change in the processes used to translate artists' drawings into printed book illustrations. During this time, the work done by intermediary craftsmen on metal, wood and stone gave place to the use of film to copy the drawings and transfer them directly onto the printing plate.

Lodge was trained as an artist and wood-engraver, and some of his engraved bird figures were among his most sensitive and satisfactory illustrations. He had full control over them, from the original design, through the drawing and then engraving on wood, to finalising of the block for the printer. But times were changing, and other methods were being tried in an effort to speed up, and so reduce the cost of, production of illustrated books. Apart from his wood-engravings, a few of Lodge's paintings were reproduced by the old hand processes of lithography and chromolithography, but most of them were reproduced by the photomechanical processes of half-tone, photogravure, collotype, photolithography, etc. Lodge was not entirely happy with these new methods, for he disliked the reduction in size which their smaller formats involved. He would have preferred to have worked within the framework of the old-style folio books in which many of the birds were drawn life-size, but he was born too late, for the era of large folio works was already passing while he was a student.

In the 1870s wood-engraving was still the commonest method of illustrating books, from the cheapest to the more expensive, so it was natural that Lodge, at the age of 16, should be apprenticed to a wood-engraver. Engraving on wood was a very skilled job and took several years to learn. Special cutting tools, called gravers or burins, were used to score grooves in blocks cut from slow-growing timber, such as box or maple, which had been dried for many years. Cutting the white lines of the design on the end grain of hardwood had been brought to a fine art by Thomas Bewick (1753-1828), and all wood-engravers, particularly those whose subject

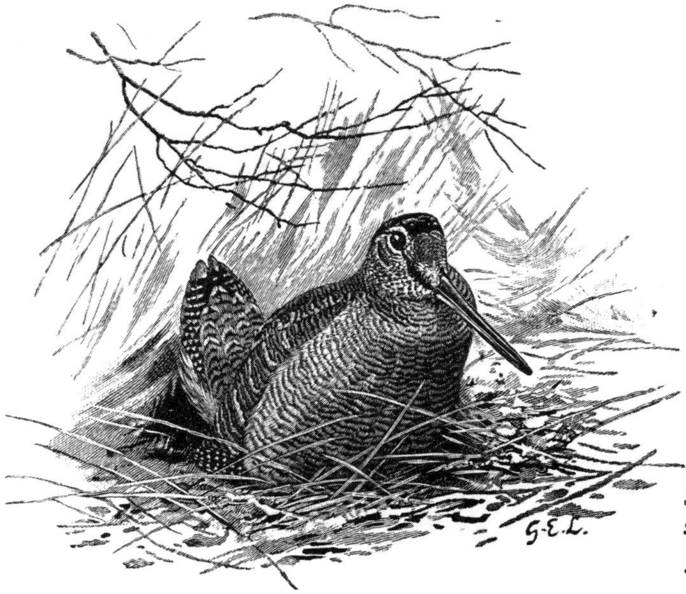

34

32. Sparrow-hawks at the nest
33. Mallard drake and woodcock sketches
34. Woodcock ready to rise

35. An original boxwood block of a peregrine, drawn and engraved by Lodge. It is composed of seven pieces joined together (some junction lines are just visible) and measures 13 × 19 cm. The white parts have been cut away with burins and the black parts coated with printing ink. This block was given by Lodge to the artist George Henry, and, judging from the unstained appearance of the white parts, it is likely that it was never used

was birds, had a high standard of artistic as well as mechanical skill to attain. Lodge acquired great skill, and though his birds always seem softer than the crisp outlines of Bewick, they show a deep understanding of the character of the subject as well as technical facility in recording this through the medium of the wood.

The first publications for which Lodge supplied figures were all illustrated with wood-engravings. For example, he both drew and engraved several for H. Seebohm's *The Geographical Distribution of the Family Charadriidae* (published in 1887 with 265 engravings), and also engraved others in the same book that had been designed by J.G. Millais. In these his initials appeared together with those of the artist, whereas his own designs were sometimes signed merely 'G.E.L.' and sometimes 'G.E. Lodge del. et sc.', indicating that he had both drawn (delineavit) and engraved (sculpsit) those blocks. In 1888 nine of his engravings were distributed through the text of J.C. Mansel-Pleydell's *The Birds of Dorsetshire*, but the most interesting feature of this book was the frontispiece. It was reproduced from a photograph by the then very new process of half-tone and was a foretaste of changes to come. The decade concluded with the publication of Howard Saunders' *Illustrated Manual of British Birds* (1889), which included some very good engravings by Lodge, and more by him were added later in the second edition (1899). Since preparation of the wood blocks was a slow and laborious business, such books were usually illustrated by several commissioned artists. A few, however, like Lord Lilford's *Notes on the Birds of Northamptonshire* (1895) and A.H. Evans' *Birds* (1899) contained large numbers of engravings which were all or nearly all by Lodge. The first of these two books also included photogravure plates by Archibald Thorburn, an early example of another new process.

From the 1890s onwards, Lodge was in great demand as artist and engraver of wood-engravings used as small text figures. However, in bird monographs these were gradually becoming used more as adjuncts to the main illustrations, which

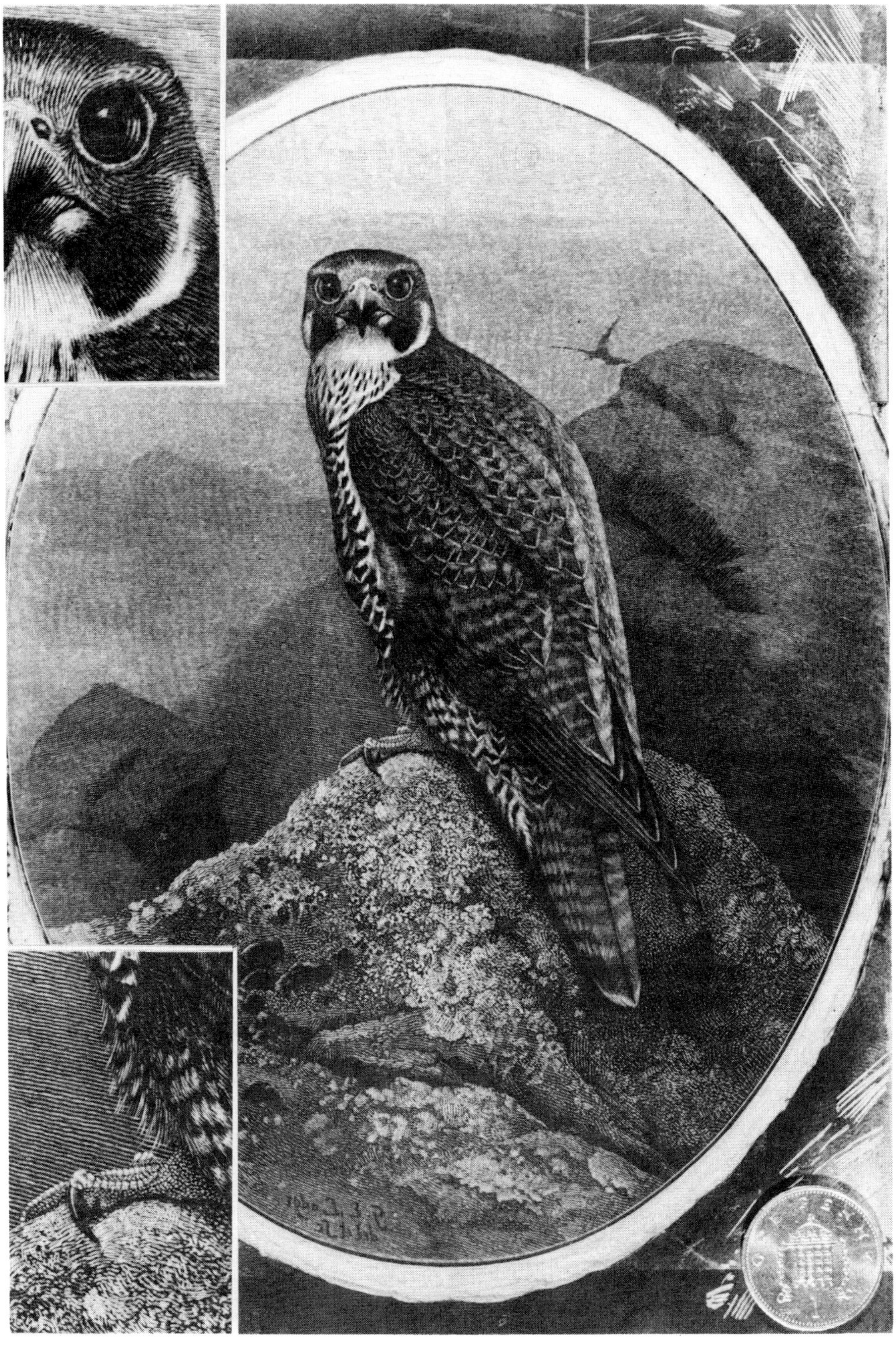

35

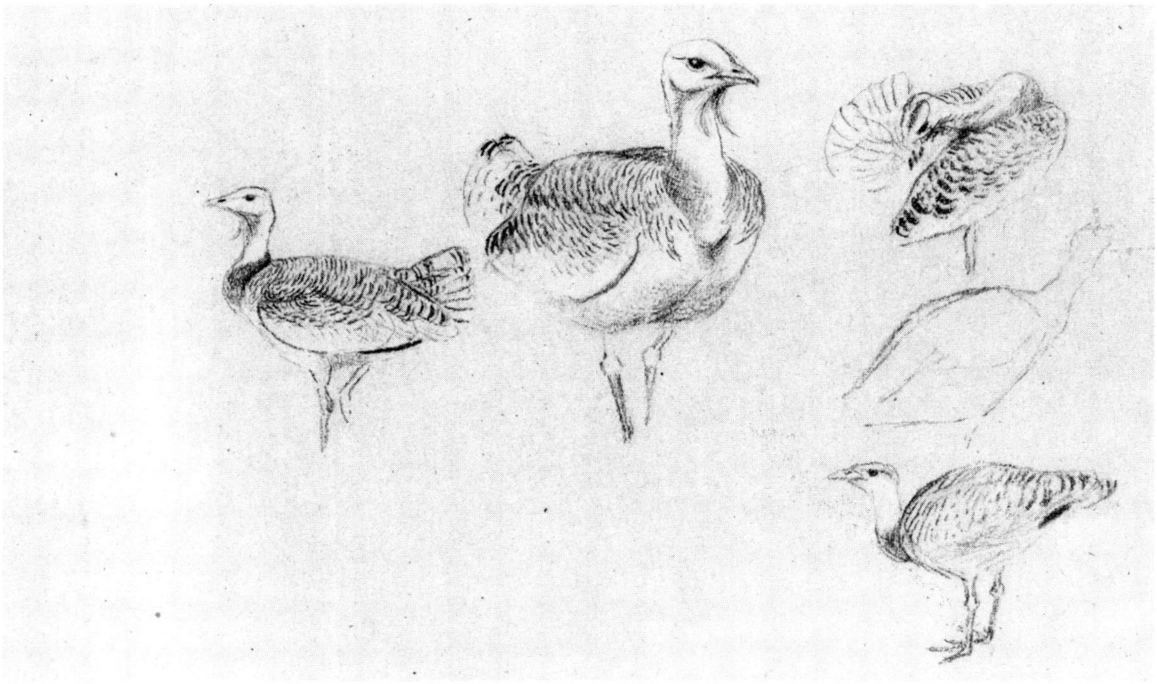

36

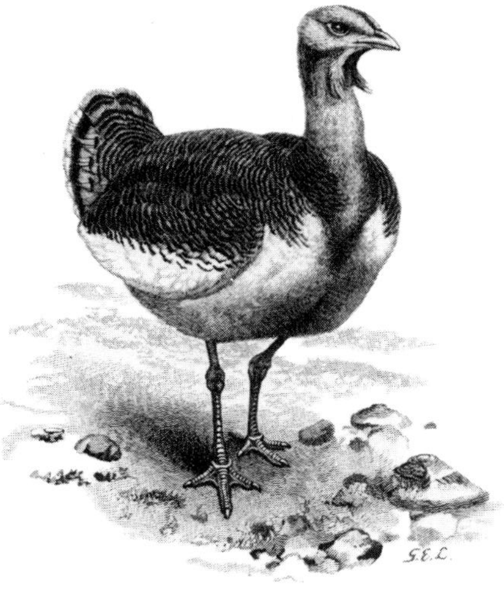

36. *Great bustard sketches and engraving*

37. *Pallas's sandgrouse, from a dead specimen found under a telegraph wire at Burnham Deepdale in October 1888*

were full-page monochrome or colour plates produced by photographic means. The method of printing the wood-engravings also changed, with increasing use of electrotyping. This technique had been invented in the 1840s but was not used extensively for many years, and it was not until the present century that it superseded printing directly from the wooden block. Electrotyping is achieved by making a beeswax mould from the engraved block, and then blackleading it to give it a metallic face and so increase its electrical conductivity. The mould is connected to a negative terminal and placed in a bath of copper sulphate solution, and pieces of pure copper connected to a positive terminal are also immersed in the bath. When an electric current is passed through the solution a thin layer of copper is deposited on the mould, and this forms the printing surface of the finished electrotype. This wax method is still used for fine grade work on wood-engravings today, though PVC is substituted for electrotypes of a cheaper quality. Electros have the advantages that there is virtually no limit to the number of copies that can be printed from them when they have been face-hardened, and they can be used with modern high-speed rotary presses.

In the same manner that wood blocks were replaced by electros to facilitate speed in printing, so the other hand processes of producing illustrations were replaced by photographic methods. All the photographic processes are based on the principle of certain chemicals being hardened by light. A transparency of the subject (which may be positive or negative, depending on the printing process) is exposed to light over a plate covered with chemicals sensitive to light. Where light passes through clear parts of the transparency the sensitive emulsion is hardened, and where it cannot pass through dark, opaque areas the emulsion remains soft and soluble and is then washed away. This leaves a hardened outline representing the image of the original subject on the surface of the plate. This method of transferring the image onto the printing surface is called 'printing down'.

The photographic process which replaced wood-engraving was called zincography since zinc was used as the printing surface. The method of producing the zinc plate, or line block, is to etch the metal after the design has been printed down photographically. This is achieved by photographing the drawing to obtain a negative. The negative is placed over a sheet of zinc coated with sensitive albumen and exposed to light. The light hardens the albumen corresponding with the lines of the image, and after washing away the soft albumen the plate is inked over. Ink adhering to the hardened albumen is dusted with powdered bitumen, and the plate

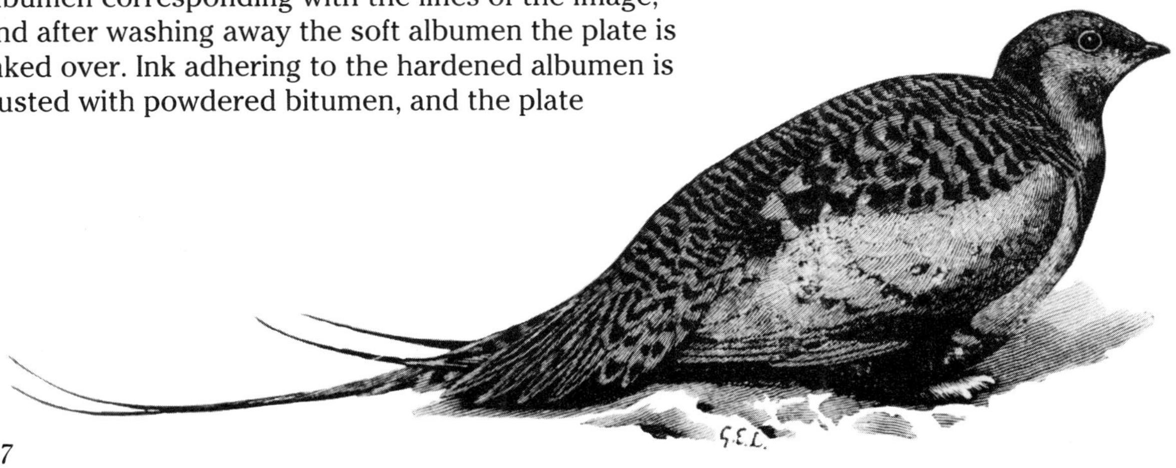

37

heated to burn it sufficiently to form an enamel-like coating. The plate is then immersed in acid which eats away metal not protected by the bitumen, so leaving the design standing in relief. The plate is mounted to the same height as the type and both can be printed together.

Zincography is an excellent method for reproducing line work, such as engravings, but suffers from the same drawback as wood-engraving in that its ability to portray tone is limited. This requirement was eventually met by using small dots of variable size which, while not being readily detected by the human eye, could create the impression of light grey through to dark tones. The picture is built up of an infinity of dots, some smaller and appearing more widely spaced in light areas and larger dots appearing more closely packed in dark areas. This process is called half-tone and was patented by Georg Meisenbach in 1882 and introduced into England in 1884. The frontispiece in J.C. Mansel-Pleydell's *The Birds of Dorsetshire* (1888) had 'MEISENBACH' printed in the lower right-hand corner. This early example of the use of half-tone must have intrigued Lodge, who provided wood-engravings for this book. Did he recognise, in this single plate, a process that would be used increasingly to reproduce his own work? Among the early titles which included half-tone illustrations from Lodge's drawings were Cox and Lascelles' *Coursing and Falconry* (1892), W.H. Hudson's *British Birds* (1895) and F.G. Aflalo's *Vertebrates* (1898).

38. White-fronted goose
39. Razorbills fighting, an example of a photogravure plate

The important feature of half-tone is the use of a glass screen, finely cross-ruled with lines, which is interposed between the lens of the camera and the unexposed film. This breaks up the negative into the fine dots which become hardened emulsion when printed down. When the plate is inked and printed, the dots reproduce the tonal quality of the original design. This breakthrough in the reproduction of tone opened the way to further processes being developed which also used the basic screen to reproduce tone, and also for colour printing.

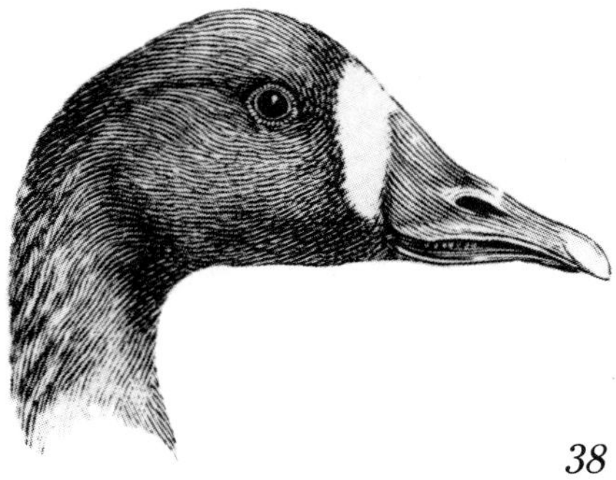
38

In the mid-1890s Karl Klič of Arnau produced successful prints from his process of photogravure

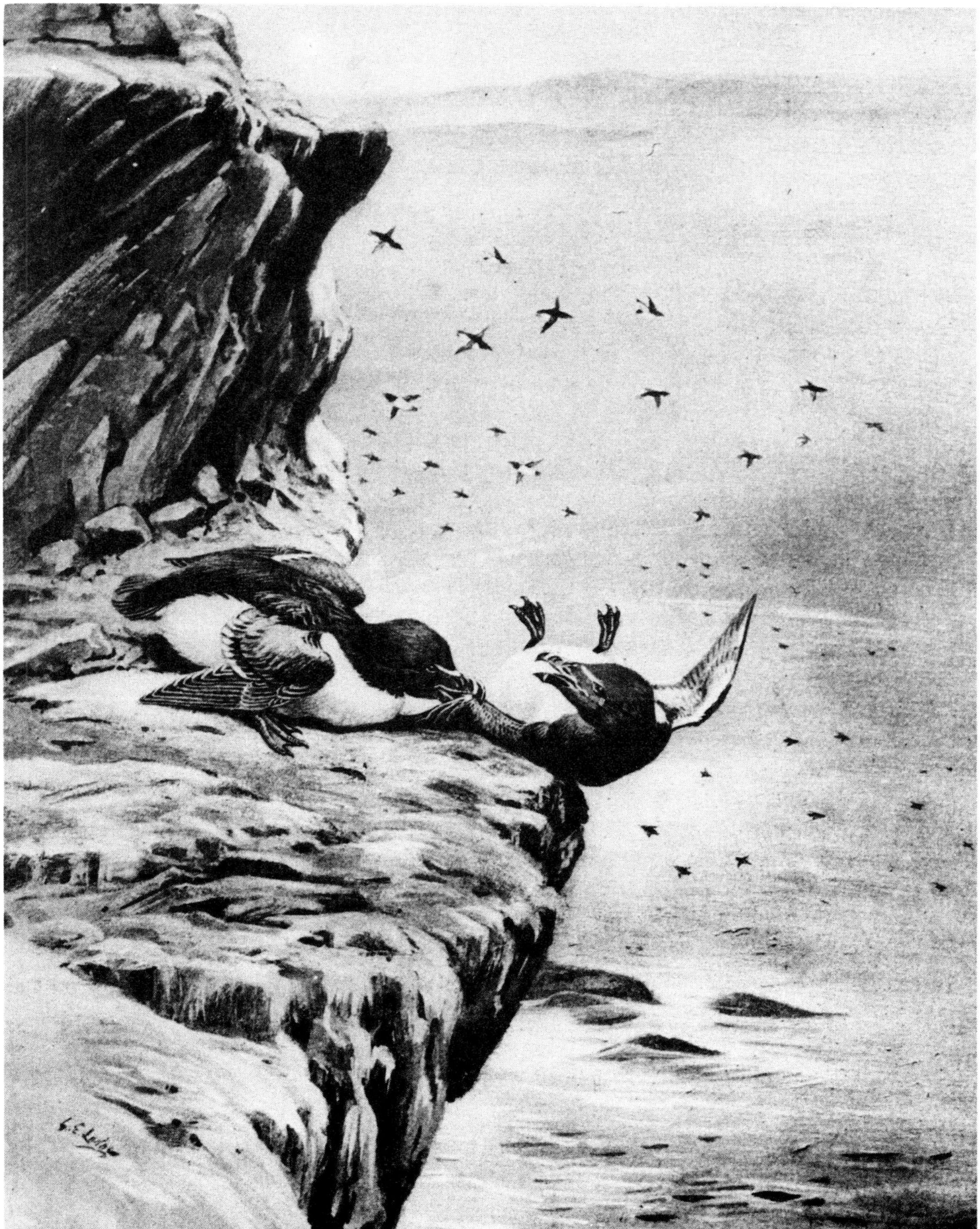

39

which he had been developing since about 1879. This was the application of photography to the intaglio methods of aquatint or mezzotint, and it was later adapted to colour printing. The process was not used much in Britain until after 1912. Klič exposed a transparent positive onto a sensitised gelatine-coated 'carbon tissue', which was then rolled onto the granular surface of a copper plate pre-ground with powdered bitumen. The thin tissue backing was washed off with hot water, and this also removed the gelatine from those parts not hardened by light. The result was that in the lightest areas the gelatine was thick and hard, with gradations down to a thin layer of soft gelatine where parts were required to print dark. When the plate was etched in ferric acid, the thicker layers of gelatine protected the copper from the acid for a longer time than did thinner layers, with a fine gradient between the two extremes. The resulting pits of varying depth in the copper plate retained printing ink in corresponding quantities, and so controlled the amount of ink transferred to the page during printing. Shallow pits transferred less ink than deep pits, producing a tonal print with barely discernible grain and no screen lines. Nowadays, a finely ruled opaque screen is used instead of bitumen texturing on the copper, but otherwise the process is the same.

Lodge's drawing of 'British wood mice' in volume 2 of J.G. Millais' *The Mammals of Great Britain and Ireland*, published in 1905, was reproduced in monochrome by the continental photogravurist Walter L. Colls. By the next time photogravure was used for his drawings a British firm had adopted the process. His monochrome illustrations in three of H.E. Howard's books, *Territory in Bird Life* (1920), *An Introduction to the Study of Bird Behaviour* (1929) and *A Waterhen's World* (1940) were all photoengraved by Emery Walker. Sir Emery Walker (he was knighted in 1930 for his services to the printing trade) was a pioneer process engraver and typographic expert who worked for the Typographic Etching Company from 1873 until 1883, when he left and founded his own firm in 1886. His signature 'Emery Walker ph. sc.' appeared on each plate in these books by Howard, which were illustrated mainly by Lodge. The heavily impressed plate line round the printed area, and the exquisitely etched birds and scenes, are characteristic of the photogravure process used to produce these fine illustrations. The three titles are valuable as examples of the combined work of an unusually perceptive writer, an excellent bird artist and an expert engraver.

Lithography, the medium which had been used in England for coloured plates, many of them folio size, from the 1820s onwards, was employed for fine specialist works for a hundred years. From the 1840s, the work of hand-colouring the lithographed monochrome outlines was sometimes replaced by printing the colours, but chromolithographs, as printed colour lithographs were called, were rarely of the same quality, which is why hand-colouring

40. Black stork

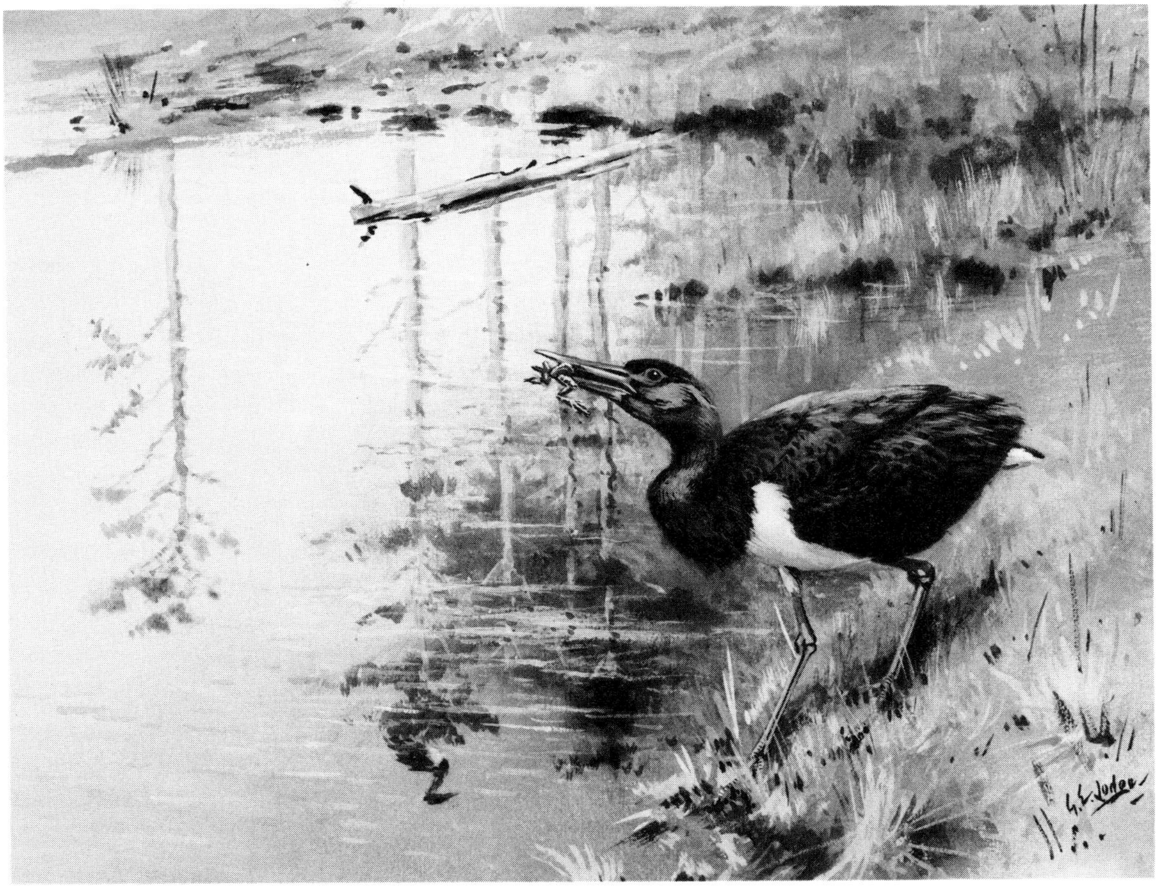

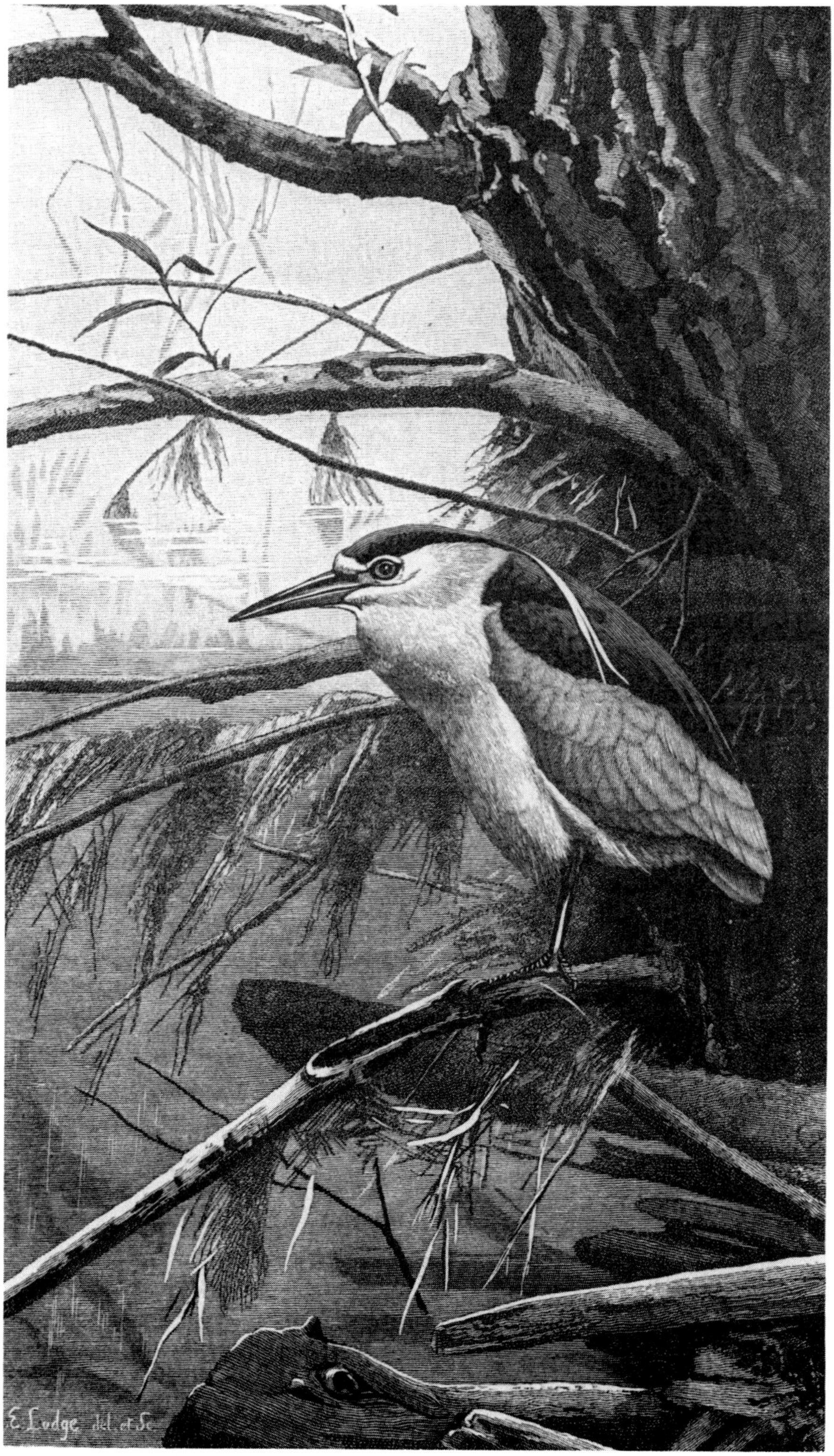

41

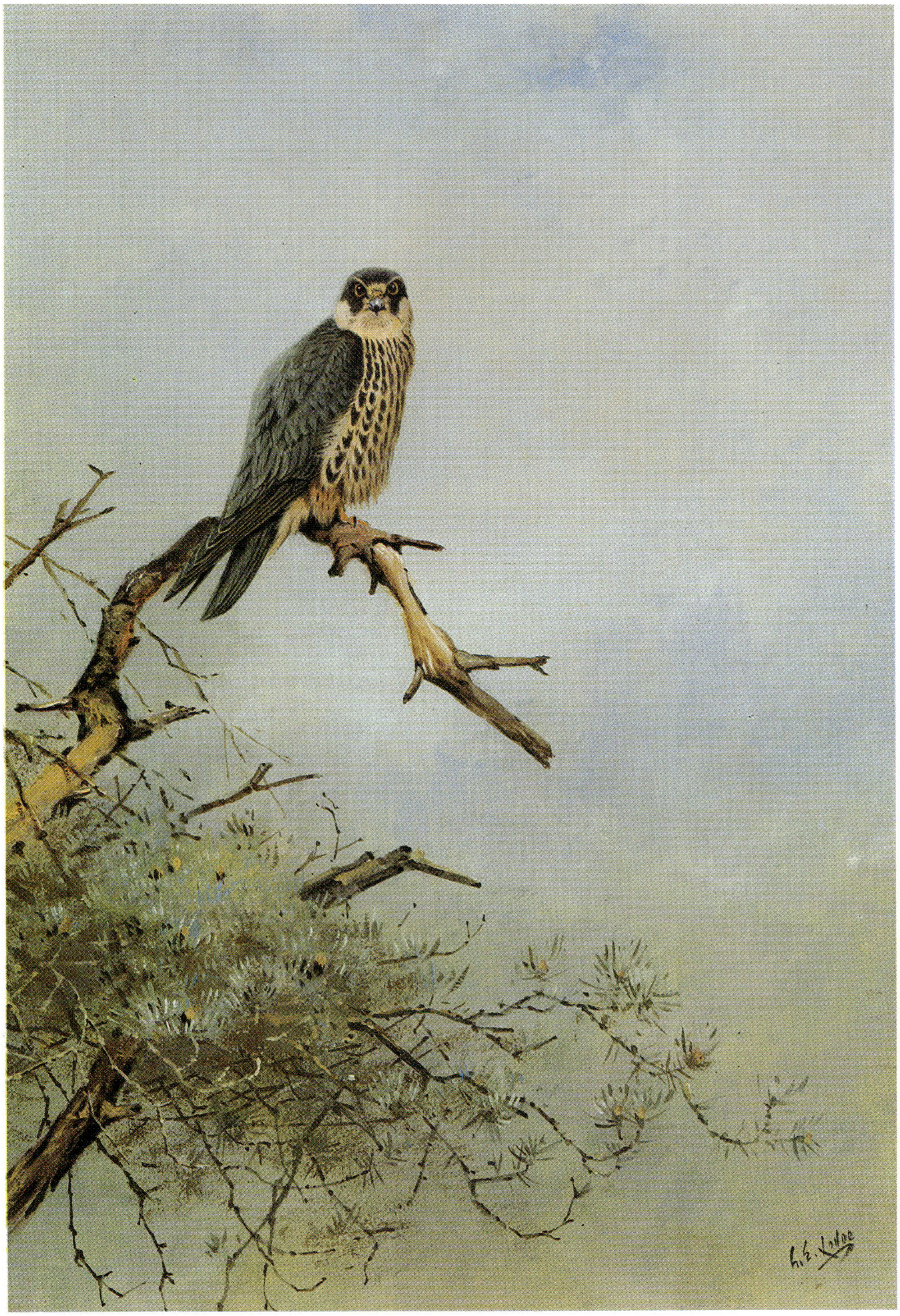

13 *Hobby*

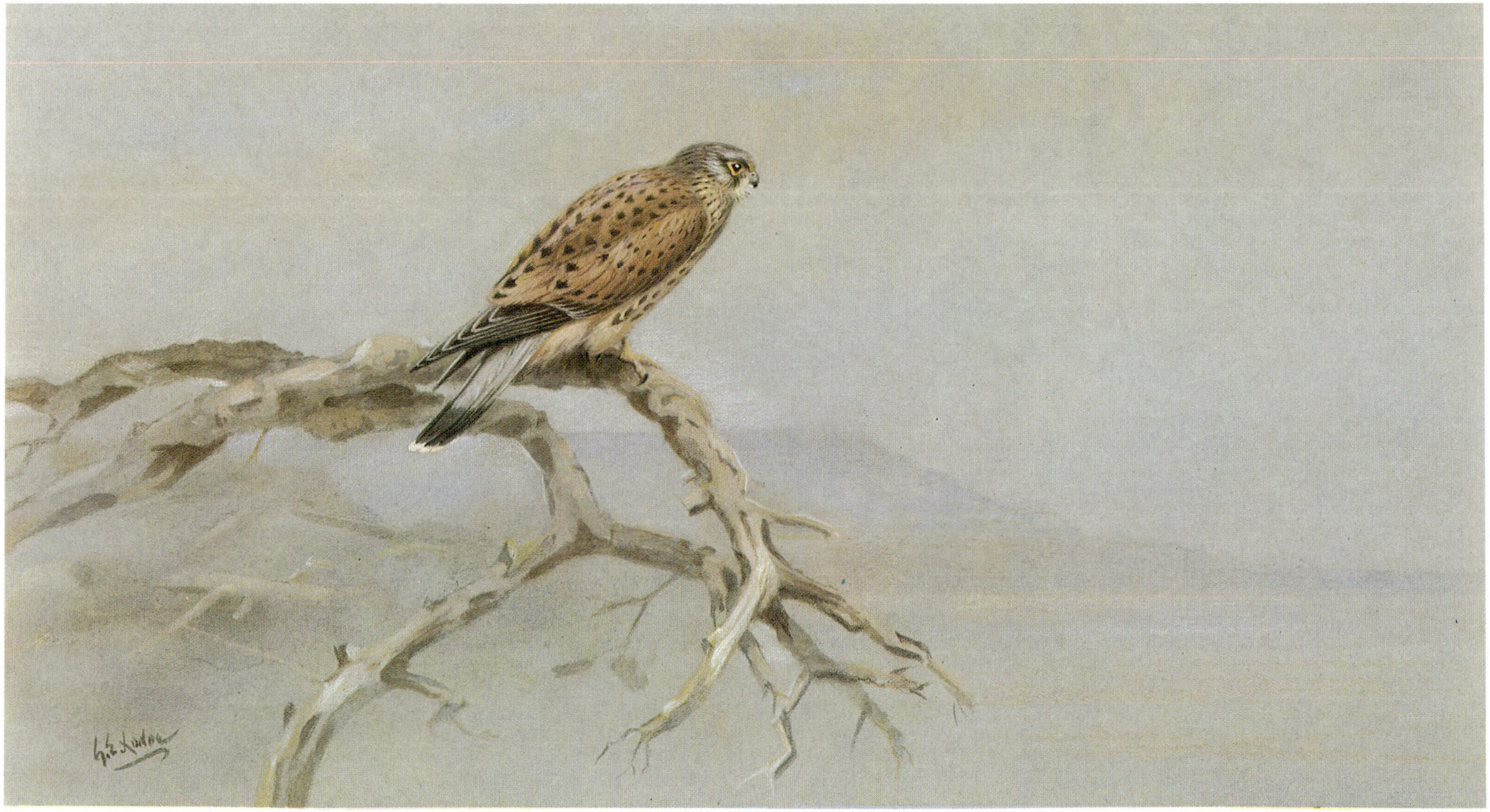

14 Kestrel

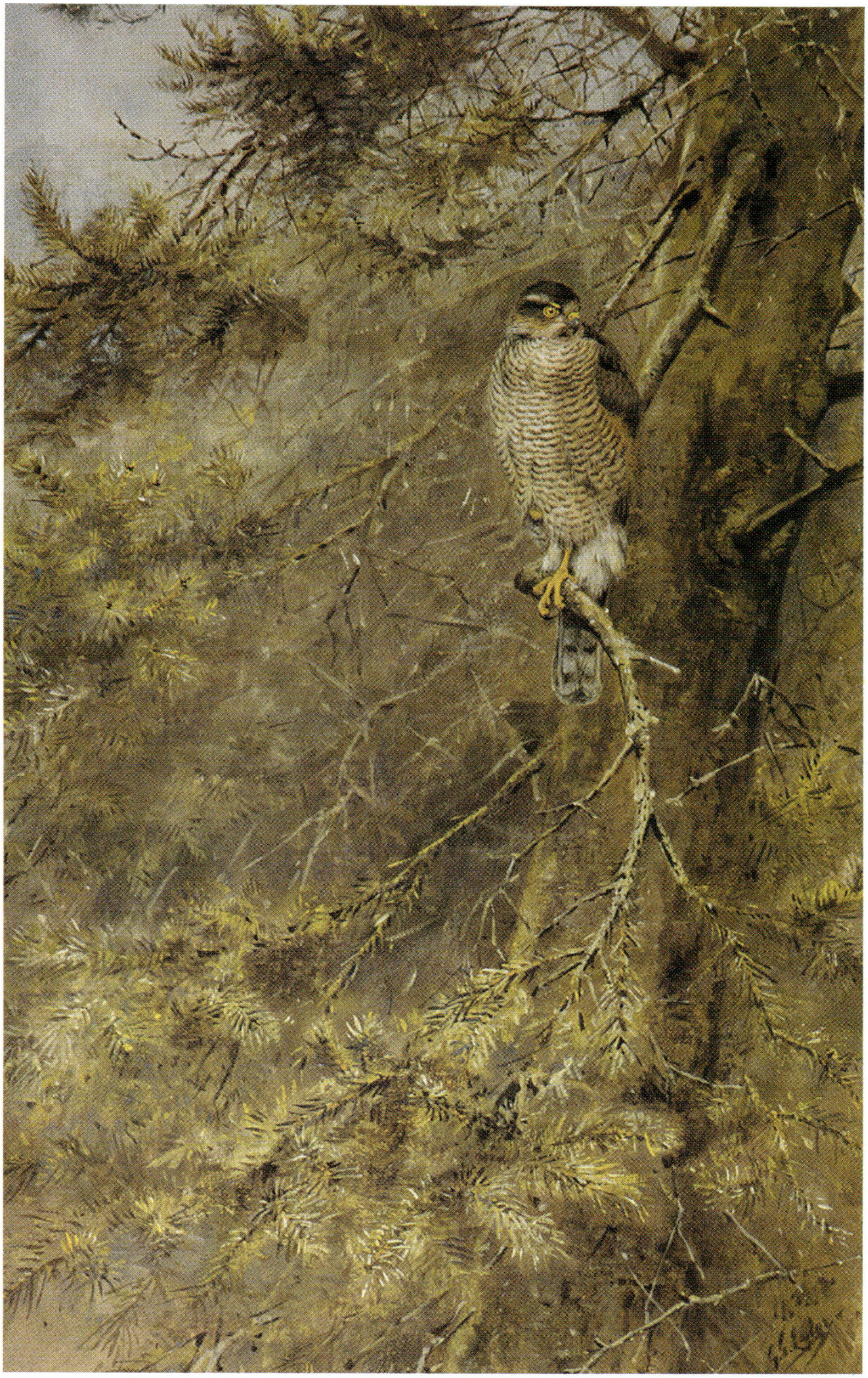

15 Sparrow-hawk

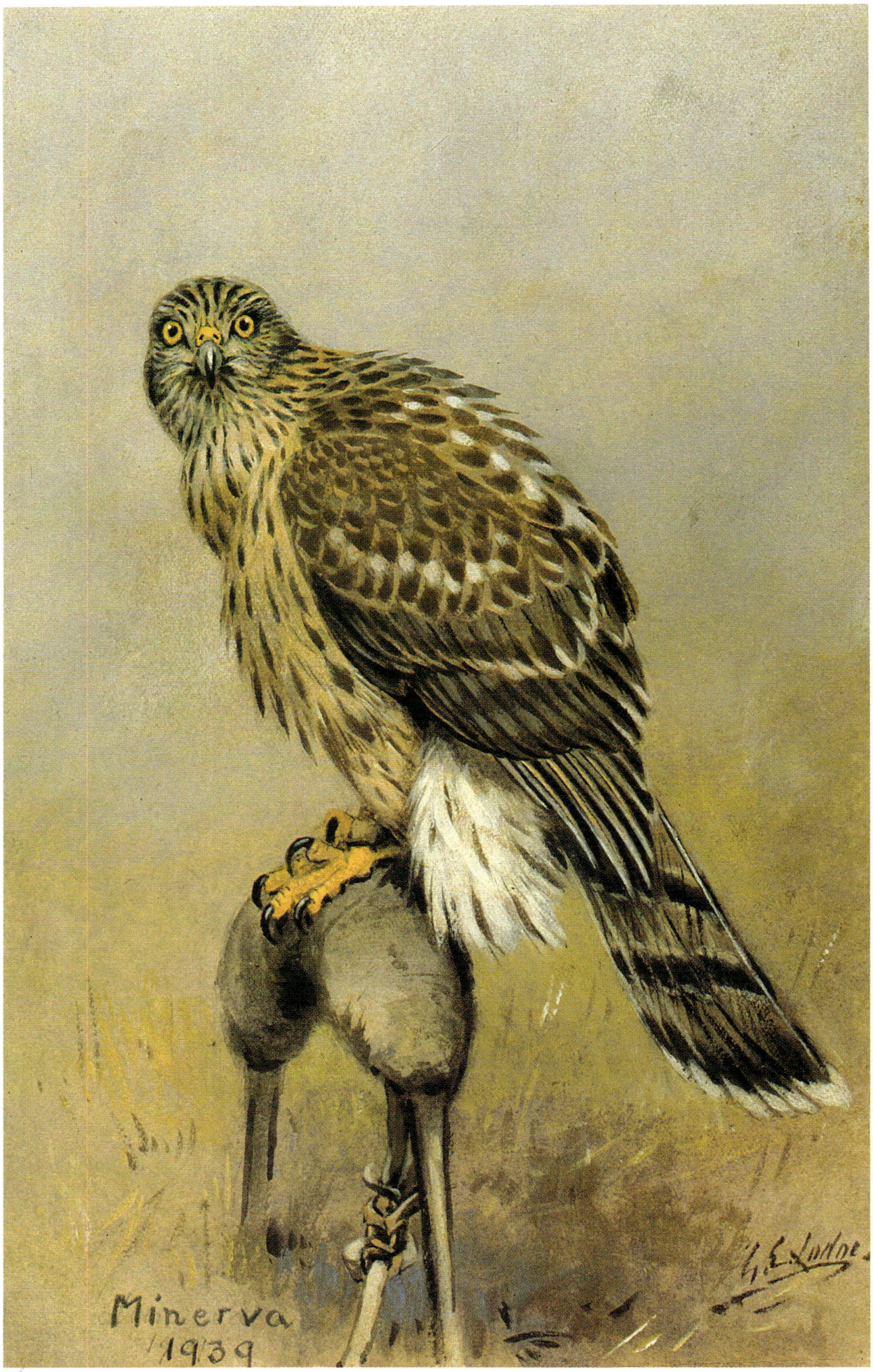

16 'Minerva', an immature goshawk belonging to Guy Aylmer

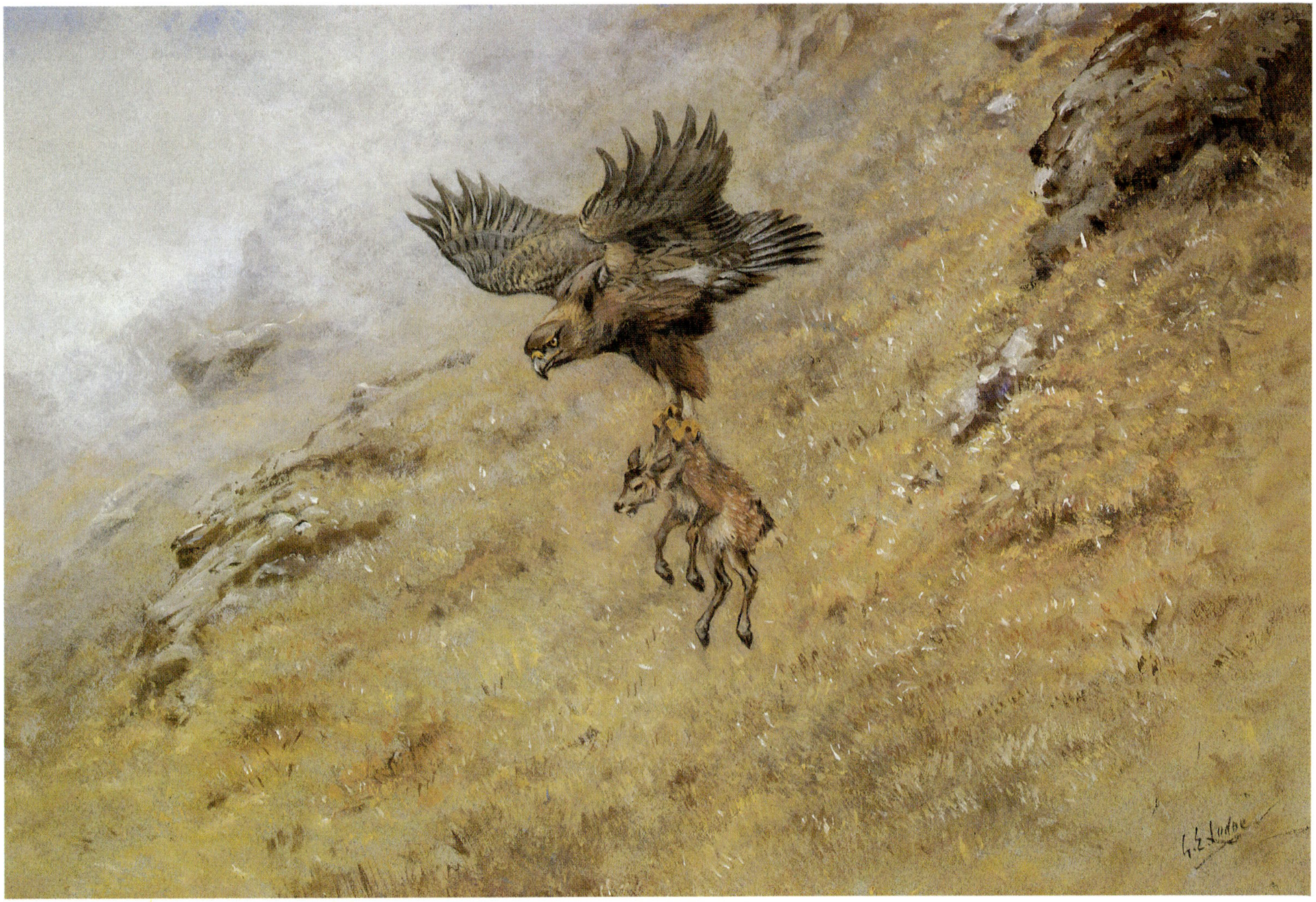

17 *Golden eagle carrying a red deer calf, an incident described in* Memoirs of an Artist Naturalist

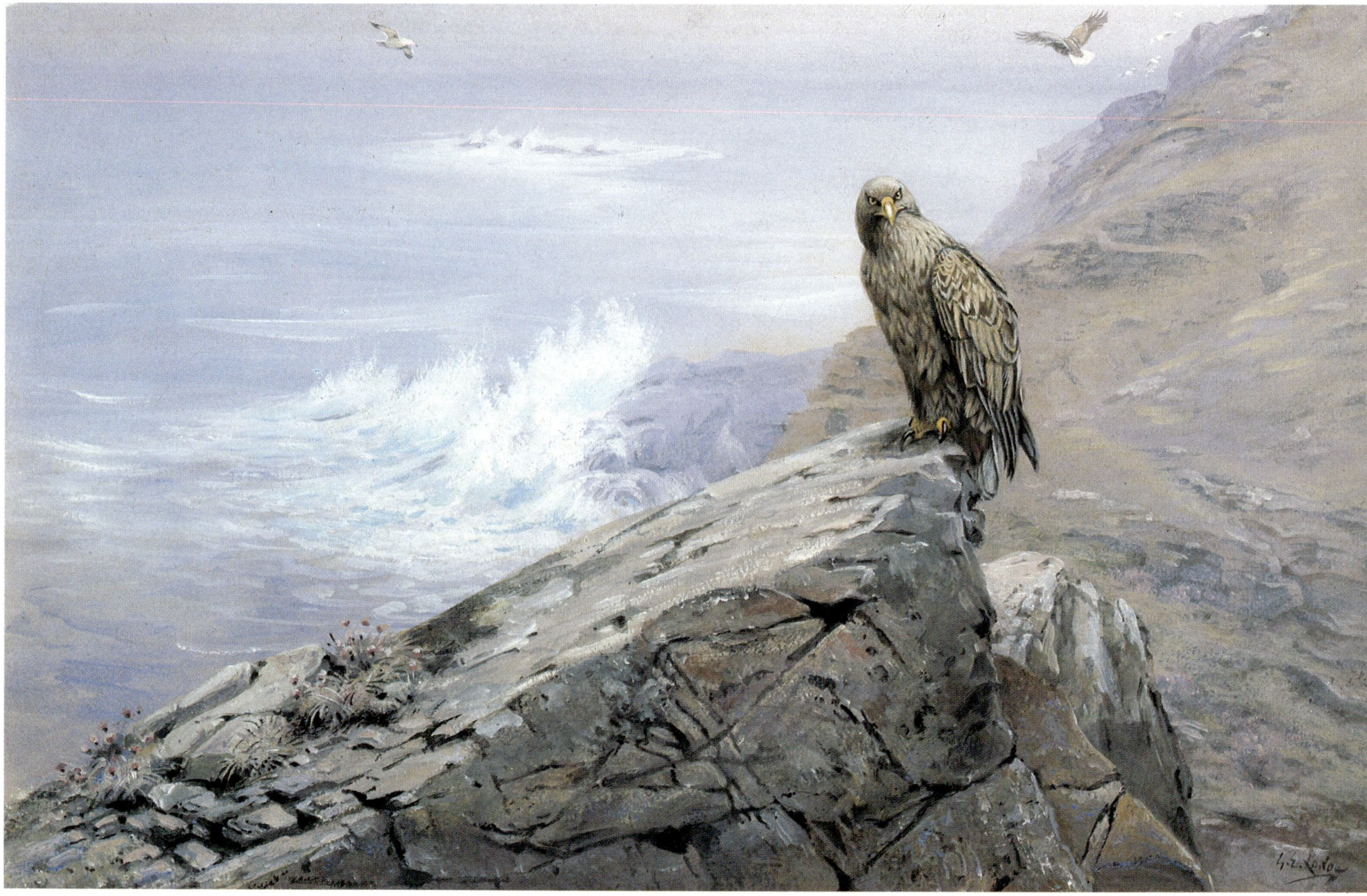

18 *White-tailed sea eagles*

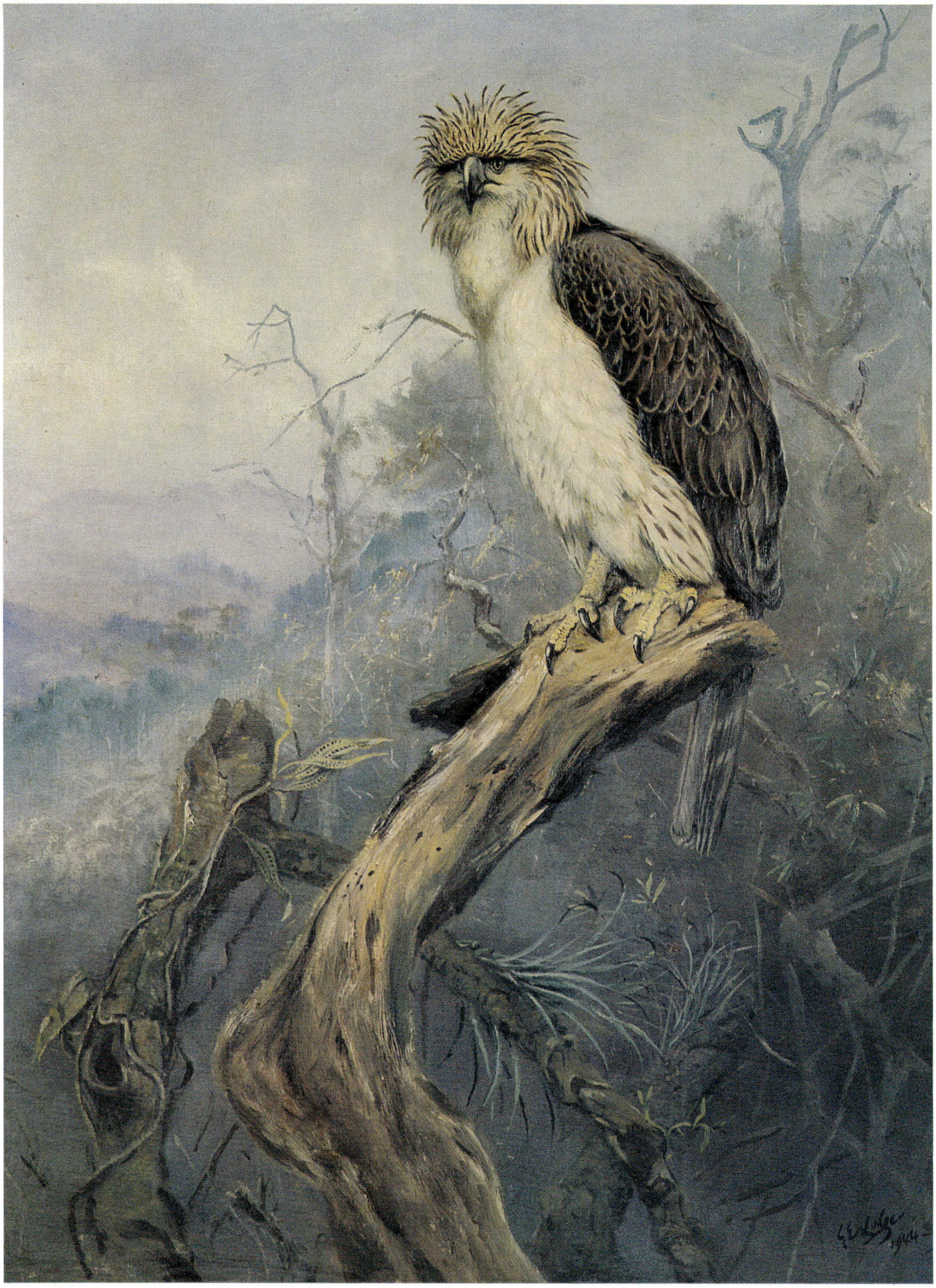

19 *Philippine monkey-eating eagle*

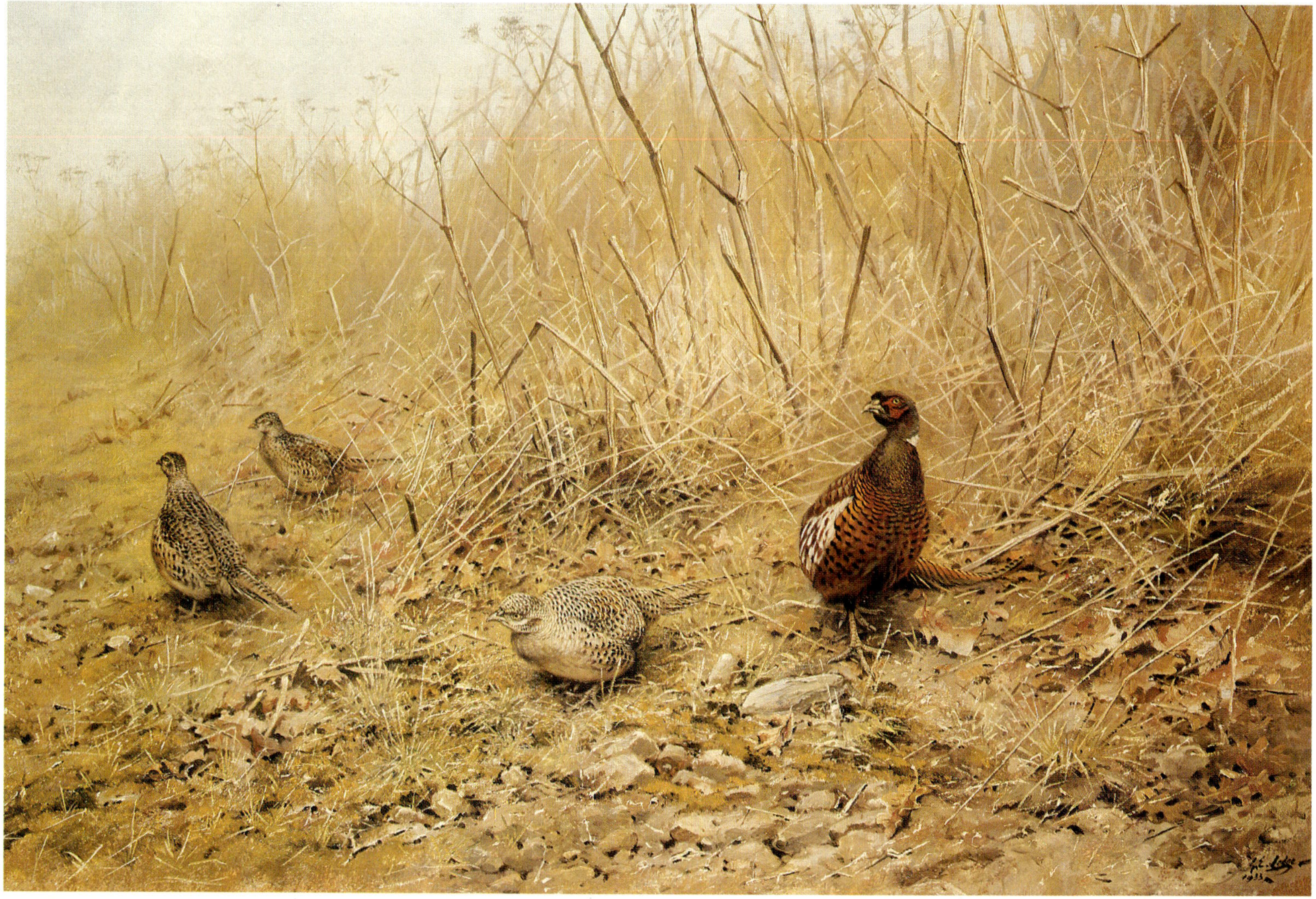

20 A pair of Mongolian pheasants and their young

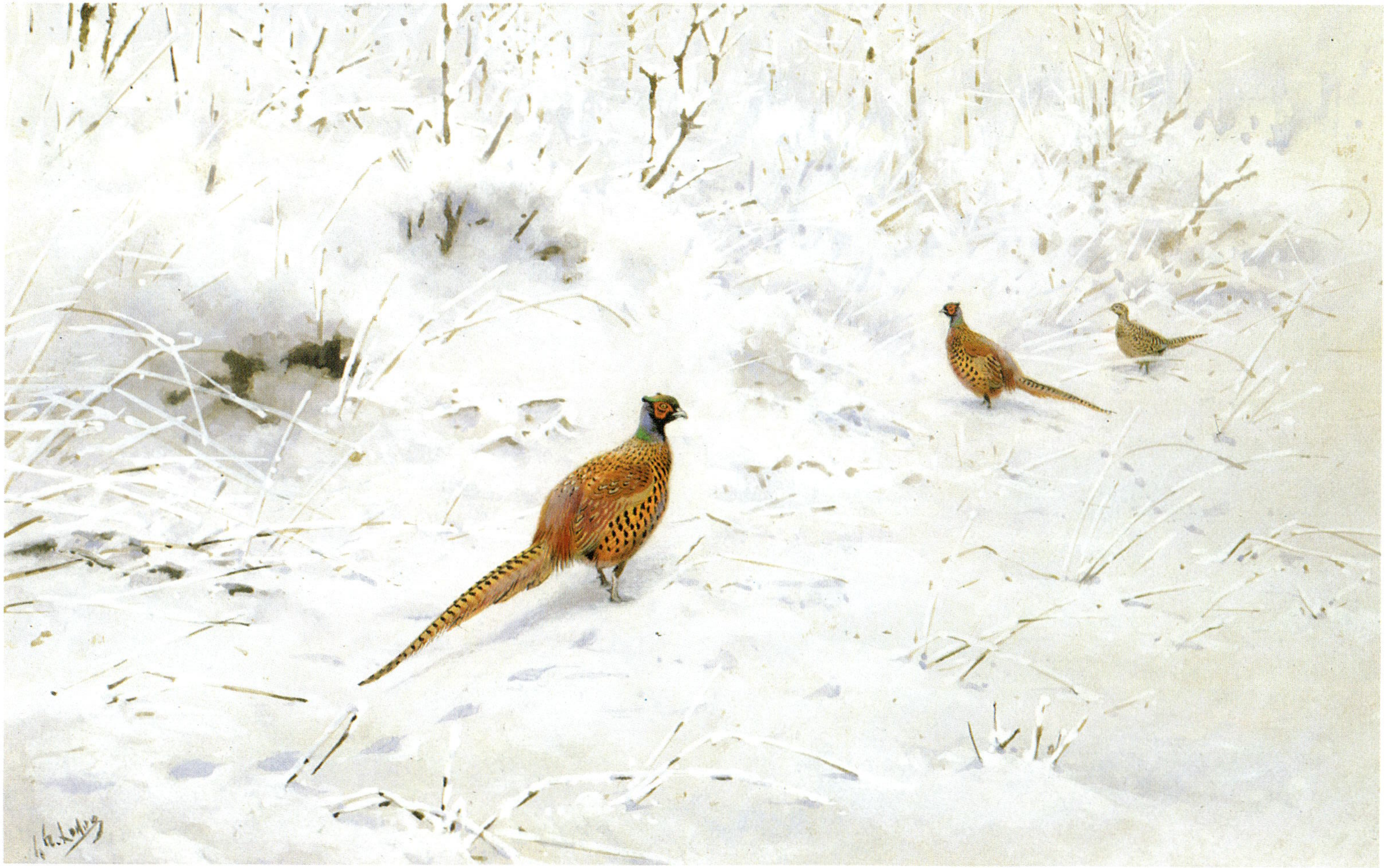

21 *Pheasants in the snow*

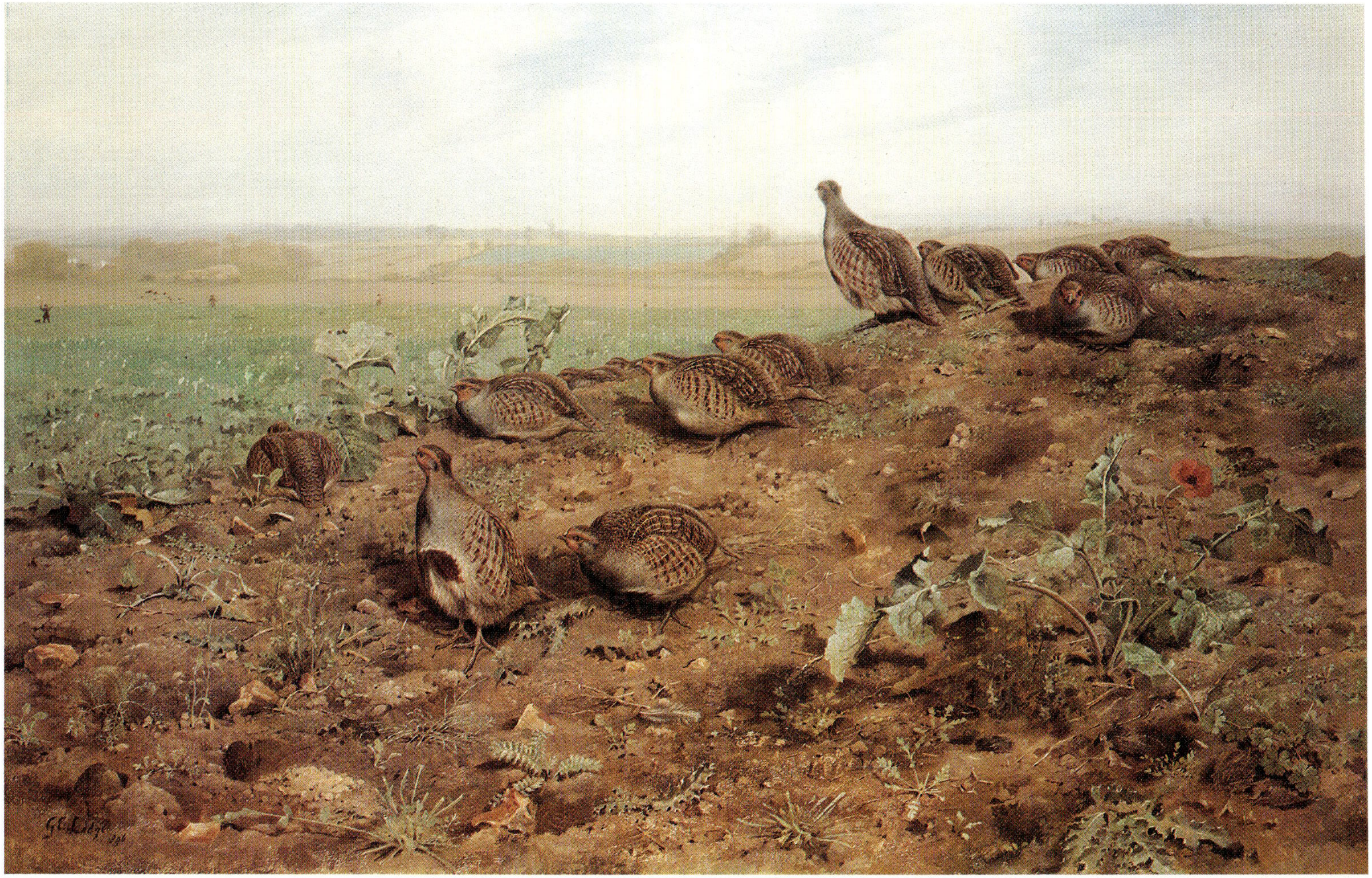

22 *Partridges in a turnip field*

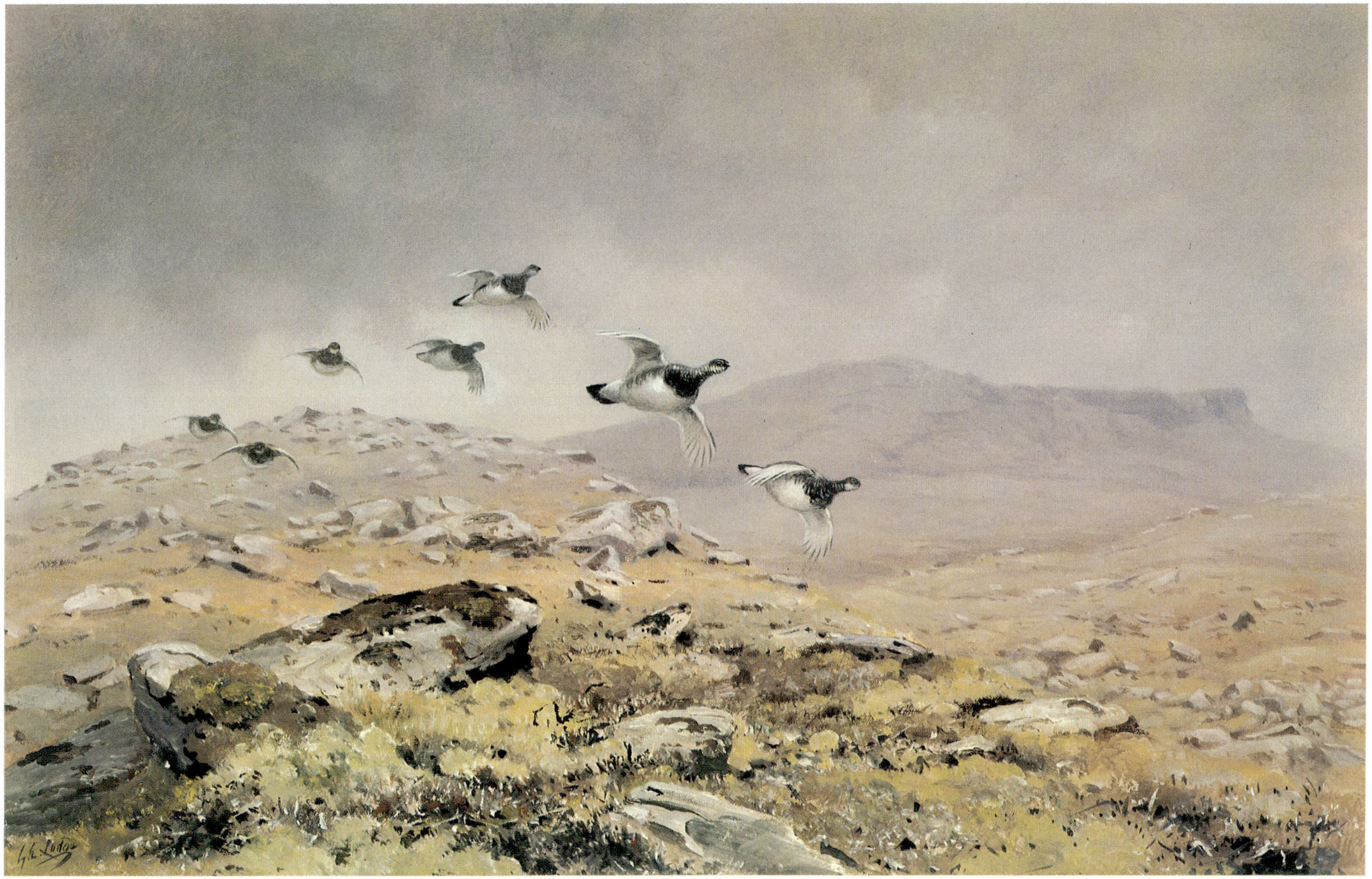

23 Ptarmigan in flight

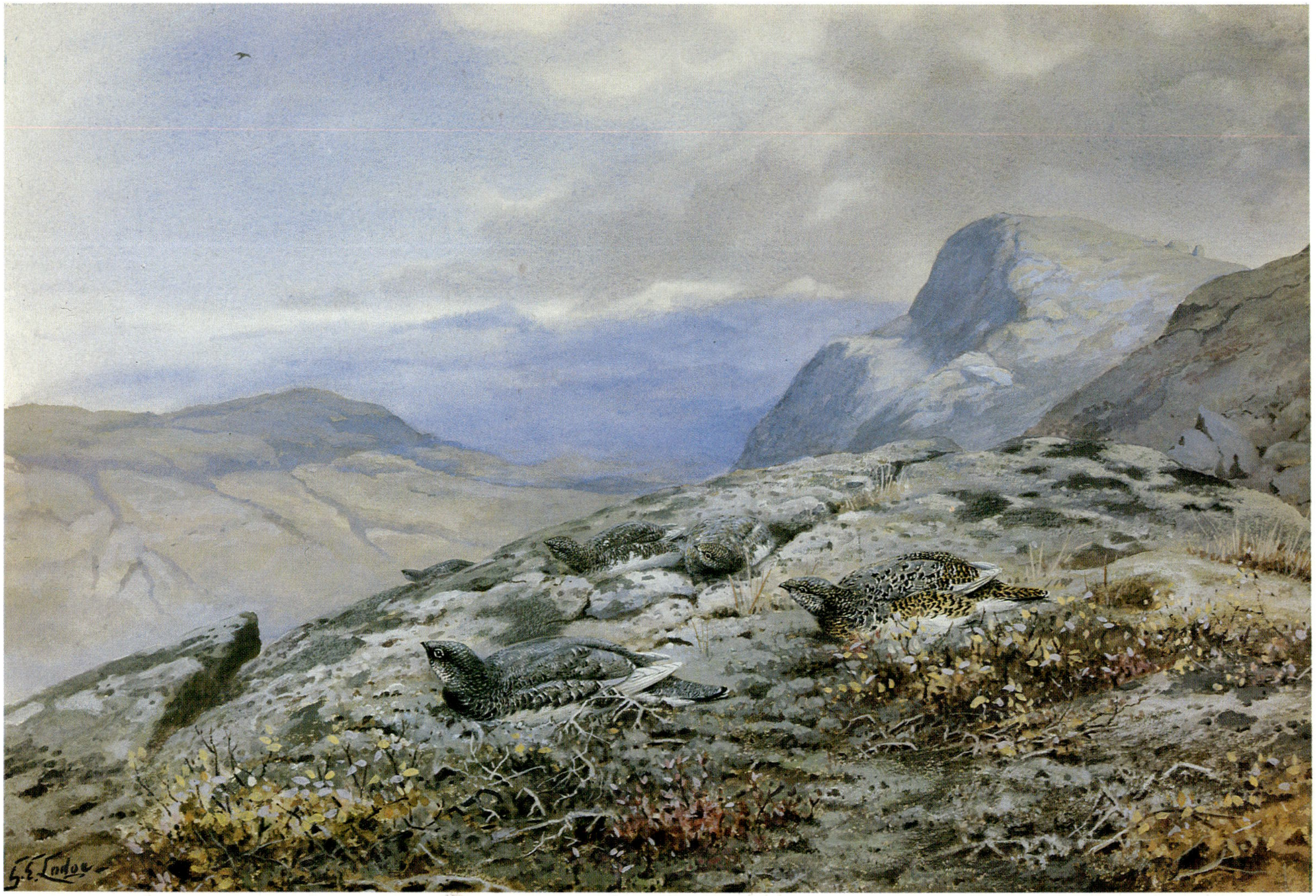

24 Ptarmigan hiding from a peregrine aloft

survived for so long. When preparing lithographic illustrations, it was usual for the outline of the drawing to be printed lightly from the stone (Greek, *lithos*) and then the artist or lithographer, or hand-colourers employed for that purpose, painted the colours in with watercolour paints. The result was a highly-finished painting, and many were very skilfully executed and formed beautiful colour plates. Lodge was unfortunate in receiving few commissions for this type of work. Perhaps, since he does not seem to have transferred his own drawings onto the printing stones, he was less keen on the medium than he might otherwise have been had he enjoyed a large commission to illustrate a whole book. As it was, he contributed but a plate or two to a mere handful of titles.

Lithography is a medium based on the antipathy of grease to water. The design is drawn with a greasy crayon on absorbent limestone, which retains the grease. When the stone's surface is moistened with water the non-greasy areas absorb the water. The printing ink is oil-based and, when applied to the surface of the stone with a roller, it is attracted to the greasy drawing and repelled by the parts which have absorbed water. Paper is then pressed onto the stone and the ink adhering to the greasy image is transferred to it. Chromolithography required a separate stone for each colour, on which the parts to be printed in that colour were marked out separately. A key stone was also used in order to ensure correct registration, or superimposition, of the separate colour printings. Chromolithographs required great skill and many show evidence of lack of that skill by imperfect registration in some part of the finished plate.

Lodge did four hand-coloured lithographs for E.C.S. Baker's *The Indian Ducks and their Allies* (1908) and two ducks for the same author's *The Game-birds of India, Burma and Ceylon* (1921-30). Of all 600 hand-coloured lithographs in G.M. Mathews' *The Birds of Australia* (1910-27) only one bears his signature, the black-cheeked falcon in volume V. He did six drawings for Lord Lilford's *Coloured Figures of the Birds of the British Islands*

41. Night heron

(1885-97), which contained both hand-coloured lithographs and chromolithographs. C.W. Beebe's *A Monograph of the Pheasants* (1918-22) was illustrated with chromolithographs and collotype plates, for which Lodge contributed a number of oil paintings.

Collotype is a photographic method of printing toned subjects without the use of a half-tone screen, and it reproduces paintings very faithfully. A glass plate covered with bichromated gelatine is exposed to a tone negative of the picture to be reproduced. The gelatine hardens in proportion to the amount of light received, and when it is soaked in a mixture of water and glycerine the softer areas (representing the highlights) absorb more liquid and rise slightly higher than harder areas. Variations in the level of the gelatine printing surface thus correspond to depths of tone, and when ink is applied more

42. Sociable plovers, a preliminary grisaille painting for an engraving

42

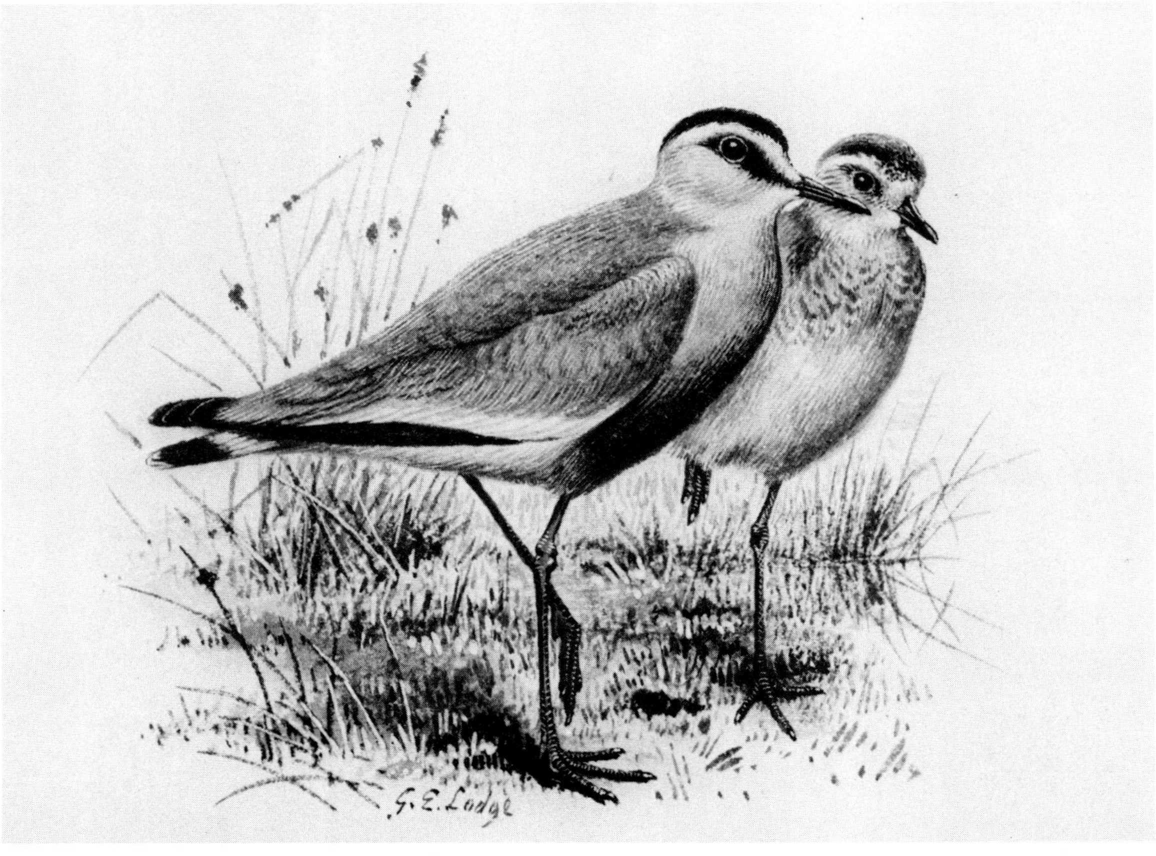

adheres to the harder parts of the image and less to the softer, moist areas.

Only about 750 prints can be obtained satisfactorily from a collotype plate before the gelatine surface breaks down. Consequently, only short runs or limited editions can be printed; Beebe's *A Monograph of the Pheasants* was limited to 600 copies. Beebe's artists' originals were done mainly in oils, and the texture of canvas and paint shows clearly in the collotype reproductions such as the magnificent Chinese Impeyan pheasant, one of 43 paintings by Lodge in the four volumes. Albert Frisch of Berlin processed the collotypes for this book, and it must have been a most satisfying publication for Lodge in that, for once, his paintings were superbly reproduced in colour.

The lithographic and collotype processes are planographic, i.e. the image is printed from the plane or surface of the plate. Photolithography is the method of printing down a photographic image onto the surface of a grained zinc plate. The grain is a light-sensitive coating which hardens in response to light, so the image is hardened onto the plate (and soft areas are washed away). When the plate is moistened, the hardened image rejects the water but the rest of the plate accepts it, and when ink is applied it adheres only to the image which is thus transferred to the paper.

The Kynoch Press was established as the printing press of ICI at Birmingham in 1890, and a succession of very fine lithographic printers there had a marked influence on the quality of printing in England and acquired the reputation of being among the best in Europe. Kynoch Press was commissioned by Oliver and Boyd to print the plates and text for D.A. Bannerman's *The Birds of West and Equatorial Africa* (published in 1953 as a condensed version of the earlier *The Birds of Tropical West Africa*) and Col. R. Meinertzhagen's *Birds of Arabia* (1954), both of which contain good illustrations by Lodge.

Photolithography is versatile in that line work or toned work can be reproduced in black and white or colour. For toned work a half-tone screen is inserted into the camera, and colouring is achieved by preparing separate negatives for the primary colours, yellow, red and blue. This is a skilled job and some firms specialise in quality separation work, e.g. Newsele Litho Ltd who did the colour separation for Vincent and Lodge's *A Season of Birds* (1980). If printed by the offset method, photolithography can reproduce almost anything already printed. It lends itself to printing type and illustrations together, and reprinting books for which the original type has been dispersed. An example of a book reissued by means of offset photolithography is *Hints on the Management of Hawks, and Practical Falconry* by J.E. Harting, first published in 1898 and illustrated with Lodge's wood-engravings, and reprinted by Nene Litho for the Saiga Publishing Company in 1981 for their Falconry Classic Reprint series.

Most of Lodge's early drawings were reproduced in monochrome, first by wood-engraving, then by its photographic counterpart zincography, and also by photogravure and half-tone. Occasionally a colour plate formed the frontispiece to a volume which he otherwise illustrated in line, but it was not until 1907 that he received a commission to work on a number of plates to be printed in colour.

Everyone likes colour plates in a book. The artist wants to see his work well reproduced in colour; the author and publisher like to have as many as possible for they help to sell the book; and the first action of the reader, on picking up the book, is usually to look for the coloured plates which receive his attention before any other part. Thus the search for an effective and cheap photographic method of colour printing greatly exercised the minds of nineteenth-century printers, and continues to the present day.

Collotype had been in use since 1855, when the Frenchman Louis Adolphe Poitvoin was granted a British patent. It was an extremely expensive process, however, because of the time it took to work through the stages involved in producing a plate for the printer. In addition, during printing humidity had to be maintained at a critical level, and the plate could give only a limited number of copies which had to be printed on a smooth, hard-sized paper. The next invention, William Griggs' photochromolithography of the 1860s, found as little favour with publishers of bird and sporting books as did chromolithography, both methods tending to result in blurred images and garishly coloured prints.

The breakthrough came after the perfection of half-tone in 1883, followed two years later by the making of a cross-line screen for half-tone photography. By the turn of the century, printing in colour by combining half-tone with colour separation was firmly established as a method of book illustration. The three-colour process was speedy and this meant it was cheaper than collotype. It was also capable of reproducing line or tone. The drawbacks are that it requires clay-coated paper for the best results and great skill in colour separation. Any faulty printing produces overlapping of colours and it is difficult to secure absolute register.

All colour printing processes are based on the three primary colours, yellow, red and blue. Any combination of colours in a painting can be separated into these elements and then put back together again to produce the original colours. By using filters to exclude the unwanted colours, the photographer prepares three negatives, representing the yellows, reds and blues. Sometimes a fourth negative is added, for printing black, to give greater depth and definition. The interposed half-tone screen breaks the negative images into dots, and the three (or four) screens used are rotated slightly so that the dots will not print on top of each other. The negatives can be used to produce plates by half-tone, litho, gravure or collotype processes, and the basic order for printing the plates is yellow, red, blue, then black (this may be varied to create specific effects).

Lodge was one of the artists whose paintings were reproduced by the three-colour process for Walter Rothschild's *Extinct Birds* in 1907, and then for F.B. Kirkman's *The British Bird Book* in 1910-13. He also produced single plates for the frontispieces in a number of other titles. His own book, *Memoirs of an Artist Naturalist*, was published in 1946 and had 16 coloured plates, but sadly many of these were out of register. Similarly disappointing results in some other books were due either to imperfect colour separation or to lack of colour correction at the printing stage.

Lodge's work is distributed over a large number of titles, most of which have only a few examples of his illustrations. His drawings were reproduced by eight or nine different processes, often in those methods' pioneer stages. Two world wars interfered with the flow of illustrated bird and sporting books which were his speciality. He waited a lifetime to realise his ambition to paint all the British birds and to see them reproduced in colour. He waited a lifetime too to be allowed to illustrate a multi-volume work with coloured plates throughout. In 1953 the first volume of David Bannerman's *The Birds of the British Isles* was published. It was finally to have two monochrome and 385 coloured plates reproduced by the 'four-colour' method (three colours and black), with illustrations of 416 species. The last of the 12 volumes appeared ten years later. Poignantly, Lodge died in February 1954, having seen only the first two volumes of what was to be the culmination of his work and achievements. He was born too late for the magnificent hand-coloured books of the nineteenth century and, though he lived for over 90 years, he died too soon to see much of his best coloured work published.

CHAPTER 3
LODGE THE FALCONER AND OTHER MEMORIES

Phillip Glasier

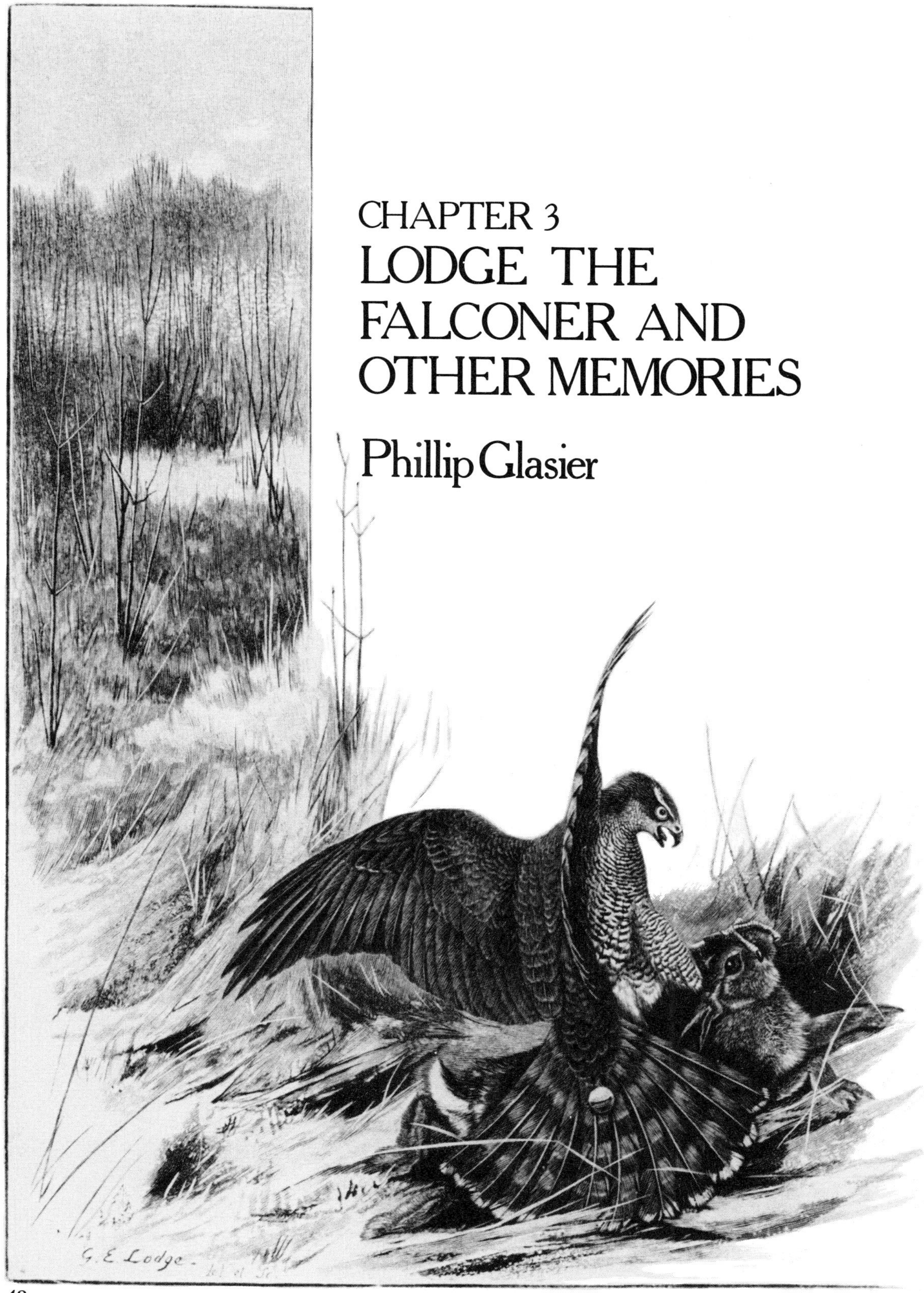

43

Extract from Lodge's notes

My first introduction to the noble sport of falconry was in this wise. In 1885, Messrs Macmillan, being the publishers of the *English Illustrated Magazine*, commissioned me to draw and engrave (on wood) the illustrations for an article on falconry, which was to be written by E.B. Michell. As I had never seen at that time anything of hawking, they gave me an introduction to Michell, so as to talk things over and see what could be done about it. Michell very wisely came to the conclusion that I ought, if possible, to see something of the sport before embarking on these illustrations; and he presently remembered that he had passed on to Mr T.J. Mann a nest of eyass merlins. The result was a most cordial invitation for us both to go down and stay for a few days with him at Bishop's Stortford, and see what sport we could with the merlins, and also see peregrines in training, flying to the lure. Thus started a friendship which lasted a lifetime.

Entries in Lodge's hawking diary

September 18th 1886 [first entry].
Went to Docking to stay with T.J. Mann for hawking. He has three peregrine tiercels, two merlins (and another last season's bird which he never flies) and a female goshawk. The goshawk today killed four rabbits, and the tiercels killed a partridge. One of them flew a kingfisher, which dived under the hawk, the latter being so close that his wings were wetted. The kingfisher ultimately escaped under the bushes. One of the tiercels is on the sick list. Two days ago he stooped at a thrush over turnips (the partridge he was flying having put in) and cut the turnip leaves off clean, and probably bruised himself badly. He went to a tree on which he settled. Now he cannot pass food out of his crop, although he has only washed meat.

January 16th 1888.
Holkham, Norfolk. By permission from Lord Leicester we spent the day on the Holkham

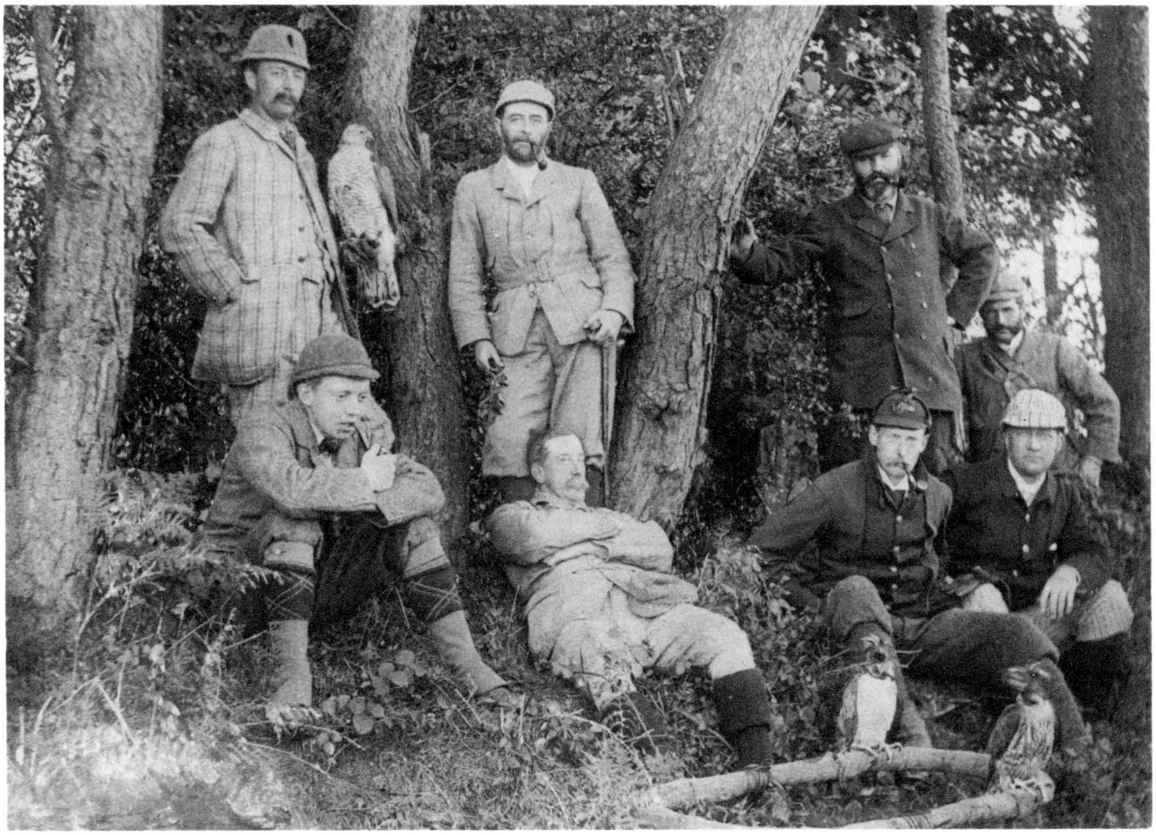

44

marshes. Shadow of Death [goshawk] killed seven waterhens, a quarry altogether beneath her, but there was nothing else to fly her at. Lundy [tiercel] flew a snipe and made a beautiful stoop, just missing it; also flew a teal, but the latter could get along in the wind better than the hawk, which had to give up. He had a lot of flying, but the wind was very strong, and although he waited on very high he did not seem to be flying at his usual pace. When taken down his wings were seen to be quite wet, which looked as if he had brushed the water while stooping at something. He made one fine flight which ended in a kill. He was waiting on beautifully at a tremendous pitch, hanging quite motionless at times in the strong wind. As the partridges, which we had marked down, got up, he singled out one bird and came down in a succession of long mighty stoops and killed the partridge about 500 yards off.

43. Goshawk with a rabbit

44. A hawking party in the 1880s or 90s. Lodge is seated second from the right, next to T.J. Mann (far right)

April 12th 1889.
Hawking today at Ickleton. Soon found rooks, and I got a good slip with Vic [falcon]. She made a couple of stoops unsuccessfully, and then the rook took the air, and she left him and started her usual game down the wind. In spite of lures she went on and was soon out of sight. We all went off in pursuit and by degrees got on to her line, hearing of her from various men working in the fields. At one place she had put a lot of rooks into a fence, and then sat on a hedge for nearly quarter of an hour close to a ploughman. I saw, at last, what I took to be her playing with a wild tiercel a long way off. I lured in vain and after they had wheeled about in a circle of some miles they went out of sight again. Frost [T.J. Mann's falconer, Alfred Frost] at last took her down in a rookery. He had also seen the wild tiercel. We had walked in a circle of about six miles in circumference, and she must have flown a lot more than that. In the afternoon we flew her again and she easily killed her rook, and was fed up. Farthingale [falcon] had three flights and killed one rook.

May 1st 1889.
Hawking today. News of Norfolk plover so hunted them up. Found one in a big field and Mann slipped Farthingale. The plover had a long start, but the hawk overhauled it and drove it down to the ground quarter of a mile ahead. The hawk went to ground too. The plover ran, and then getting onto the wing again, had another good start on the hawk, who hunted it to one of the farm buildings, where the plover was said to have gone in. This part of the flight I did not see as the buildings and stacks hid them from my view. When I next saw them, the hawk was coming back from the farm at a tremendous pace and about 150 yards in front of her was the plover, whistling and making every effort to escape. The hawk was gaining rapidly and when about a third of a mile ahead I stooped down to catch sight of them on the skyline, I saw the falcon stoop at the plover, and as I saw neither falcon nor quarry again I concluded it to be a kill. When I struggled up I found this to be the case. The hawk

had knocked the plover over into a sand-pit, and Frost took her up there with the quarry in her foot. This was a long hunting flight; the quarry very game and the hawk sticking it out splendidly. They must have been flying for about eight minutes. Afterwards Mann slipped her at a lot of rooks and she went straight up to them and took one first stoop. Later on I slipped her at a rook on passage, which she took right in a hedge, after missing her first stoop.

September 22nd 1913.
[With Gilbert Blaine in Caithness] The hawks killed 13 grouse today. During one flight when Sylvia [falcon] was up, a wild falcon came and joined in. Sylvia was flying a covey which went over a cottage on a smallholding, the wild hawk following hard after. One of the grouse put into some cabbages and this we got as we ran after. By this time they were all out of sight so we ran on in the direction they had gone; and before long found the wild hawk sitting on a fence post. She went off again pretty wild, and we scouted around feeling sure that Sylvia must be on her quarry in the vicinity; and we soon found her among the grasses and rushes, pluming her grouse.

August 26th 1939 [last entry].
Had to cut short our holiday on Salisbury Plain [with Kim Muir], as, owing to the imminence of war, Blanford [Dr H.O.] had a wire recalling him back to his Sanatorium. So we packed up and went off. On the way we cut off the bells and jesses of our hawks [merlins], and enlarged them half way between Heytesbury and Chitterne, each with a good lump of beef, and trusted to luck.

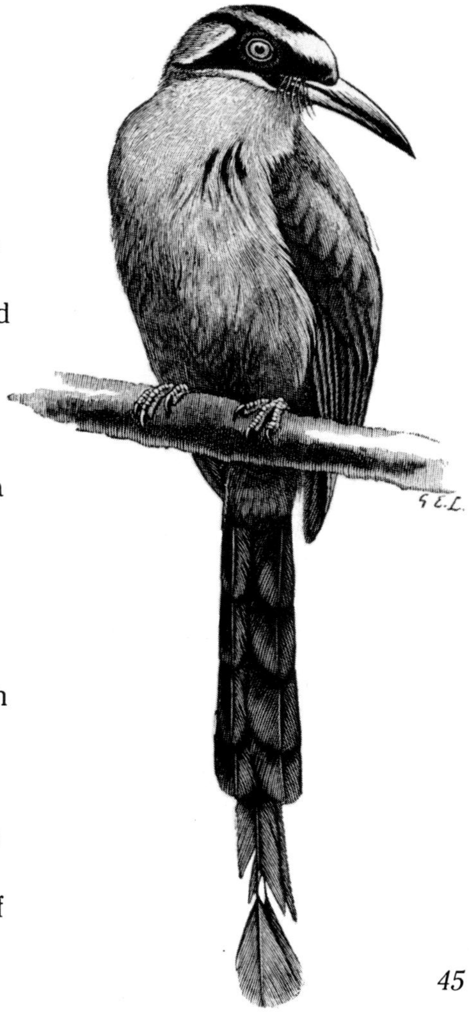

45

* * *

I first met George Lodge sometime in the late 1920s. I had gone to Camberley with my uncle, the late Captain Charles Knight M.C., F.R.P.S., who was showing one of his films. He was one of the earliest pioneers of nature cine-photography, the first man

45. Motmot

to film golden eagles and ospreys at the nest, and later on the large African crowned hawk- and martial eagles. Lodge, whose great speciality was portraying birds of prey, came along to see the film.

A few years later I met him again. In the early 1930s a number of friends and relatives, all interested in falconry, used to take their various hawks and falcons down to Salisbury Plain to fly them. The then open country there was ideal for rook hawking and for flying merlins. There were rabbits in abundance for goshawks, and starlings and other birds for those who flew sparrow-hawks. Game-birds were very scarce on the Plain then, so it was fairly easy to obtain permission from the local farmers and landowners to fly our birds over their ground.

We stayed at Avebury, some of us at the Red Lion and others at the house next to it, which had some empty stables where we could keep the birds at night or in bad weather. At the back of the house was a field with a long line of large elm trees along one side, and in fine weather and during the day the birds were put out there on their perches when they were not being flown. Here each fine morning they would be bathing, preening and exercising, 'upwards jumping with wings flapping sideways', as the Swedish drill instructors would have termed it. Lodge would be there sitting on his folding camp stool, busy sketching away in one of the small sketch books that he invariably carried in one of the capacious pockets of his green hawking jacket with the shining brass buttons of the Old Hawking Club.

As soon as the birds were ready for action the hawking parties would set out. Peregrines would jump to their owners' fists, have a small reward and be hooded up. Their party would set off on foot or by car in one direction and the merlin party in another. It is most unwise to have merlins flying anywhere near peregrines since the peregrine, having perhaps missed a rook after flying it into cover, might well see a merlin in the distance and have a crack at it. Lodge would accompany whichever party he fancied, armed, of course, with his sketch book. I don't remember his ever having

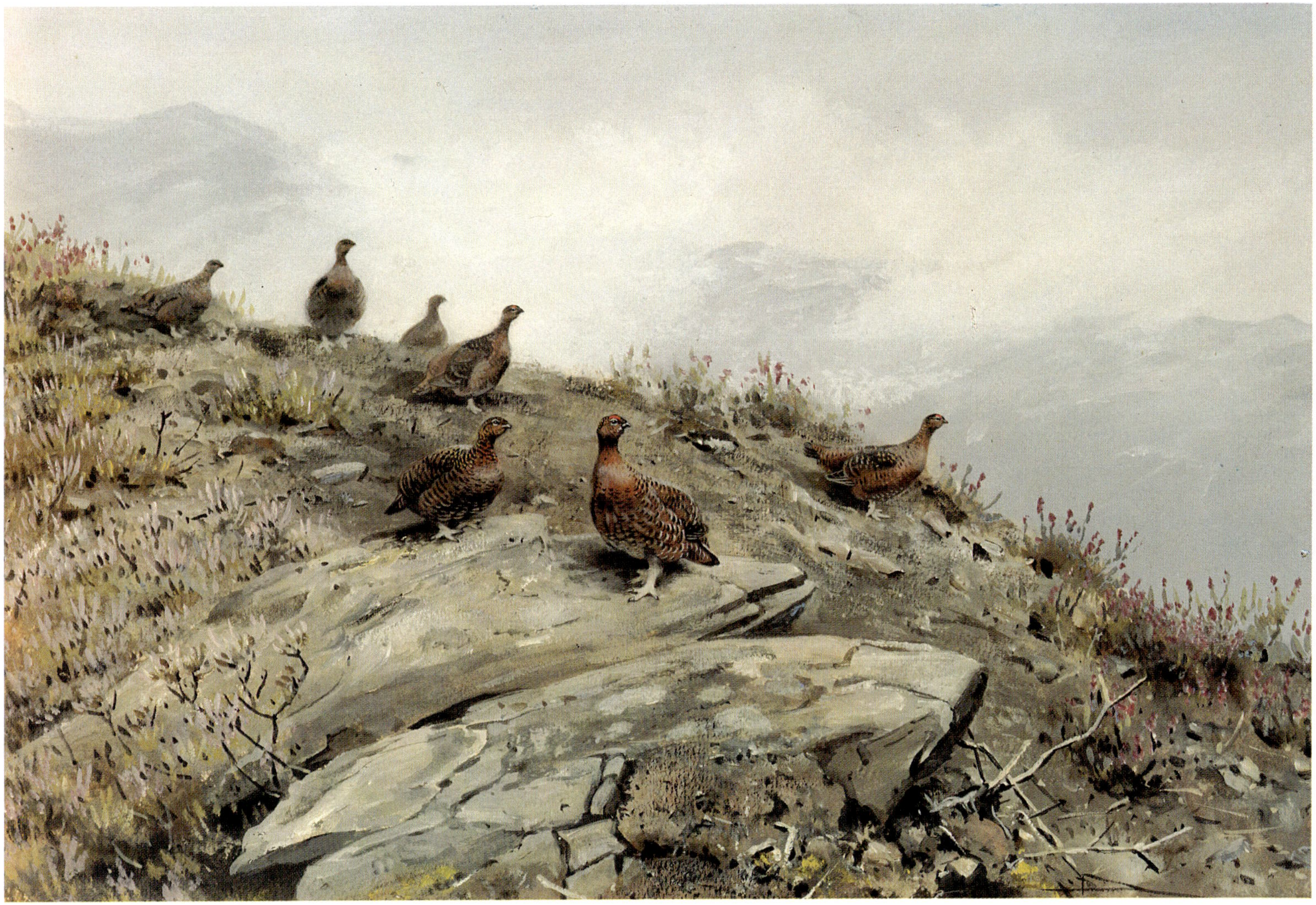

25 *A covey of red grouse*

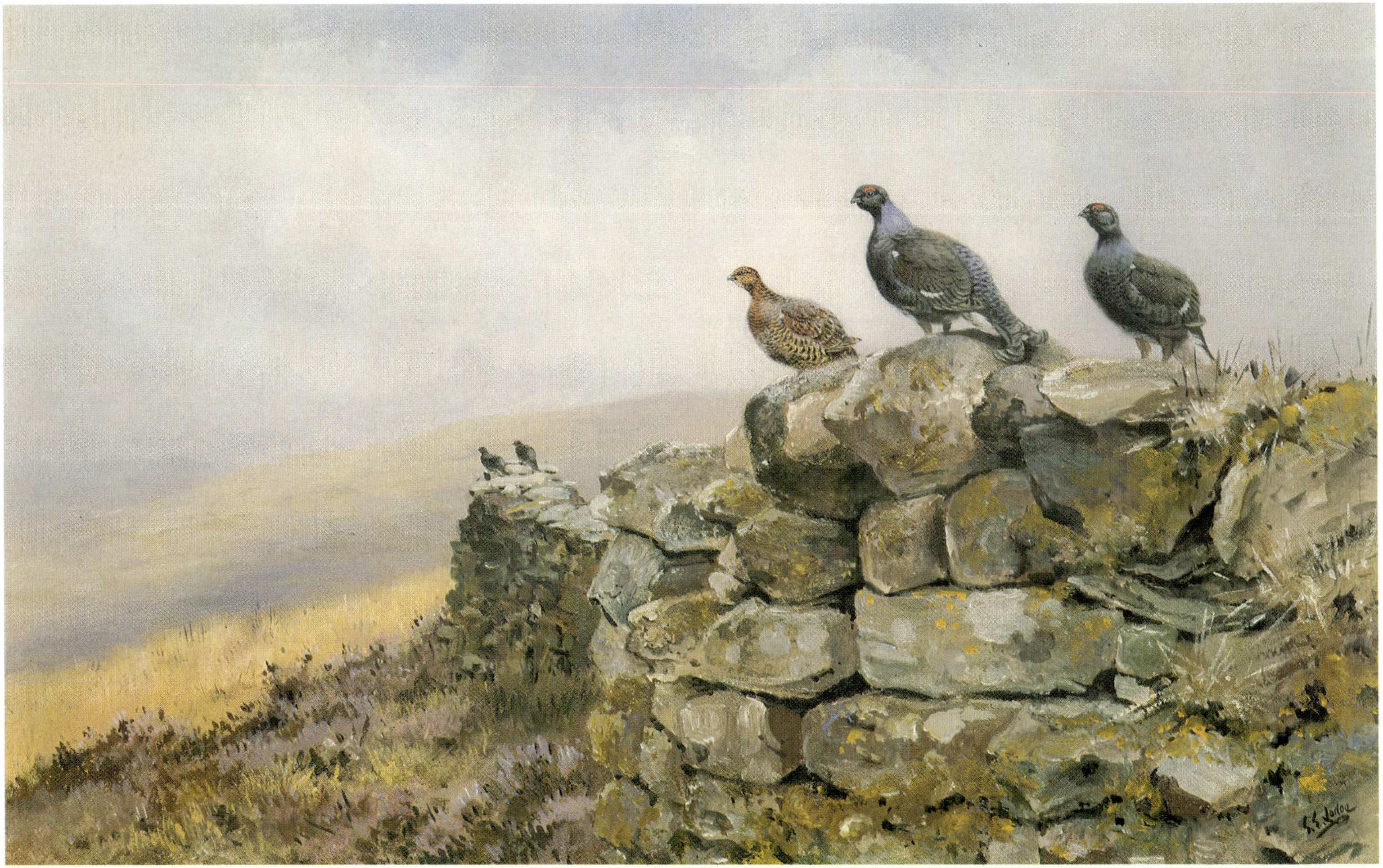

26 Black grouse on a moor

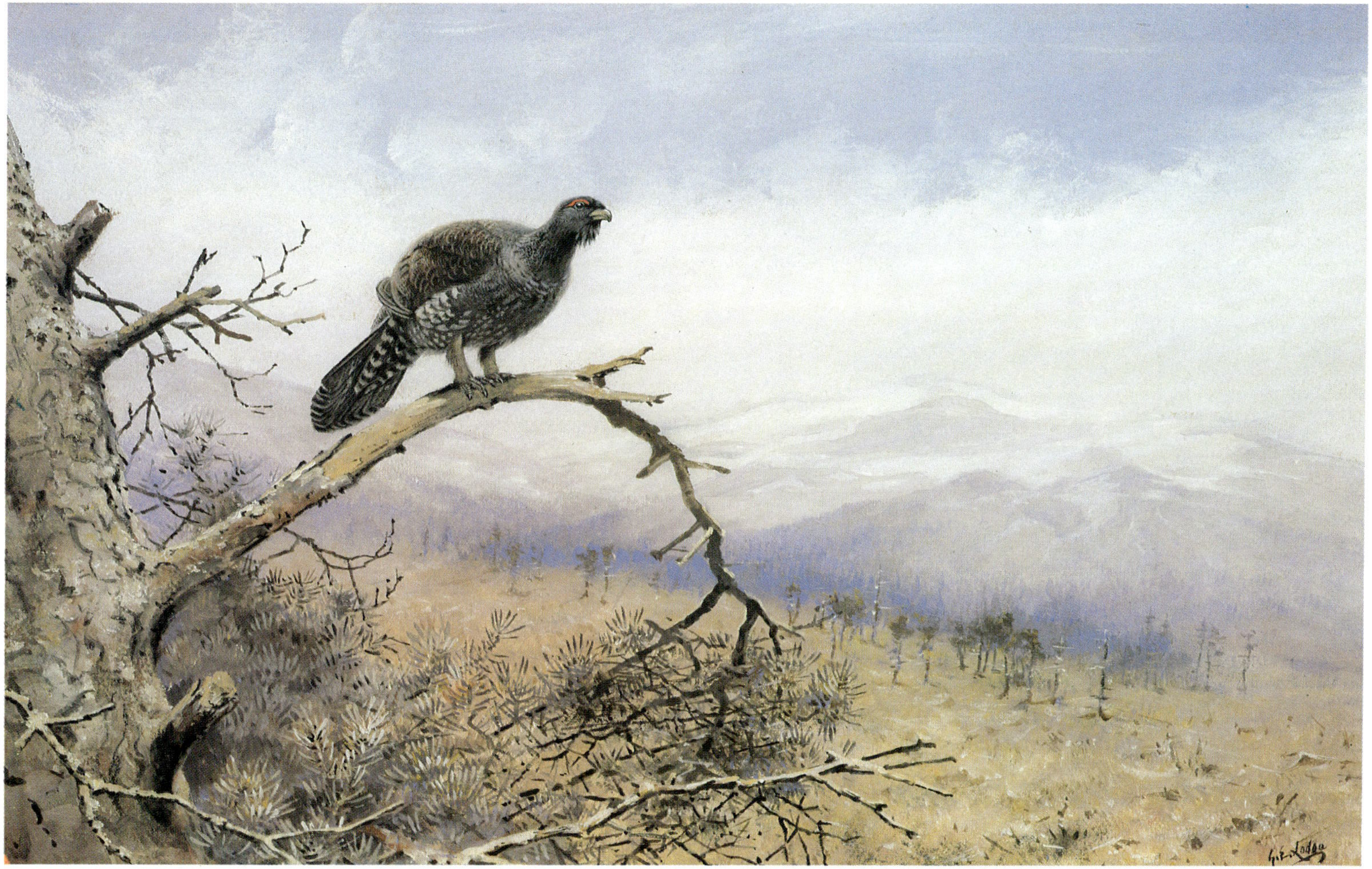

27 *Cock capercaillie, 'the sentinel'*

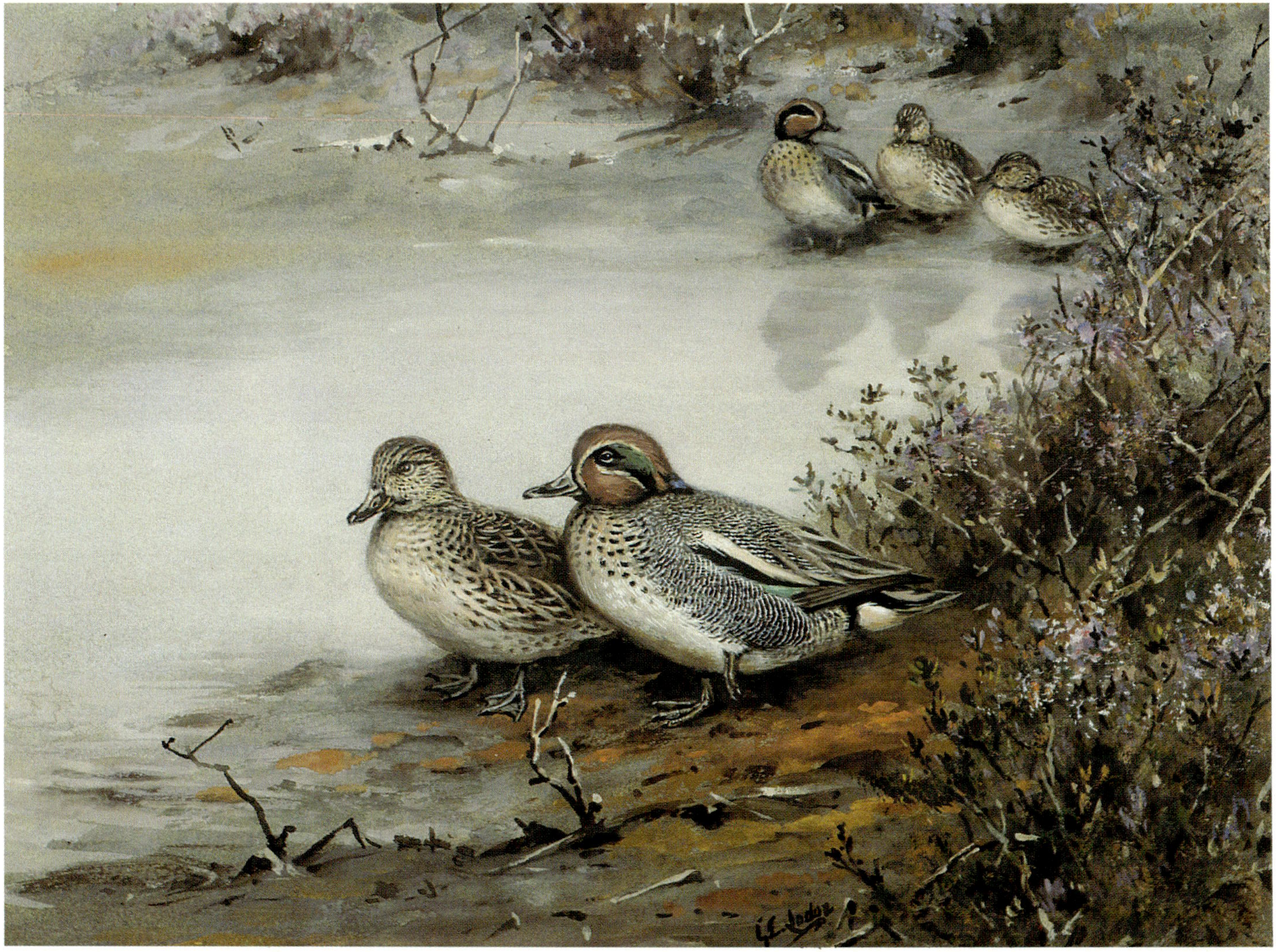

28 Teal

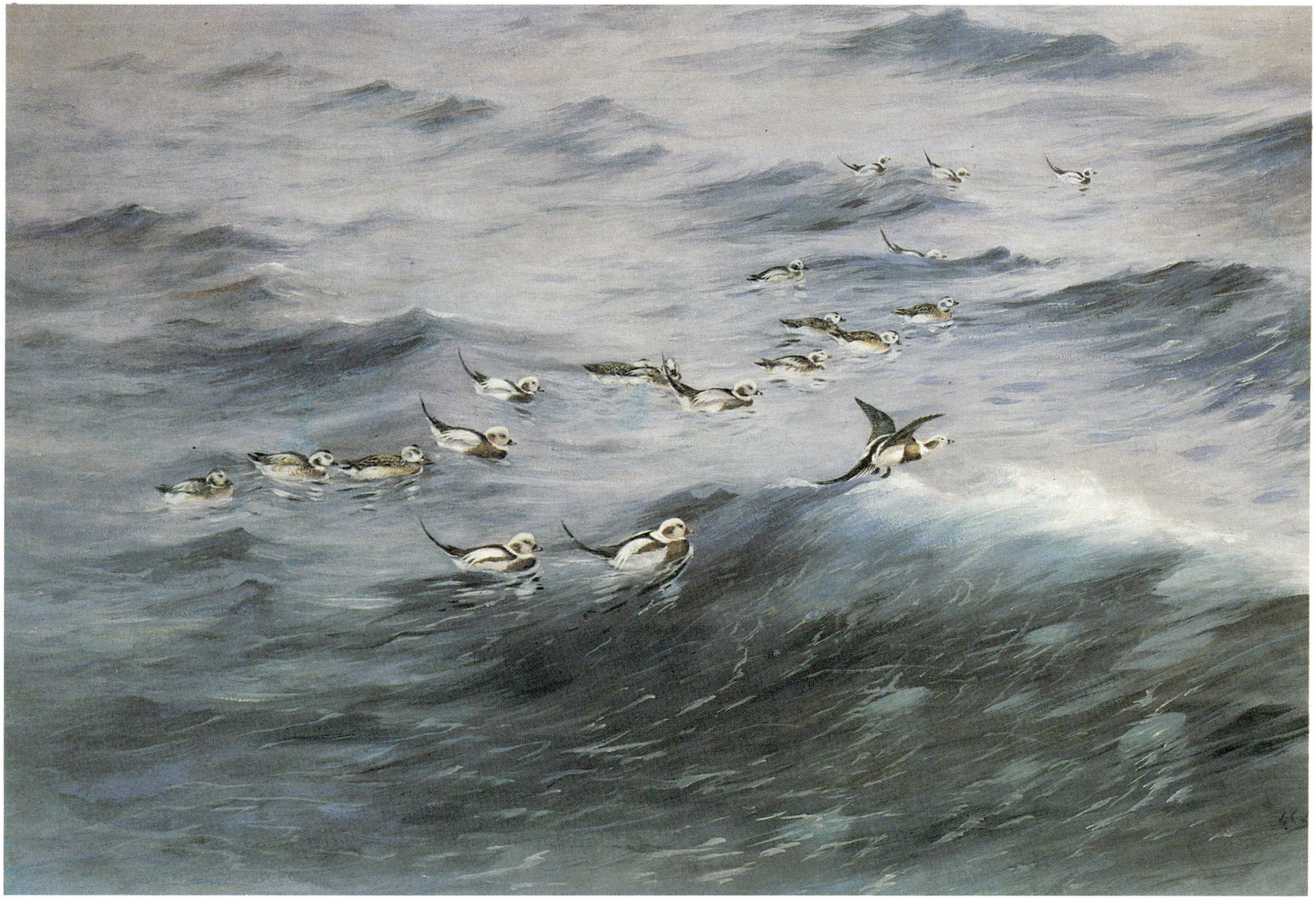

29 Long-tailed ducks at sea

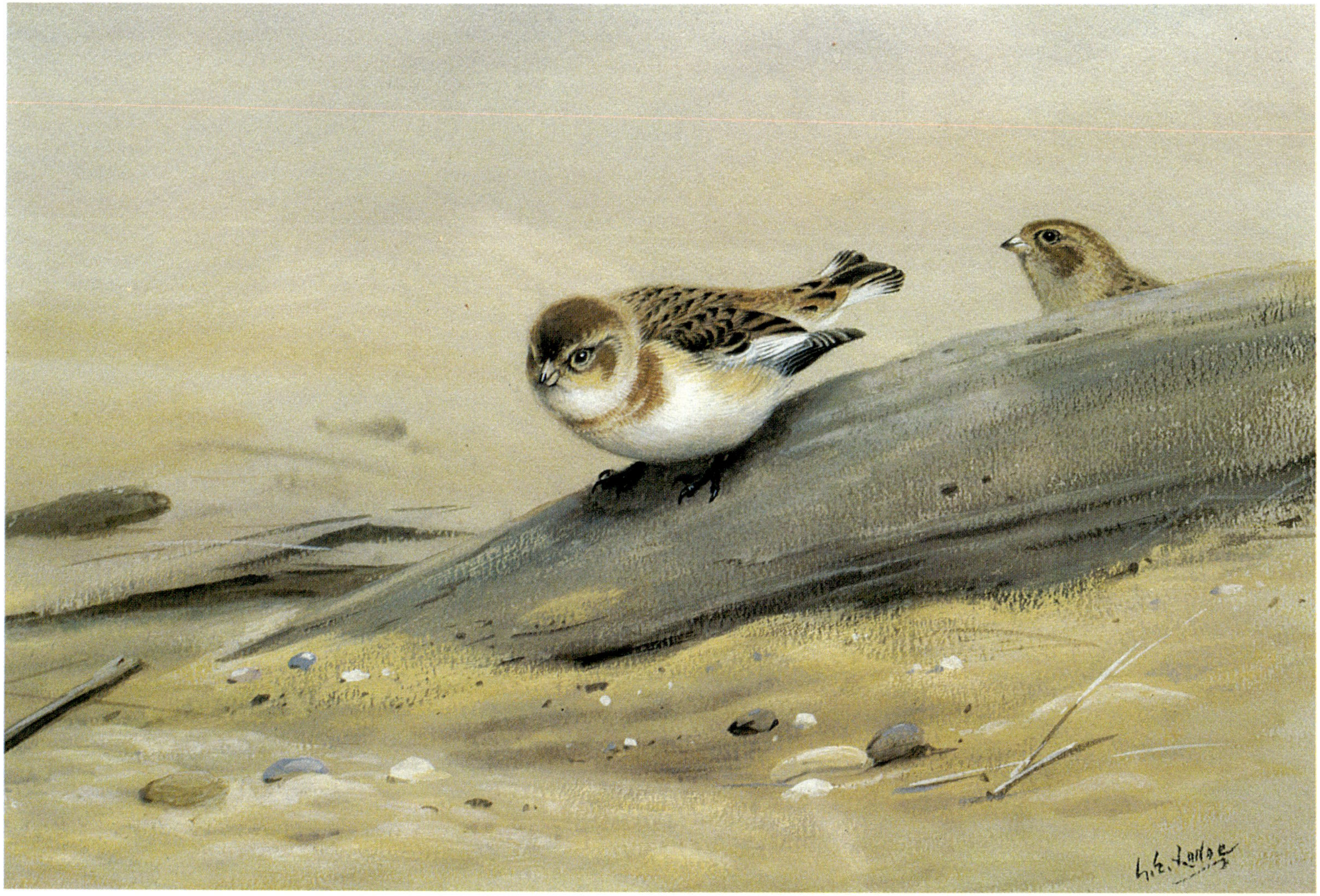

30 *Snow buntings*

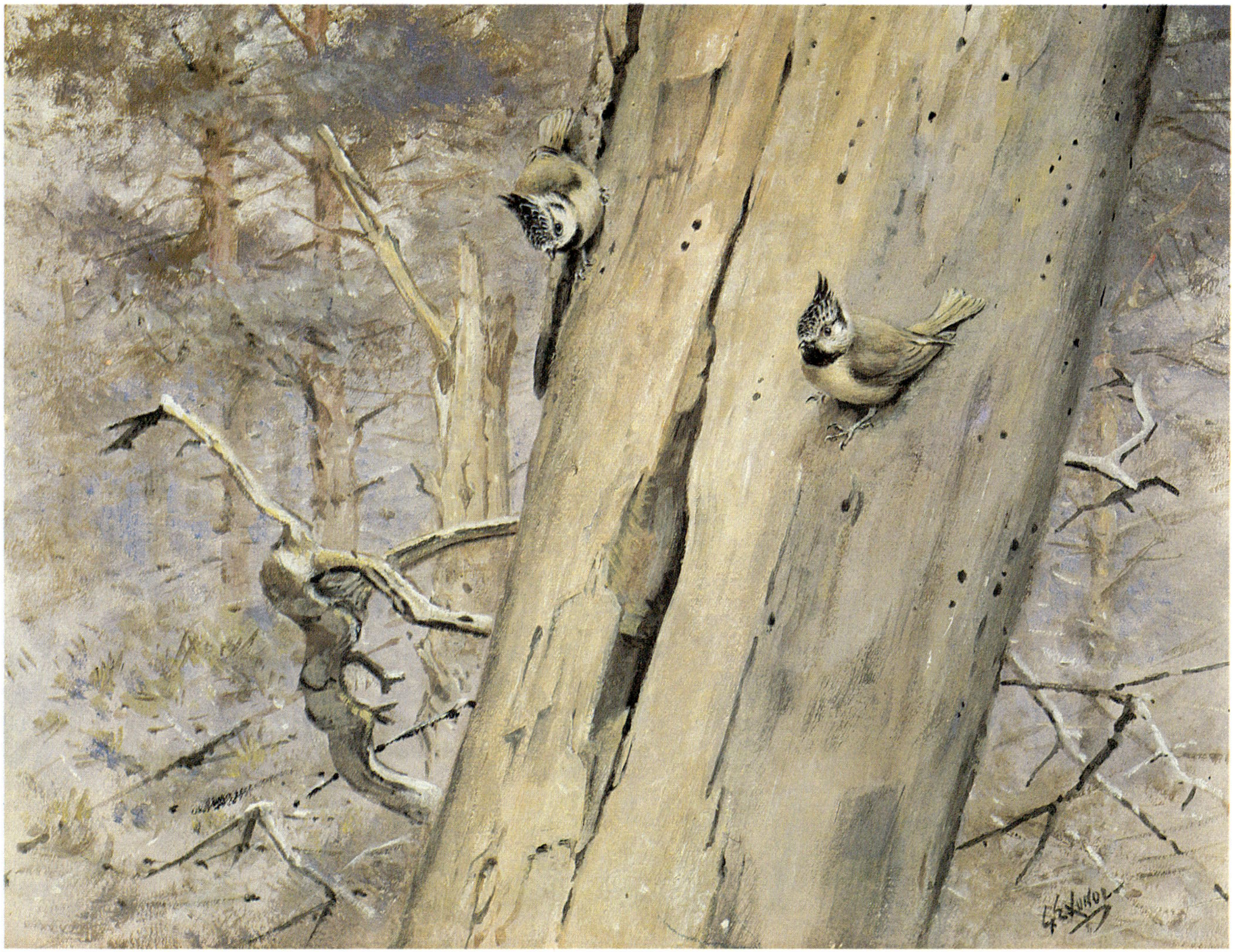

31 Crested tits

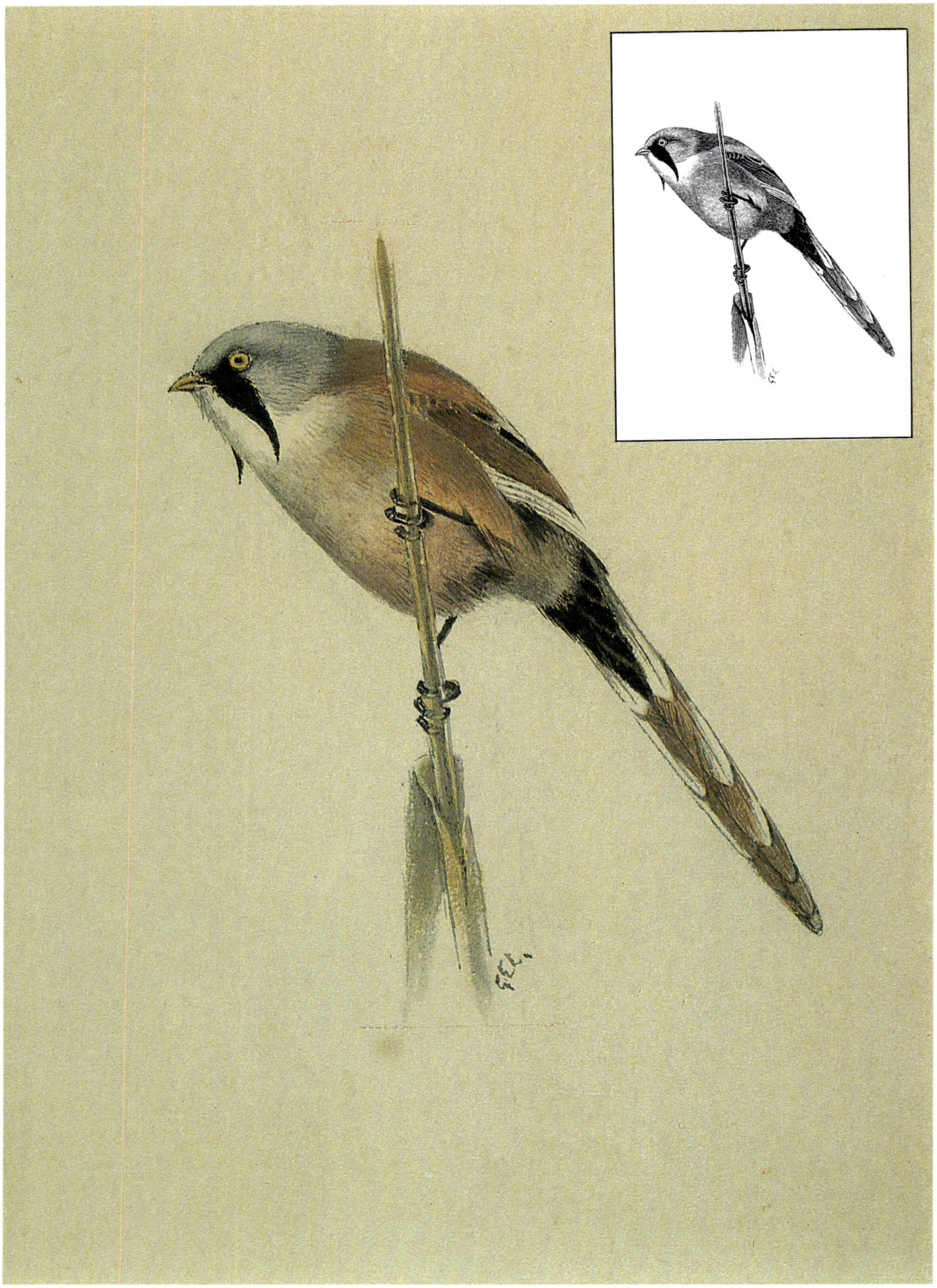

32 Bearded tit (with engraving)

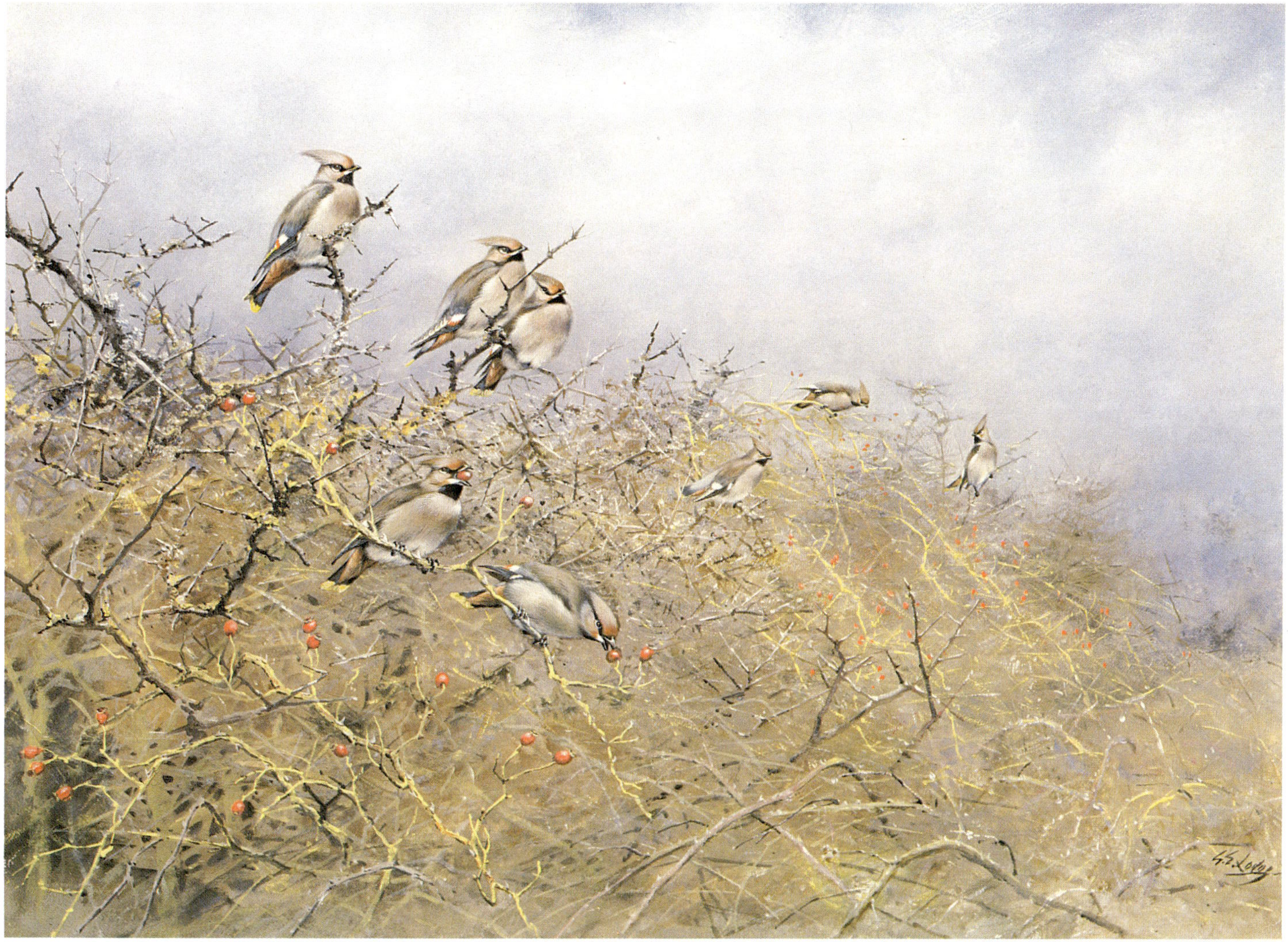

33 Waxwings

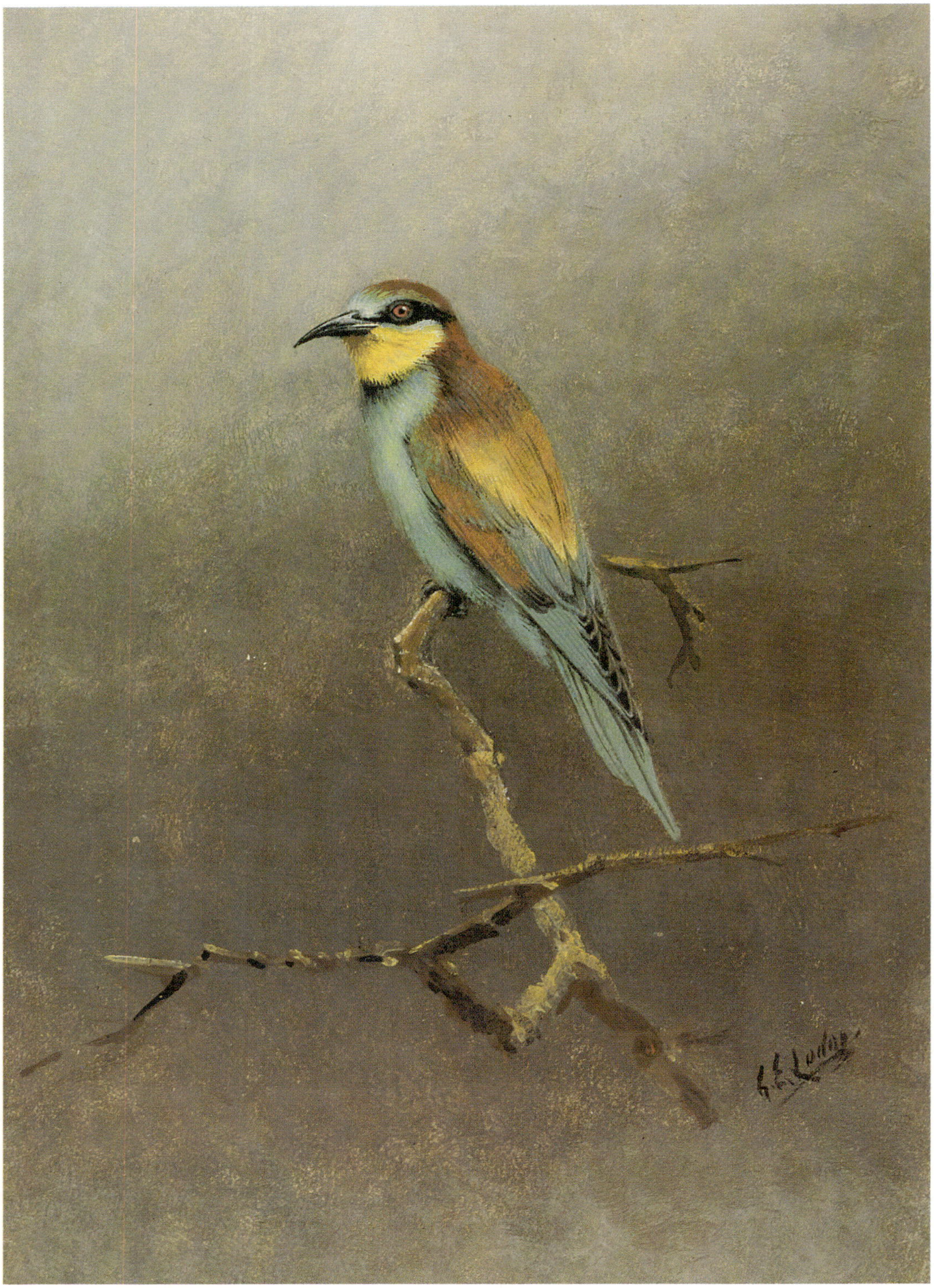

34 European bee-eater

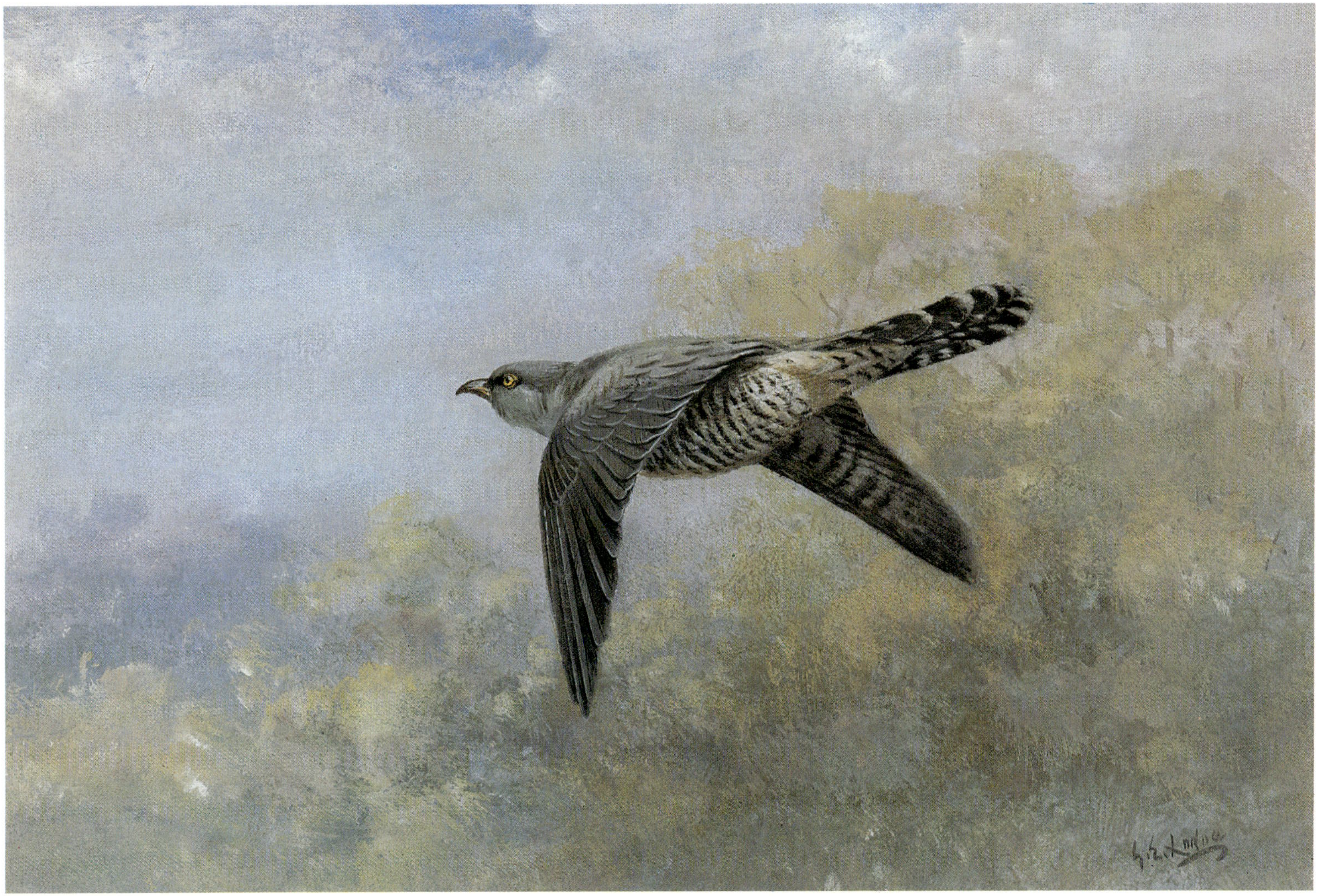

35 Cuckoo in flight

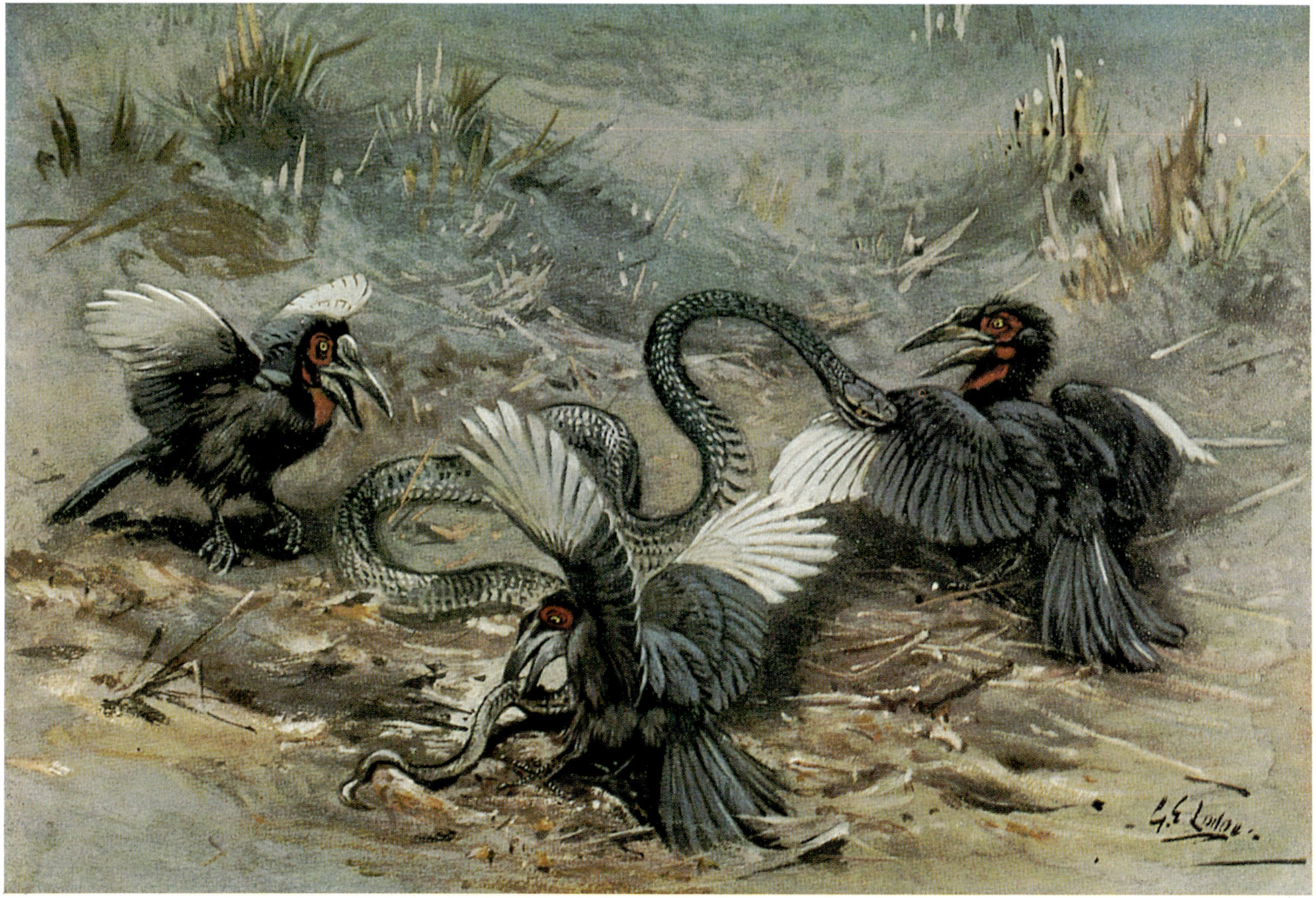

36 Ground hornbills and black mamba

any of his own birds there, although he was a competent falconer and had seen more birds flown than most of us. He would at times take one onto his fist and feed it up, and one could see by the way he handled it how proficient he was.

In the afternoons more parties would go out and often in the evenings as well, for the holiday was only about a fortnight and we wanted to get the birds going well. Evenings were a good time for the goshawks to be flown and they caught a great many rabbits which helped provide food for the less successful hawks and for ourselves as well. Lodge sketched not only the birds but anything else he came across that he thought might be useful later on — a branch whose shape caught his fancy, a rock, and views for backgrounds or for his rather rare landscapes. He always said he could never draw people, though at times one or two did appear in his pictures.

These hawking holidays were a great opportunity for people to see birds of prey both in action and in repose. They consisted mainly of the four species that were the main stem of falconry in those days: peregrines, merlins, goshawks and sparrow-hawks. Sometimes someone would bring along a buzzard, and one year a young hobby, not yet flying, was brought to us after a gale had blown it from its nest. I remember Lodge pointing out to me that a really well manned sparrow-hawk, when at rest and fluffed out, has white spots on its back the size of a sixpence. The moment it gets nervous or is about to fly its feathers tighten up and the spots are hidden.

When flying for the day was over we would gather in the Red Lion to discuss the day's events and to refresh ourselves. Sooner or later someone would say 'Come on Mr Lodge, let's see what you've done today', and he would obligingly let his sketch book be passed around. The amazing thing to me was not that they were extremely good sketches of birds of prey — and you must remember that falconers are just as critical of drawings of raptors as jockeys are of drawings of racehorses — but that these sketches had something extra, for one could easily recognise the individual birds. 'Look that's Mavro's spar Olga, there's Robert's merlin, and that's Silver Wings in the background preening', such were the sort of comments these sketches produced. Of course to the uninitiated one merlin looks much like another, as alike as sheep to all but the shepherd, and for an artist to catch the different characteristics in a quickly drawn pencil sketch was really something.

Looking at some of Lodge's hawking notes it is interesting to see that he was on Salisbury Plain with some of the members of the Old Hawking Club as early as 1890, sketching away just as he did in the 1930s. He used to tell us all about the horse-drawn van in which falcons were carried to the field in the old days, and how men had been employed to stand a mile or so downwind of the flying ground to act as markers if the falcons should come their way. It was all carried out in high style and was very different from our 'throw the falcon off and hope she goes' methods. He was not the only artist to come with us to Avebury. Henry Williamson was writing his book *The Peregrine's Saga* (1934) at the time, and he brought Charles Tunnicliffe, who was doing the illustrations, down one year to see our peregrines at close quarters.

During the next few years I met Lodge occasionally, but it was not until the latter part of World War II that I really came to know him well. I was in the army then and was stationed at Sandhurst as a gunnery instructor, and in my spare time I would often go and call on him at his home, Hawkhouse, in Camberley. Both he and his sister were extremely kind and in spite of food rationing they always produced a delicious tea, which after the dreary army fare was a great treat. I would be asked in and the maestro would usually be in his studio at the side of the house. Sometimes we went for a short walk together but more often we sat in front of the fire and talked about wildlife and the countryside in general, and of course about hawks in particular. He would talk of seeing the falconer of the Old Hawking Club bring back passage hawks from Holland, where they had been trapped by the hawk-catchers at Valkenswaard, of rook and partridge hawking with Tom Mann, of his other

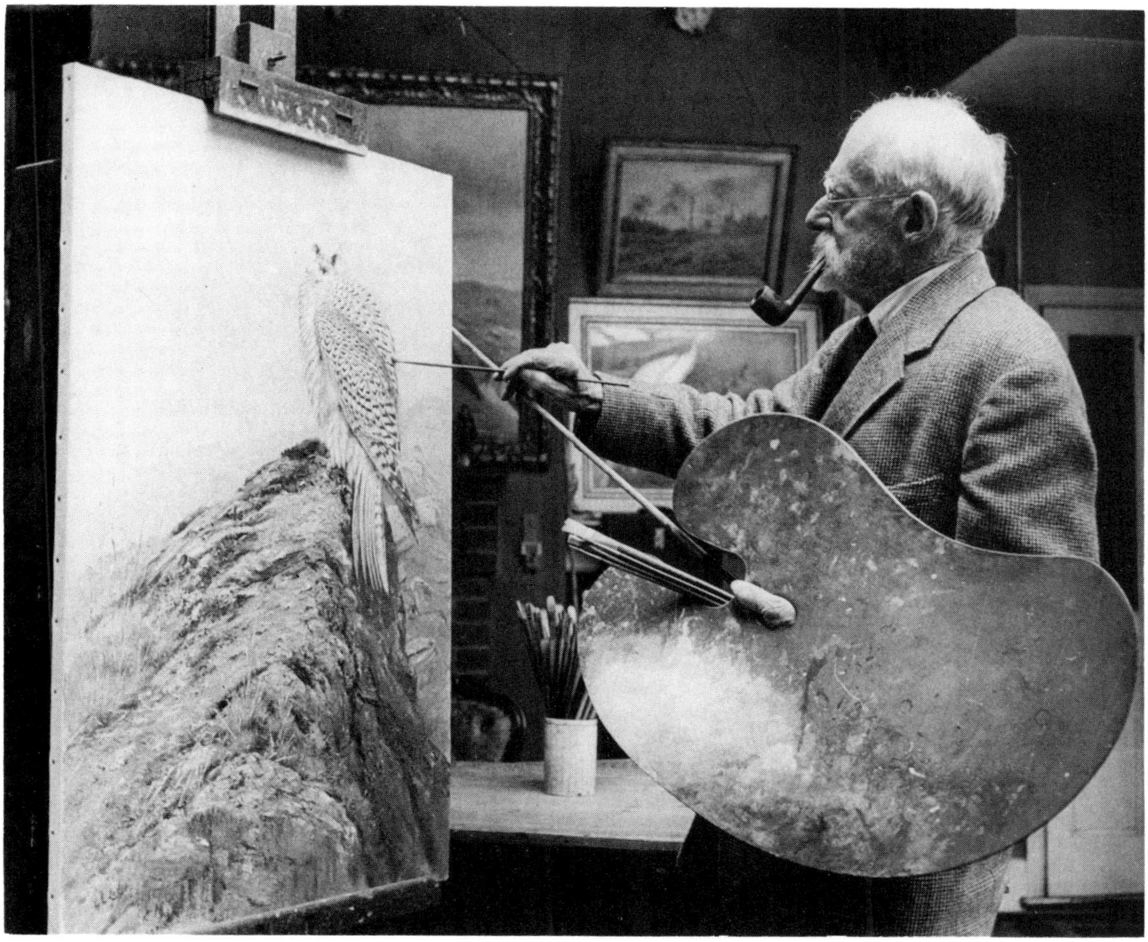

46

46. *The artist at work in his Camberley studio, circa 1942*

sporting interests, and of painting birds on his travels abroad. He would bring out a beautiful little gold tie-pin with a hood at its head, or his silver mustard pot in the shape of a hood with the spoon made like a lure.

Out in his garden we would watch crossbills feeding on pine-cones, and he would bring a discarded cone indoors to use as a model. He was a perfectionist and liked to have every detail correct in any picture he painted. His countless sketches of items of interest were all gathered in and stowed away, perhaps for years, till he had a particular use for them. At his request I brought back such things as a branch of a walnut tree, some viper's bugloss, or a root of wood sorrel, all models for his painting.

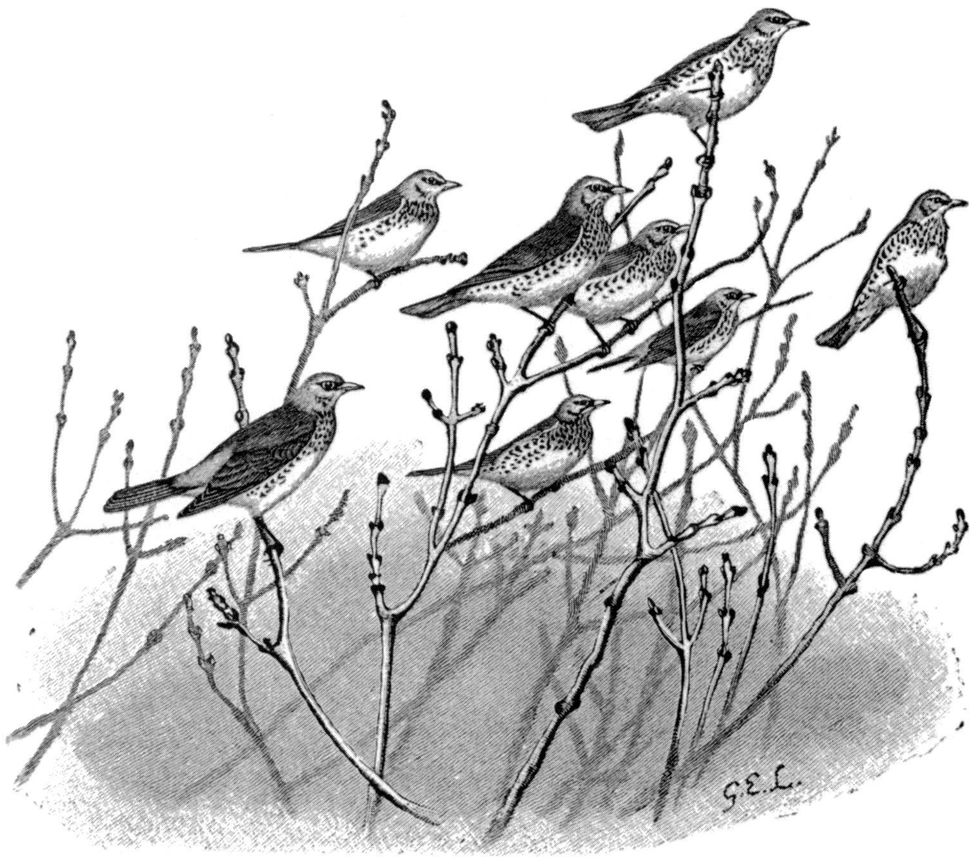

47

47. Fieldfares
48. Fieldfare sketches

Lodge never drew from photographs, and how right he was. Since those days I have met artists who came and took photographs of my hawks for use in their pictures and what a great mistake this generally proves to be, for the average artist has little idea of how to photograph even trained birds. They will use cameras with standard lenses, and because of this they get too close and all they get is a picture of a camera-shy bird. They also tend to make their own pictures far too photographic, with pin-sharp detail everywhere. Lodge himself remarked that in some paintings by fellow artists the birds seemed 'petrified'. If one examines his pictures one will often see that quite a lot of detail is left out simply because it is not necessary. I have a tempera painting by him of an Icelandic gyr falcon on a rock looking for a ptarmigan which has taken refuge underneath the same rock. The leaves of the arctic birch by the rock are not joined to the stems at all and yet, viewed from the correct distance, this does not show and the effect is great. One almost feels that one could peel the lichen from the rock, it is so lifelike.

Whilst at Sandhurst I happened to go into Guildford on a day pass, and in a secondhand bookshop there I noticed a large crayon sketch of a gyr falcon on a mallard drake. The sketch was on old yellowed paper on a wooden stretcher and was split in places, and I bought it for 30 shillings if I remember rightly. I took it straight to Lodge in Camberley and he confirmed what I had thought: it was by Joseph Wolf and was one of the many preliminary sketches that he did for a finished picture. I photographed the sketch and gave it to Lodge, and a few weeks later he gave me a small copy of it in oils that he had signed 'G.E. Lodge, after J. Wolf'. Lodge was a great fan of Wolf and told me that Wolf's early paintings made a lot of birds

48

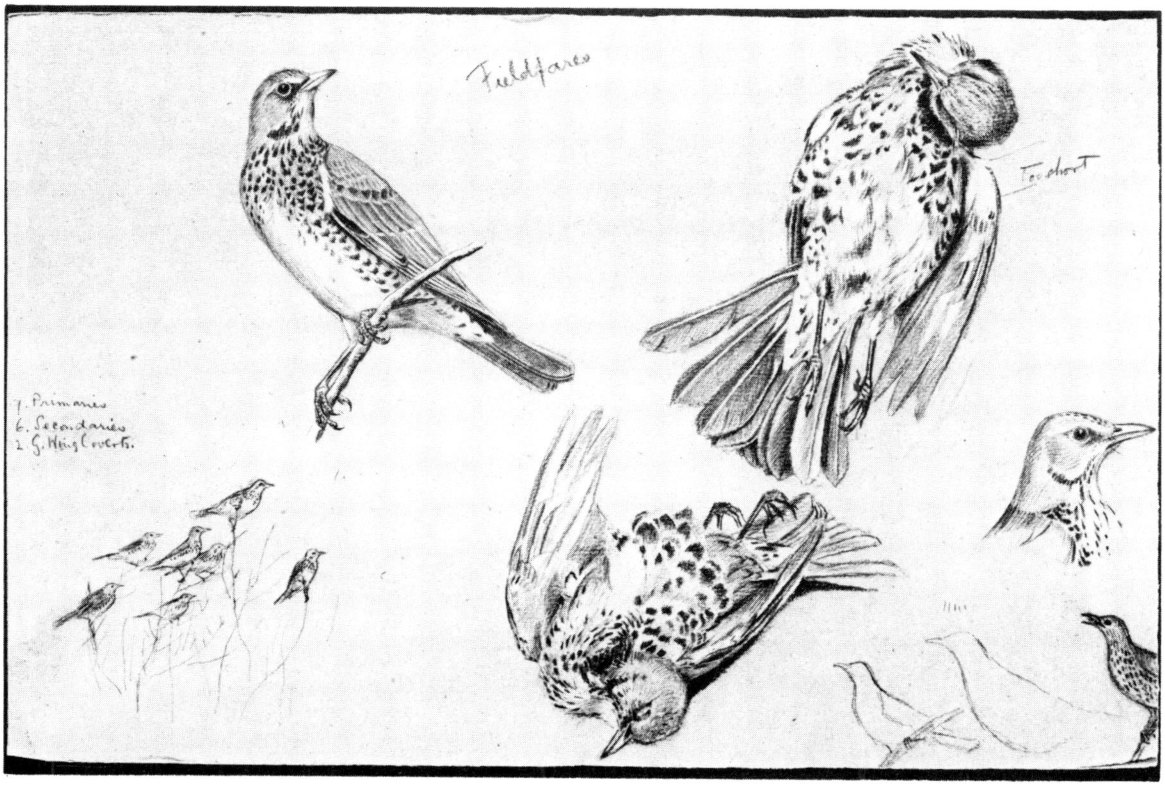

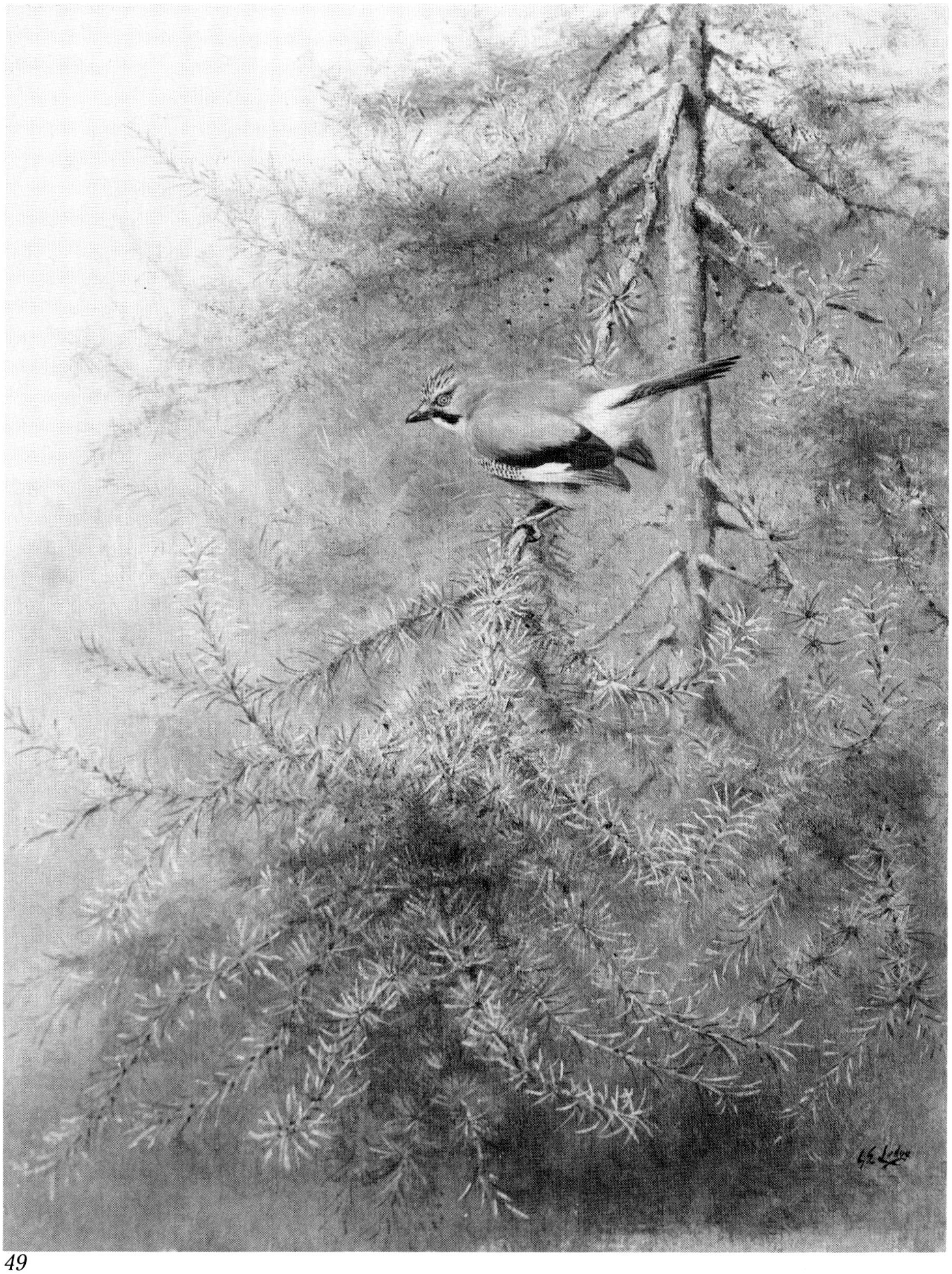

49

look too tight-feathered and frightened, but that later on he changed his style and became a far better artist.

At that time Lodge was working on the last few pictures for Bannerman's *The Birds of the British Isles*. This work was Lodge's great ambition and it is a pity that some of the birds of prey are not as good as they might have been. The reason was that people often wanted to buy a picture intended for the book and so he would say to himself 'Well I can always do another one', but his eyesight was going and he was no longer at his peak. Because of the war he found it difficult to obtain good brushes and had resorted to some rather strange ones that had been given to him many years before when he was in Japan.

His studio was full of paintings, stuffed birds and study skins. One would have tea with an ivory-billed woodpecker at one elbow, the skin of a harpy eagle sharing the same table as one's cup, and with a Scandinavian elk wending its way through some windblown timber as though to have a nibble at the toast. He set up the mounted specimens himself with great care. After measuring and skinning a bird he would cure the skin with arsenical soap and spend a long time loosening the feathers at their roots, and when he had made the body based on a lump of peat he would add bits of cotton wool here and there to conform with his original measurements. He told me that so many taxidermists worked under great difficulty because they had rarely seen their subjects when they were living. They often turned out specimens with sunken eyes because they failed to put something in place of the little pieces of flesh removed from the skull. He once said to me of such a bird: 'You'd call in the vet if it was your bird, it looks ill.' His study skins were used as guides for feather detail but not for colour, for as he rightly said, they not only fade but handling removes the bloom from feathers just as it does from a grape.

But the pictures were the main attraction: some hanging, large numbers stacked against walls or in portfolios, one in progress on an easel, a cupboard

49. Jay

with its panels painted with falcons, and shelves in one corner full of sketch books. It was a real 'Aladdin's cave' and others were obviously as enchanted as I was. One Sunday afternoon I was having a quiet chat with Lodge in his studio when Field Marshal Lord Alanbrooke came to see him. His arrival somewhat embarrassed me as he was more than a little higher in rank, and I thought I had better make myself scarce. However, George and the Field Marshal insisted that I stay, and we all three sat by the fire talking birds and painting for the rest of the afternoon.

He was kindness itself to me, and later on when I flew hawks and stalked in Scotland I was better able to appreciate what a great artist he was. For one of the great joys of Scotland is the constantly changing light on the hill, and Lodge was able to capture this in a way that I have never seen any other artist do. Just before his death I had suggested to Max Hastings, then editor of *Country Fair*, that Lodge was an ideal subject for one of a series of articles the magazine was running at that time. Max sent down a photographer but a week or so before publication Lodge died. The article was not scrapped, but instead was turned into a tribute to 'the veteran artist, naturalist and falconer'. The last line summed it up nicely: 'The old hawk is gone back to his eyrie.'

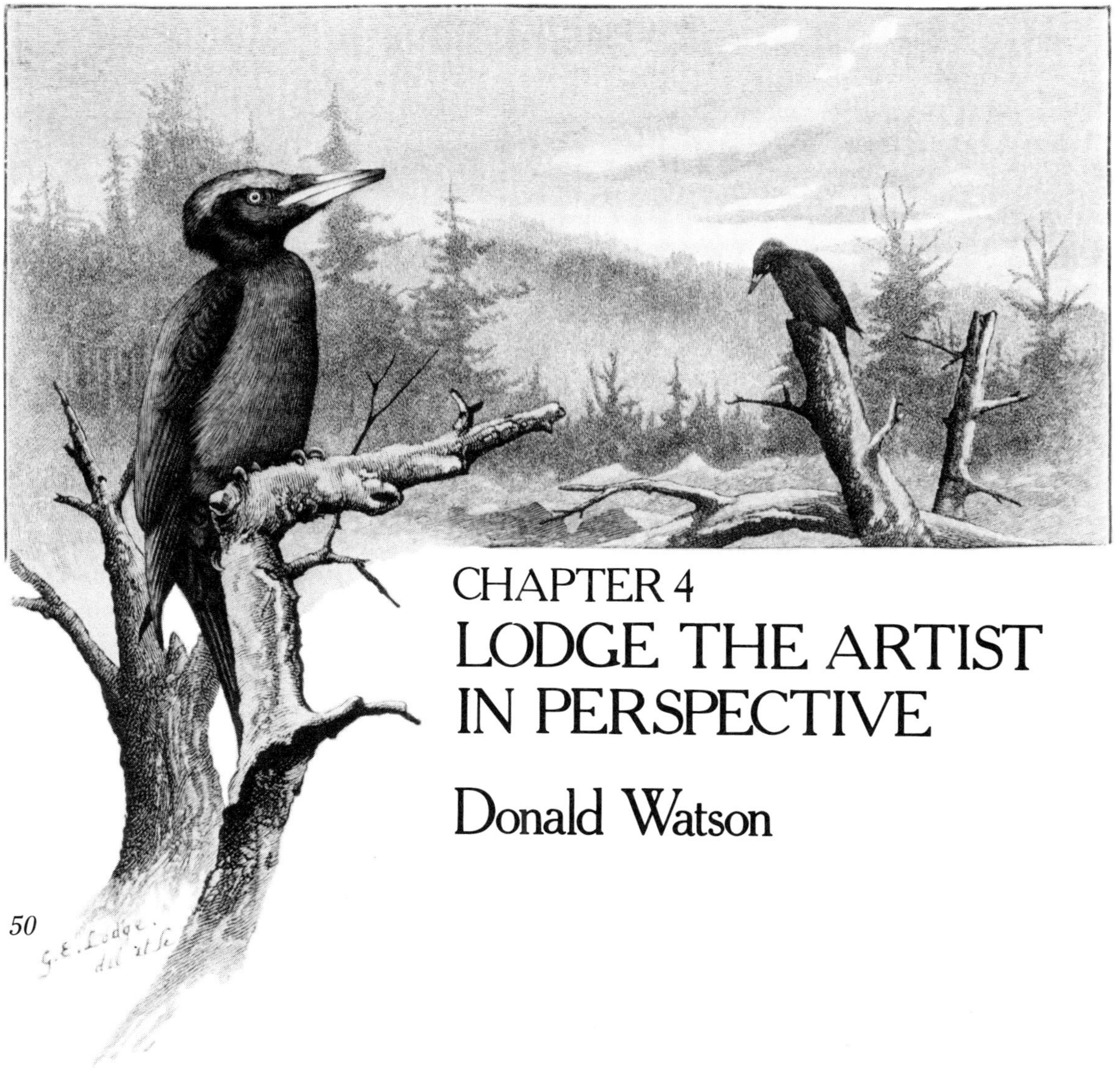

50

CHAPTER 4
LODGE THE ARTIST IN PERSPECTIVE

Donald Watson

In this book, thanks to John Savory's research, the full range of George Lodge's art is shown as never before. Like many bird artists, Lodge had to face the dilemma of finding his way between the rather arid requirements of identification plates and his natural inclination to paint pictures of wildlife in its environment. It is a tribute to his great skill as a wood-engraver that his black and white illustrations are generally of high artistic quality. Indeed some will say that these are his finest work, but my own view is that his most original and delightful achievements were his landscape paintings in which keenly observed birds or mammals, often on rather a small scale, were the focus of interest. In the best of these he excelled in mastering problems of scale and composition and, above all, conveyed the atmosphere and spaciousness of wild country. As young bird illustrators, both he and Thorburn revered Wolf who had been described by Landseer as 'without exception the best all-round animal artist

50. Black woodpeckers

51. Chough sketches and engraving

51

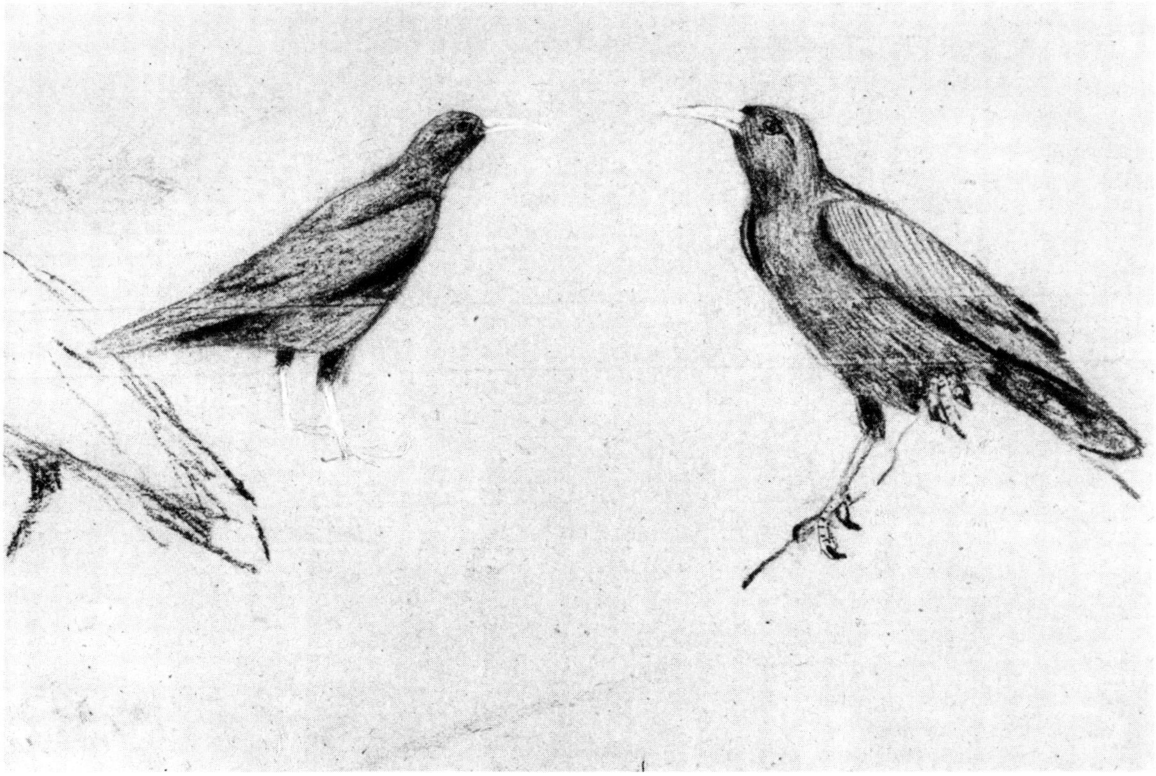

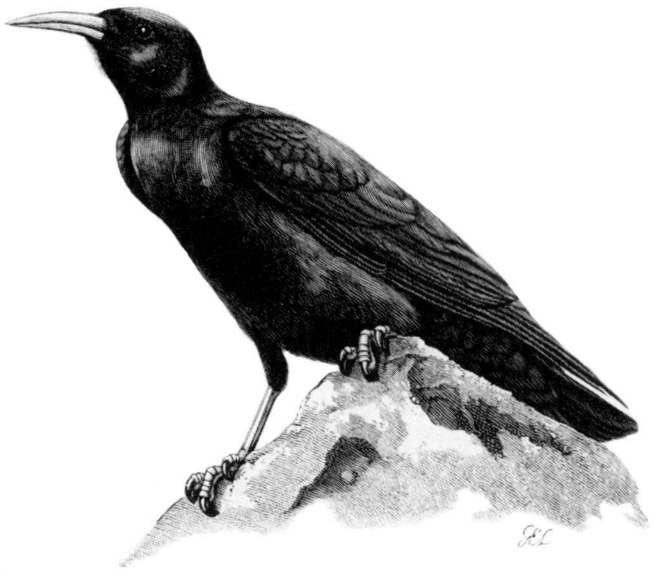

51

who ever lived'. Wolf was a very fine draughtsman but to modern eyes his major pictures tend to be heavily laden with sentiment, a quality which Lodge avoided. Few before Wolf had drawn birds in convincing living postures, although some like Edward Lear and Landseer himself had made fine studies from live models in zoos, especially Lord Derby's menagerie. The great decorative art of Audubon in the early nineteenth century of course owed much to knowledge of birds in the field, but for active postures he used cunningly devised arrangements of dead birds to simulate life. Wolf heralded a new era of drawing from life. One little-known artist of the mid-nineteenth century who was a pioneer in drawing birds from life was Jemima (Mrs Hugh) Blackburn. Her delightful lithographs of West Highland birds she had observed amply justify the title of her book *Birds Drawn from Nature* (1868).

When Lodge's fine wood-engravings were first appearing in books in the 1880s the long domination of bird illustration by John Gould and his team had ended, though Wolf, the most gifted, was still active. It has been said that Lodge's wood-engravings did not achieve Bewick's mastery of this medium, but they have wonderful richness of tone and far excel

Bewick in ornithological grasp. As Christine Jackson explains, developments in colour reproduction opened up new possibilities and artists like the Dutchman Keulemans and the Dane Grönvold were in demand for colour plates. For a long time little of Lodge's work was reproduced in colour. Grönvold was always a meticulous museum man and hardly related birds to their surroundings, but Keulemans' work for Lord Lilford's *Coloured Figures of the Birds of the British Islands* (1885-97) is not entirely eclipsed by that of Thorburn who took over when he fell ill. Keulemans painted some attractive pictures in a freer style than his book plates. Thorburn's plates for Lilford and in his own and other major books showed a special mastery in subordinating feather detail to the overall form and feathered appearance of his birds. His delight in colour and decorative floral touches combined to make him the most popular bird artist of his day. The coloured figures reappeared in reduced format in Coward's admirable *The Birds of the British Isles and their Eggs* (1920), but there is some loss of definition in the printing and signatures are indecipherable or absent in some plates. It is therefore all the more fun spotting Lodge's few distinctive contributions. So lowly was the artist's status that Keulemans, Lodge and Smit are referred to as 'others' on the title page of Coward's book.

While in Britain the demand for bird books with coloured illustrations greatly influenced the careers of Thorburn and Lodge, their contemporary Bruno Liljefors in Sweden was hardly touched by this discipline. Liljefors' large, often dramatic and always broadly painted canvases were the antithesis of Thorburn's gentle but very personal watercolours. Where did Lodge fit into this trio? Both Liljefors and Lodge were keen shooting men and were fascinated by avian predators in pursuit of prey, while Thorburn disliked all killing in spite of being greatly admired as an artist by the sporting public. I think this difference in attitude goes some way towards explaining why Lodge's wildlife art is closer to Liljefors than Thorburn. If Liljefors was more of a 'painter's painter' than either of the others, Lodge at

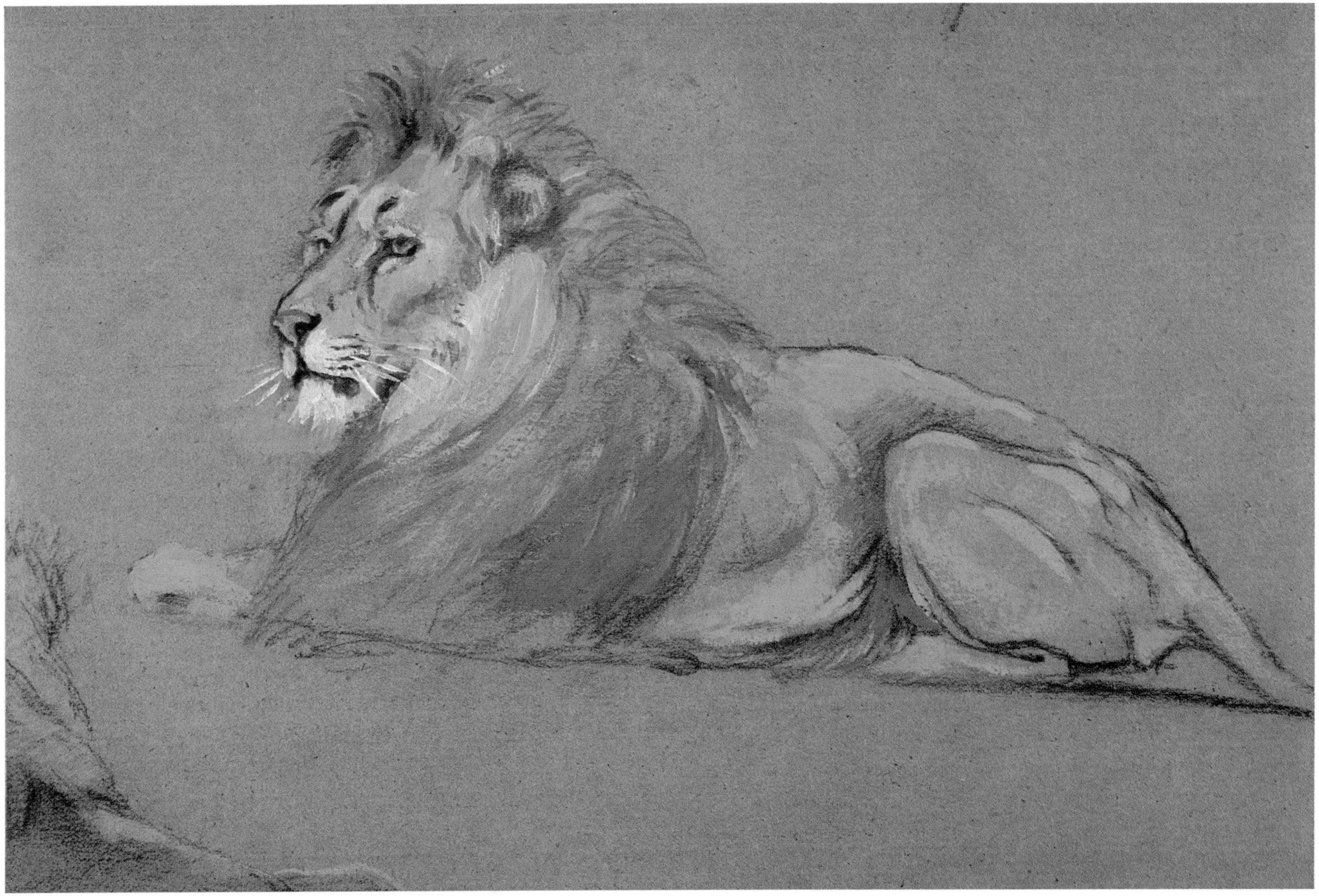

37 Lion sketch

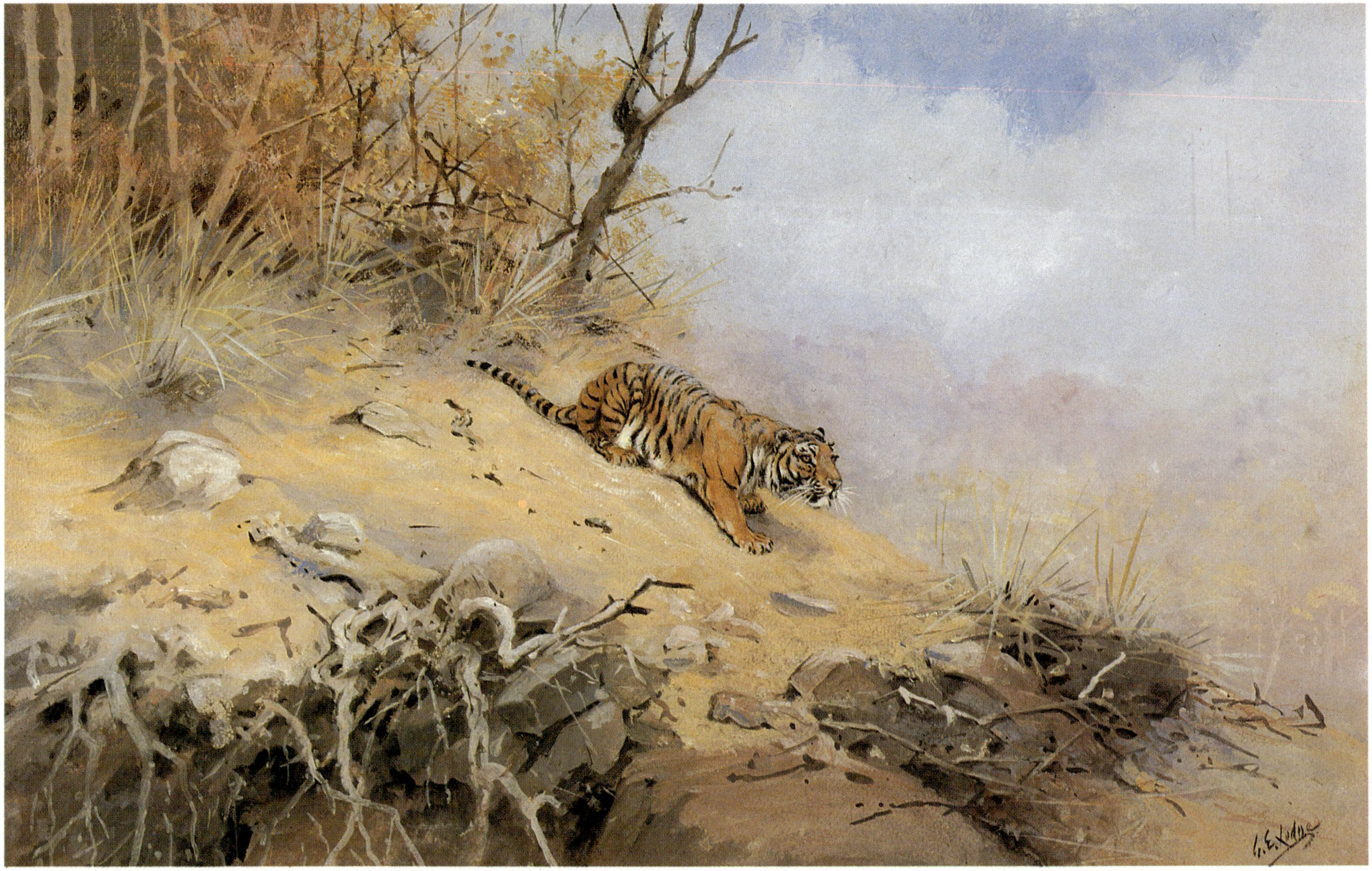

38 *Tiger crouching*

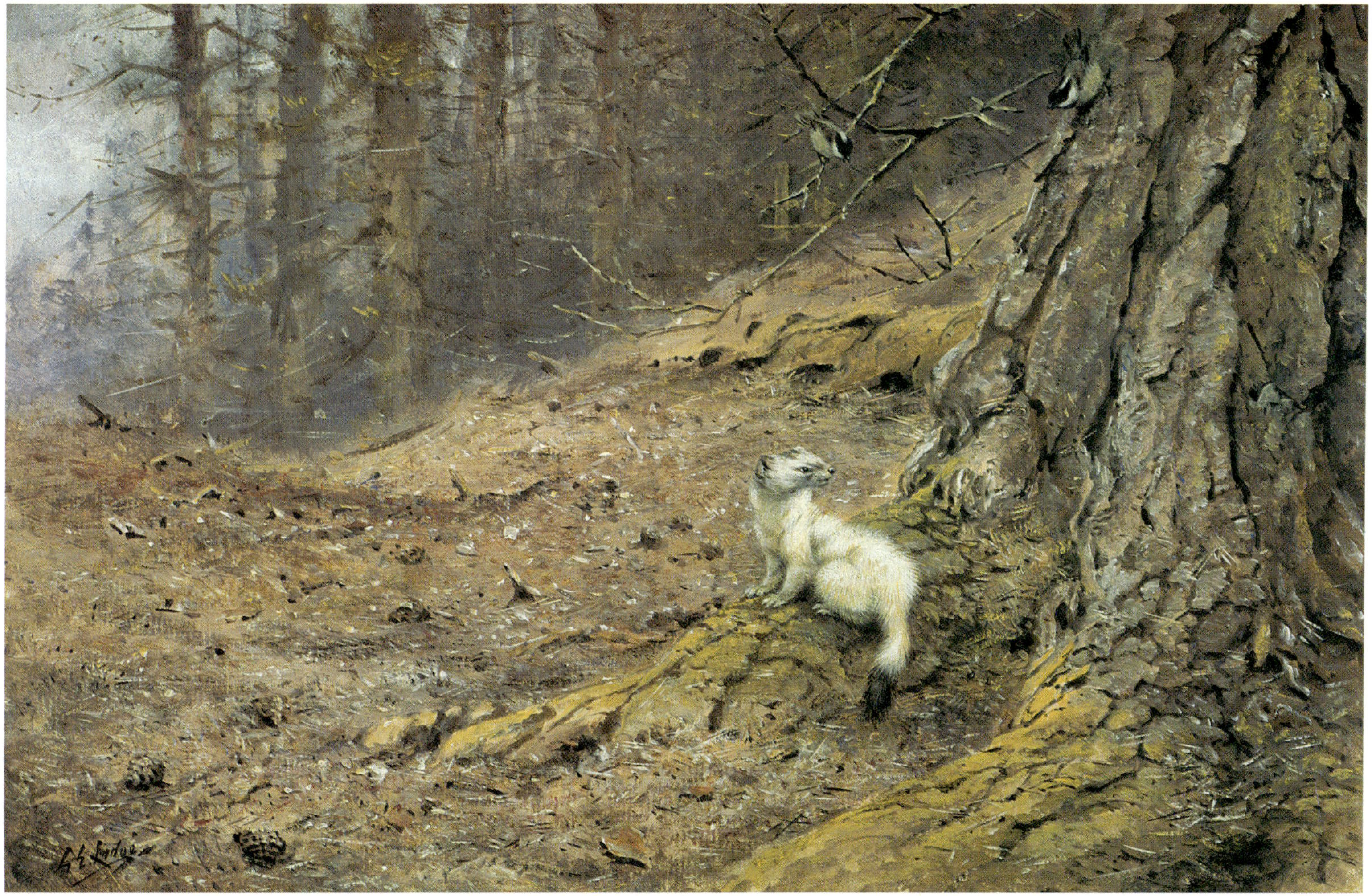

39 *Stoat in ermine mobbed by coal tits*

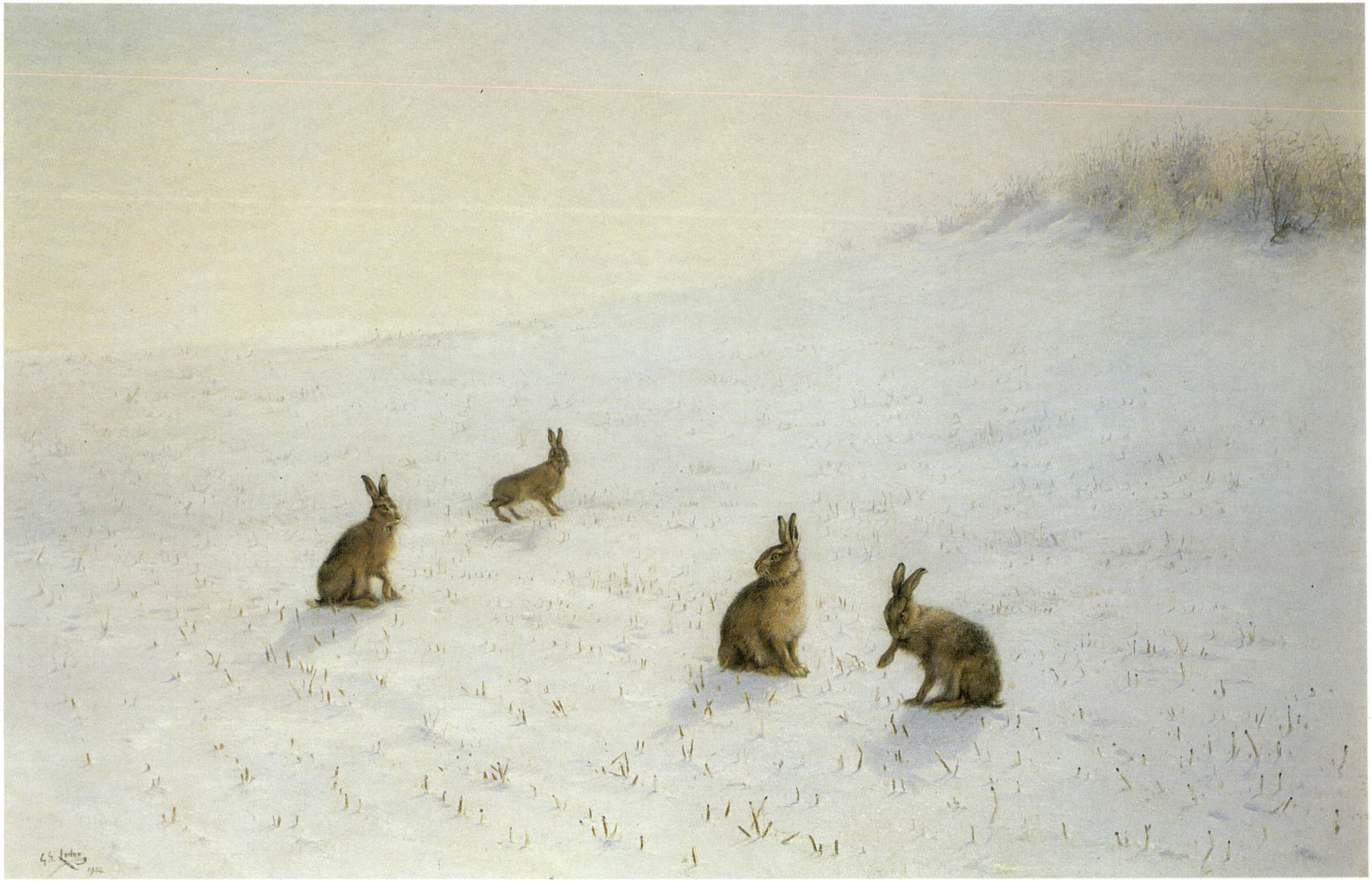

40 *Brown hares in winter stubble*

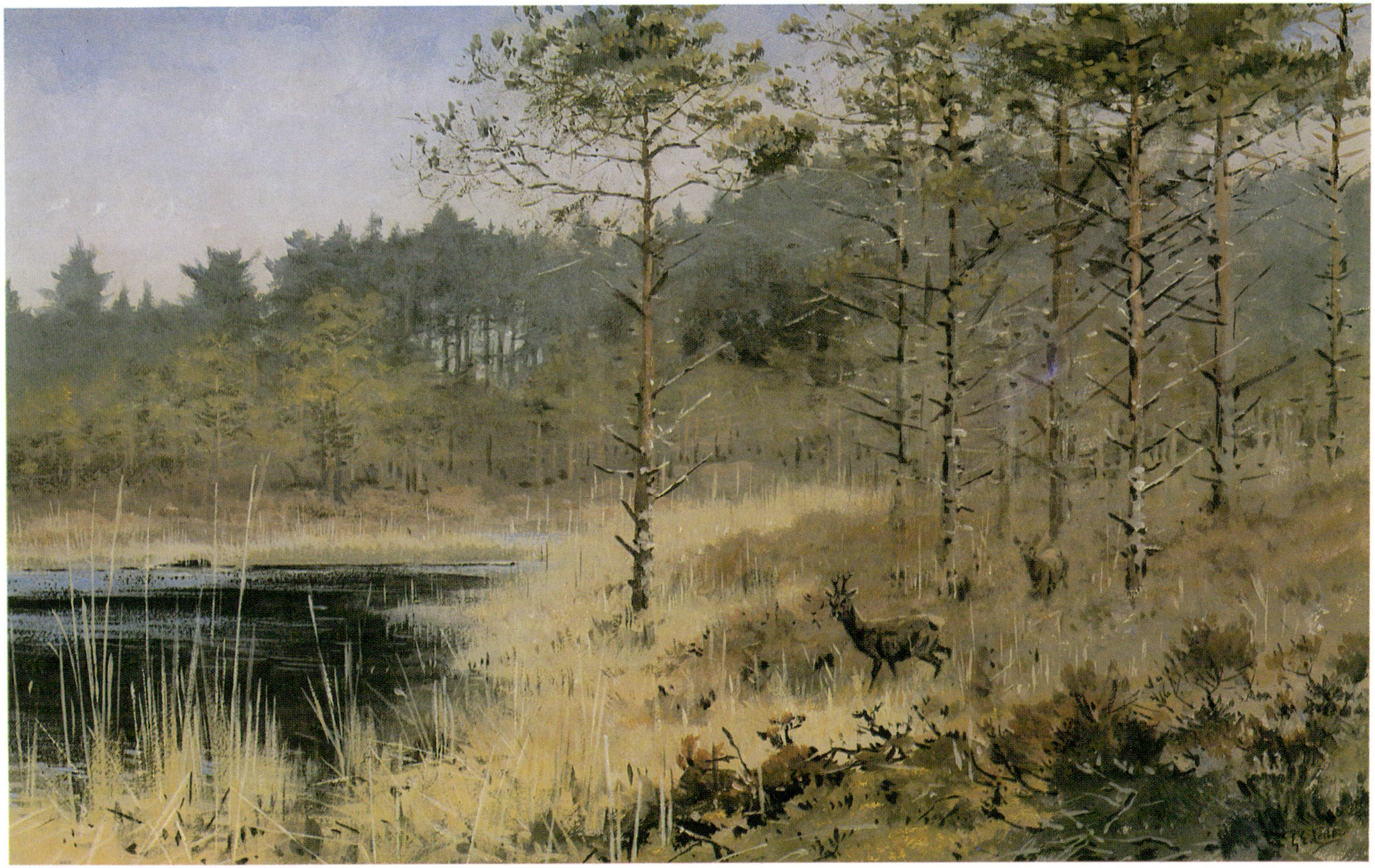

41 *Roe deer at a lochan in Rothiemurchus forest*

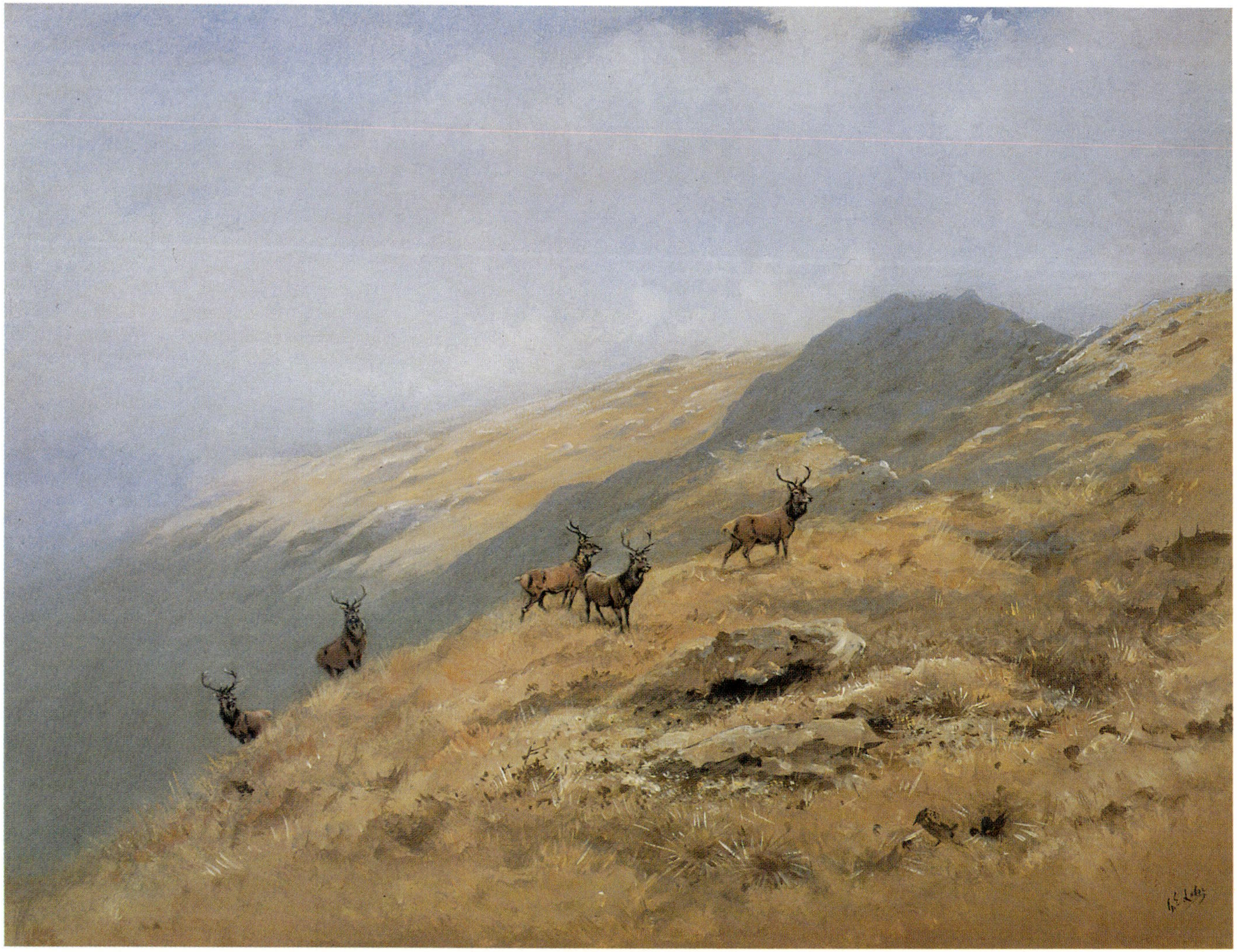

42 Highland red deer

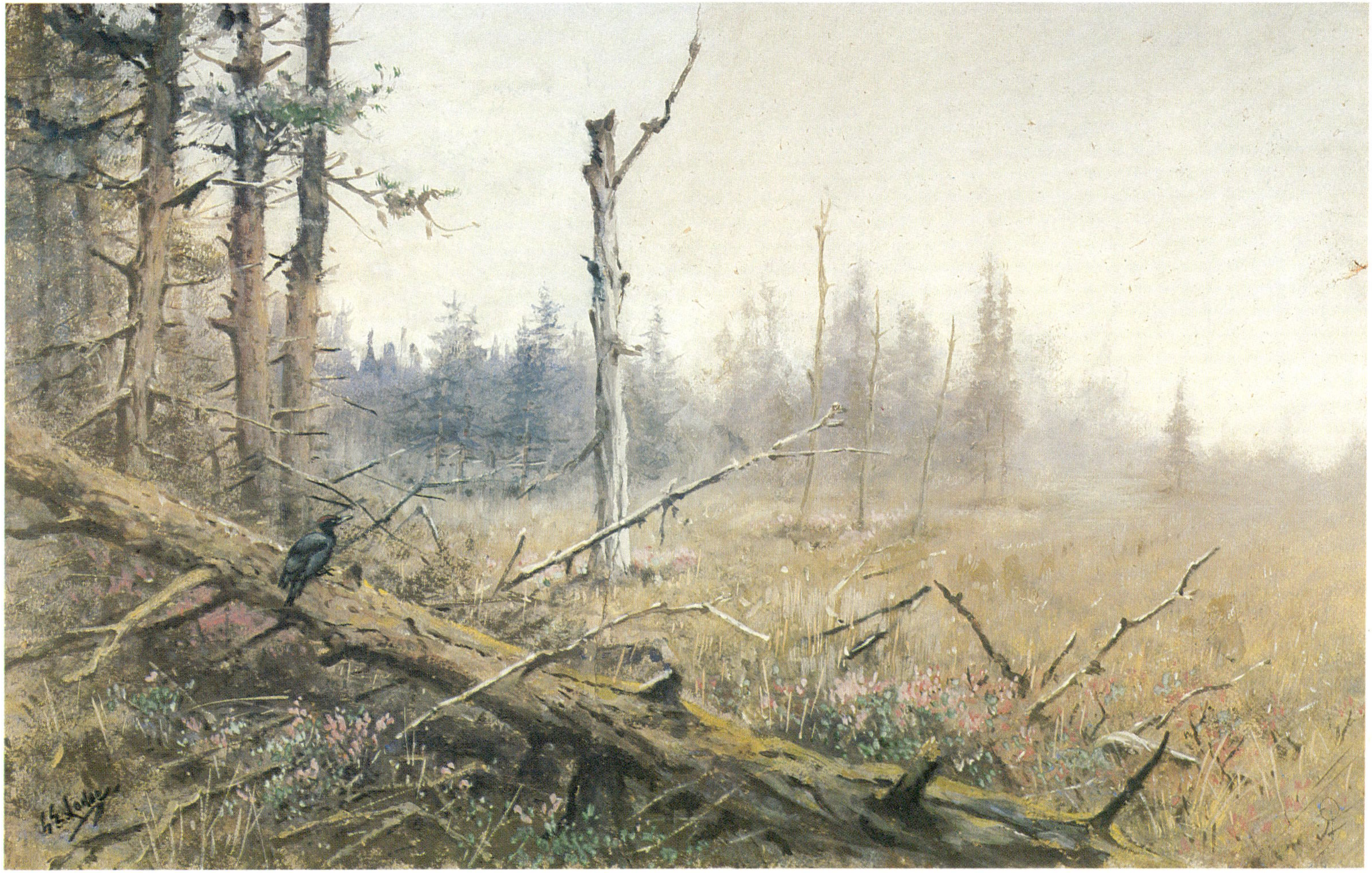

43 *Black woodpecker habitat*

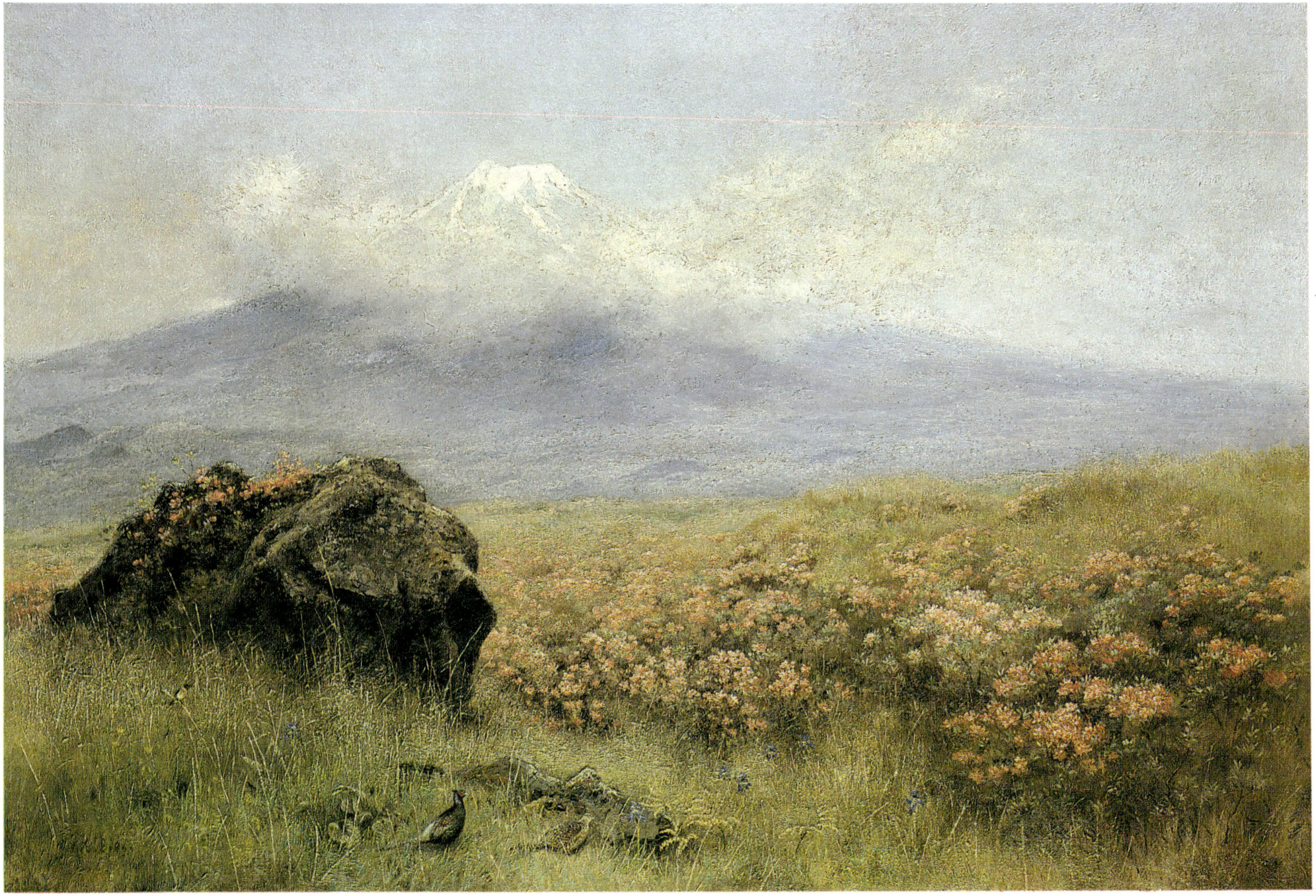

44 Pheasants and stonechat, view of Mt Fujiyama from Shogi (Japan)

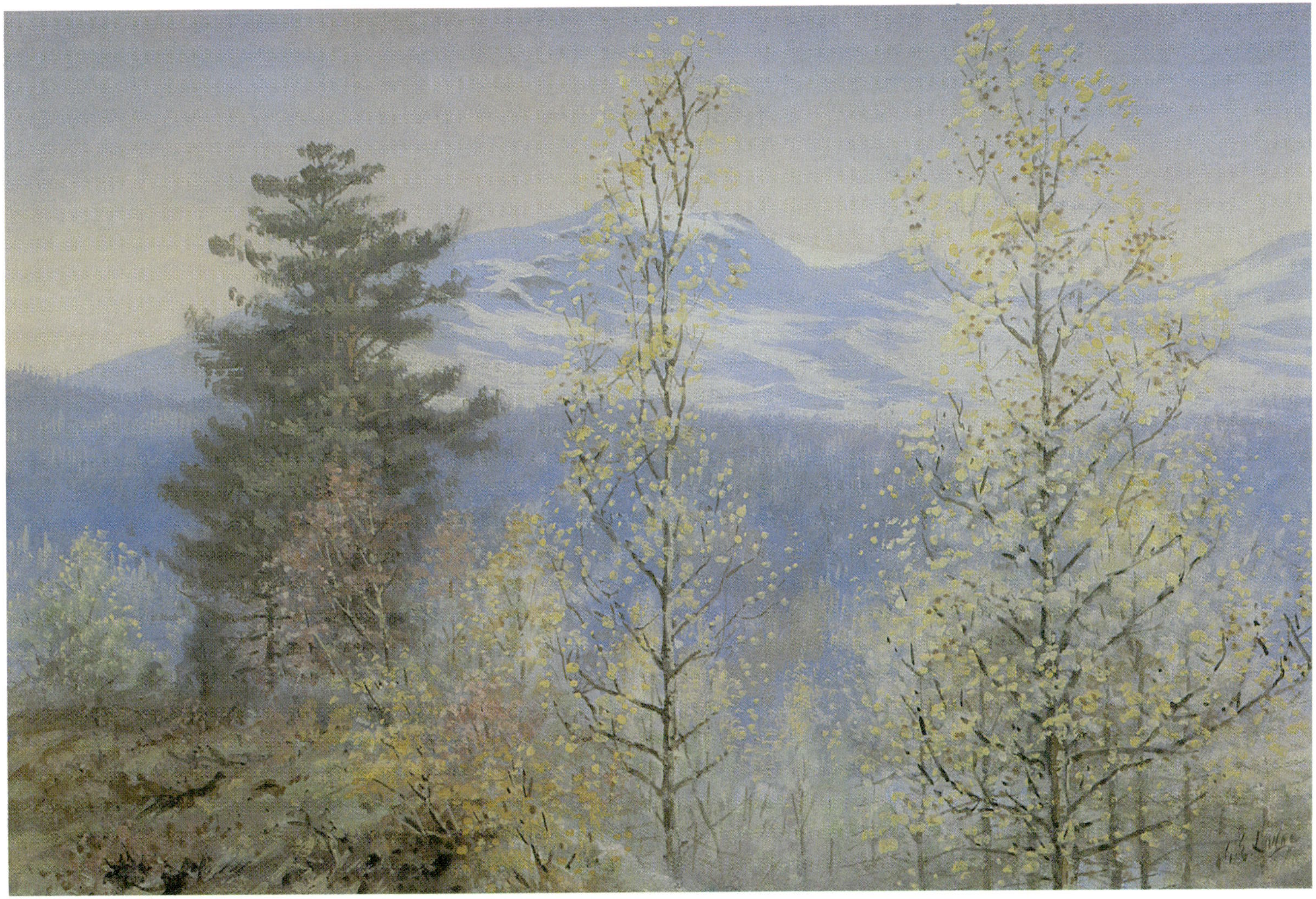

45 *Silver birches, Norway*

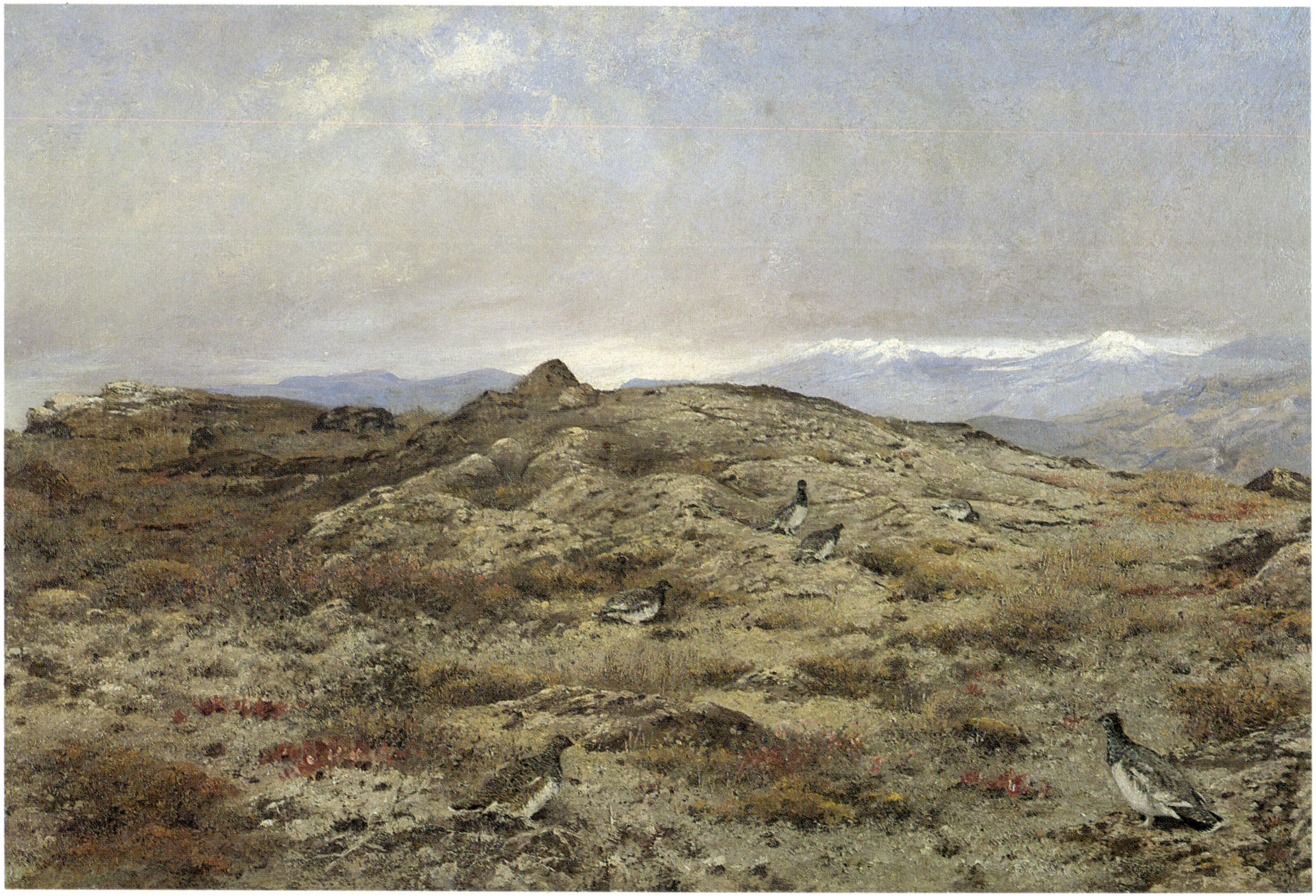

46 Ptarmigan ground, Norway, exhibited at the Royal Academy in 1905

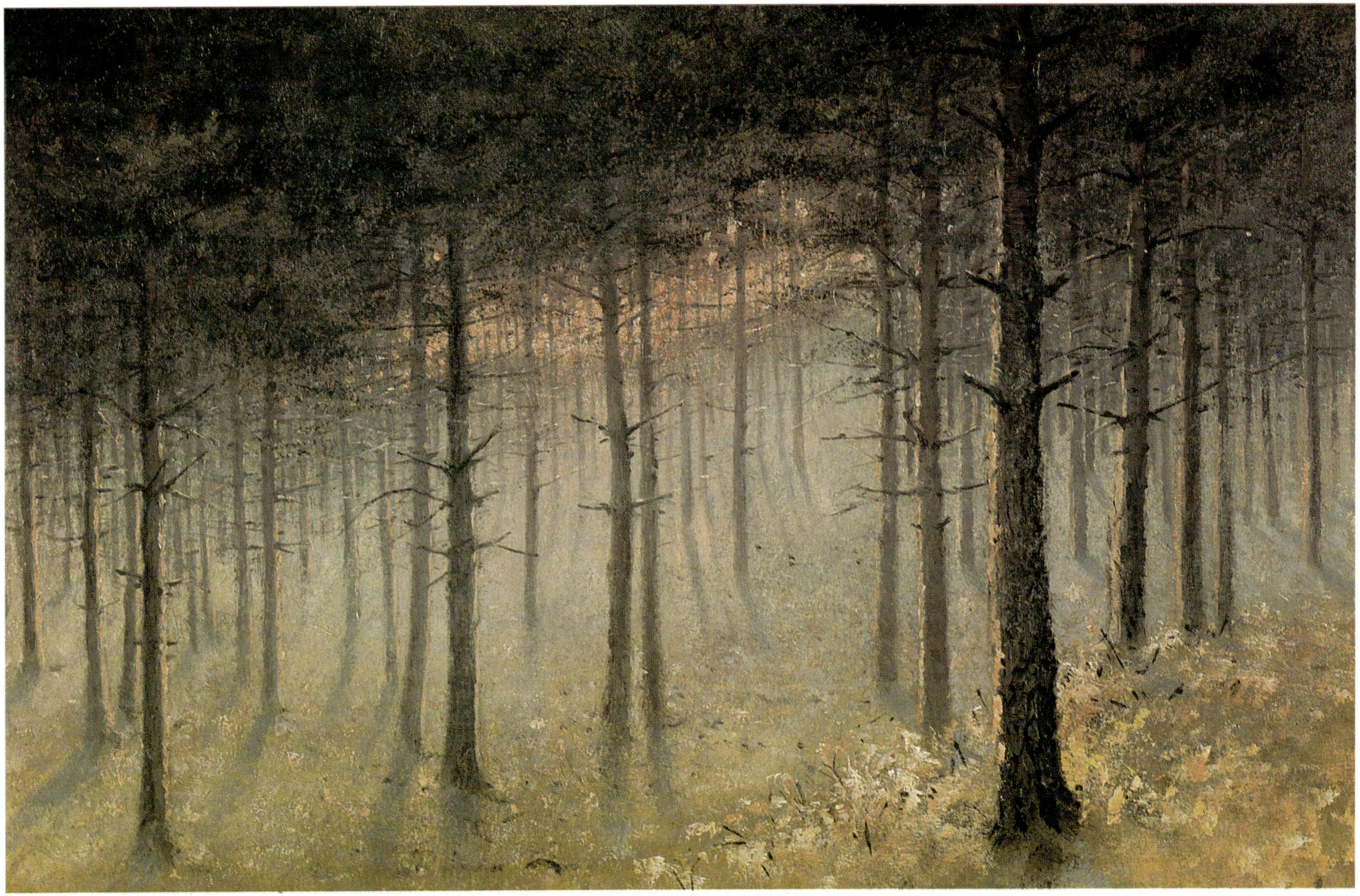

47 *Sunshine through trees, a plantation near Camberley*

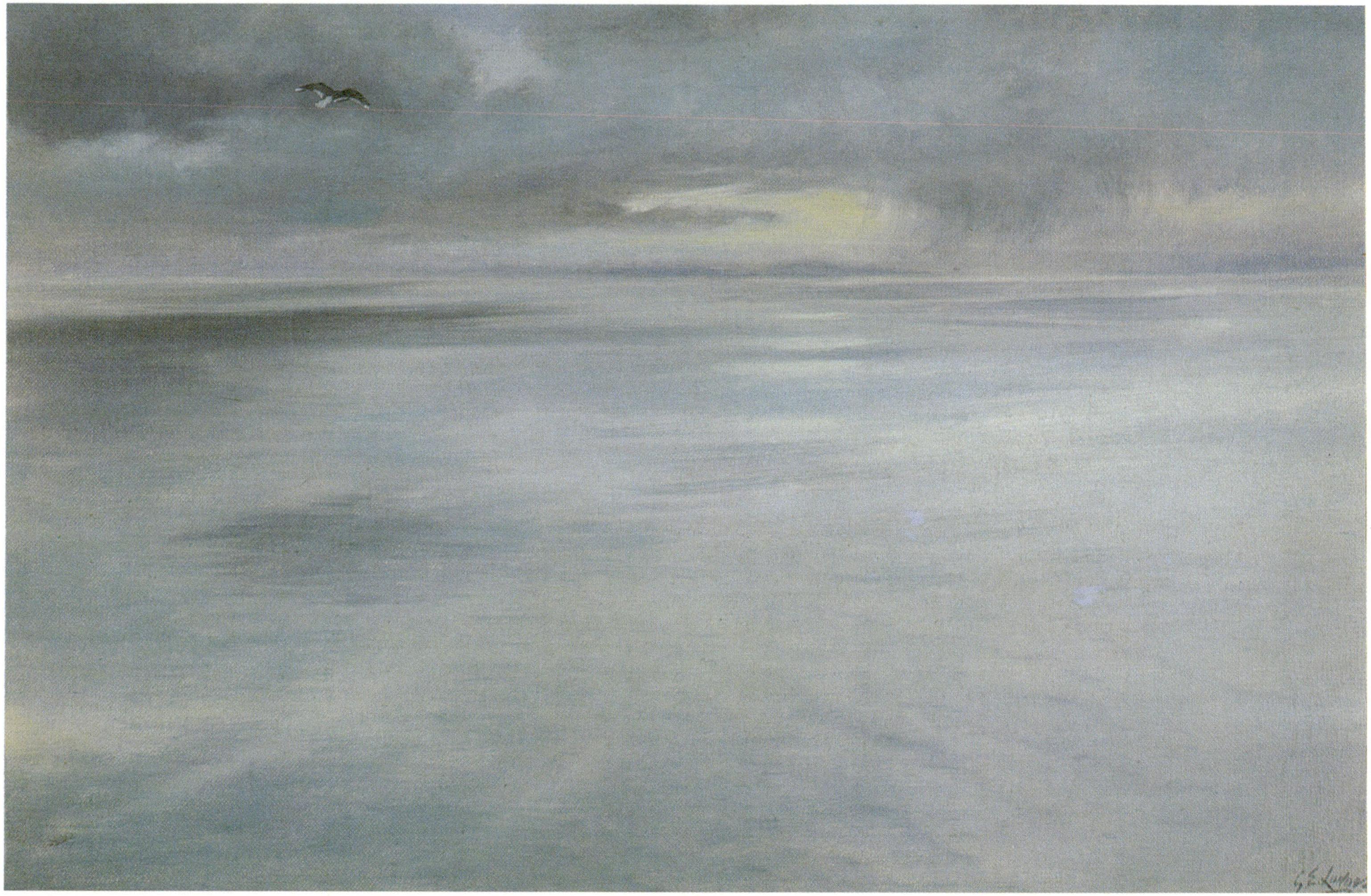

48 *Seascape with a lone gull*

his best was no less good at evoking the landscape environment of his subjects. Working in tempera or oils, Lodge generally surpassed Thorburn at birds of prey by making them more truly raptorial and by his superior drawing. Many years ago, when my brother and I were very young, we spent a glorious afternoon with Thorburn in his studio. He told us that some drawings on a side table were by his friend George Lodge and that he regarded him as the master at birds of prey. Both Lodge and Thorburn were exceptionally good at painting game-birds, but in some of Lodge's finest pictures, like partridges in a turnip field (Pl. 22), it is the union of birds and landscape that is so good. In this picture do I detect an affinity with the Hague School of landscape painters, especially Roeloffs, who was also a naturalist? Lodge must have known the work of the contemporary German wildlife artists, Kuhnert, Rungius and Friese, famous for their pictures of large mammals in their environment. Even with all her African and Asian territories Britain was well behind Germany in painters of 'big game'. Thorburn admired the sensitive and discreet watercolours of Edwin Alexander, a fine Scottish painter of birds, insects and flowers whose work appeared in only a few books. Lodge had some good, characteristic plates in Kirkman's *British Bird Book* (1910), but to my mind the most exciting pictures in that book are by A.W. Seaby. Both Alexander and Seaby must have been aware of the art of Joseph Crawhall who was influenced by seeing Japanese prints. There is an example in this book (p. 43) of Lodge's collaboration with J.G. Millais who, among many accomplishments, wrote and lavishly illustrated *British Diving Ducks* (1913), though one of the best plates in that book is by Otto Murray Dixon, tipped as a successor to Thorburn before he was killed in the 1914-18 war. Frank Southgate, another war casualty, was a splendidly atmospheric painter of East Anglian wildfowl, much admired by Eric Ennion (1900-81).

It is tempting to write about more of the fine bird artists born near the end of the century like Winifred Austen, George Henry, Philip Rickman, J.C. Harrison,

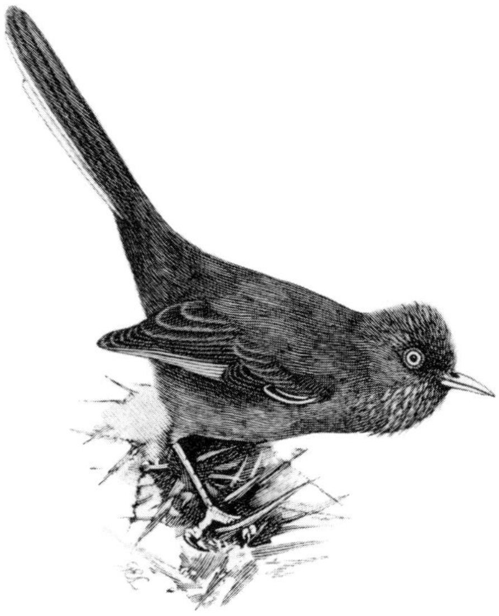

52. Dartford warbler

Roland Green and R.B. Talbot Kelly, but that would lead me too far from my brief! Mention must, however, be made of Fuertes (b. 1874), the brilliant American. In correspondence published recently in the fascinating *To a Young Bird Artist: Letters from Louis Agassiz Fuertes to George Miksch Sutton* (1979), he advised the aspiring young Sutton of the excellence of 'some of those Europeans', showing him work by Liljefors and Thorburn.

Lodge was clearly less happy at some groups of birds than others, and some of his illustrations of passerine birds have been particularly criticised. His reputation suffered to some extent because many critics were unfamiliar with the true range of his work, so much of the best being done early in life and never reproduced. I hope that the present selection will be a revelation to younger generations.

Drawing birds in flight is a special challenge to bird artists. Today we have all absorbed a great deal of knowledge of wing actions from modern photography, though this does not provide the secret of suggesting rapid movement in a drawing. I doubt if any of Lodge's contemporaries made much use of photographs and Lodge himself has said (p. 100) that he never did. Liljefors daringly blurred the wings in paintings of fast-moving eider flocks, but most artists of the period had no answer to this problem which they usually avoided when doing close-up portraits of birds for book plates. Lodge, perhaps inspired by Wolf, was undaunted by such subjects as stooping peregrines. The results show his acute observation, but I think it is fair to say that the impression of rapid flight is better conveyed in some of his sketches from life than in his finished pictures with more feather detail than the eye would see. He was aware of the danger of 'petrifying' a bird with too much detail, but feared that to blur the wings would result in a 'daub'. He has given an interesting account of how he watched a party of ravens mobbing a pair of eagles (p. 94) but found the birds' movements far too rapid for the eye to register. Nowadays, with modern binoculars or telescope, an experienced bird artist would probably

53. Red-backed shrikes and larder

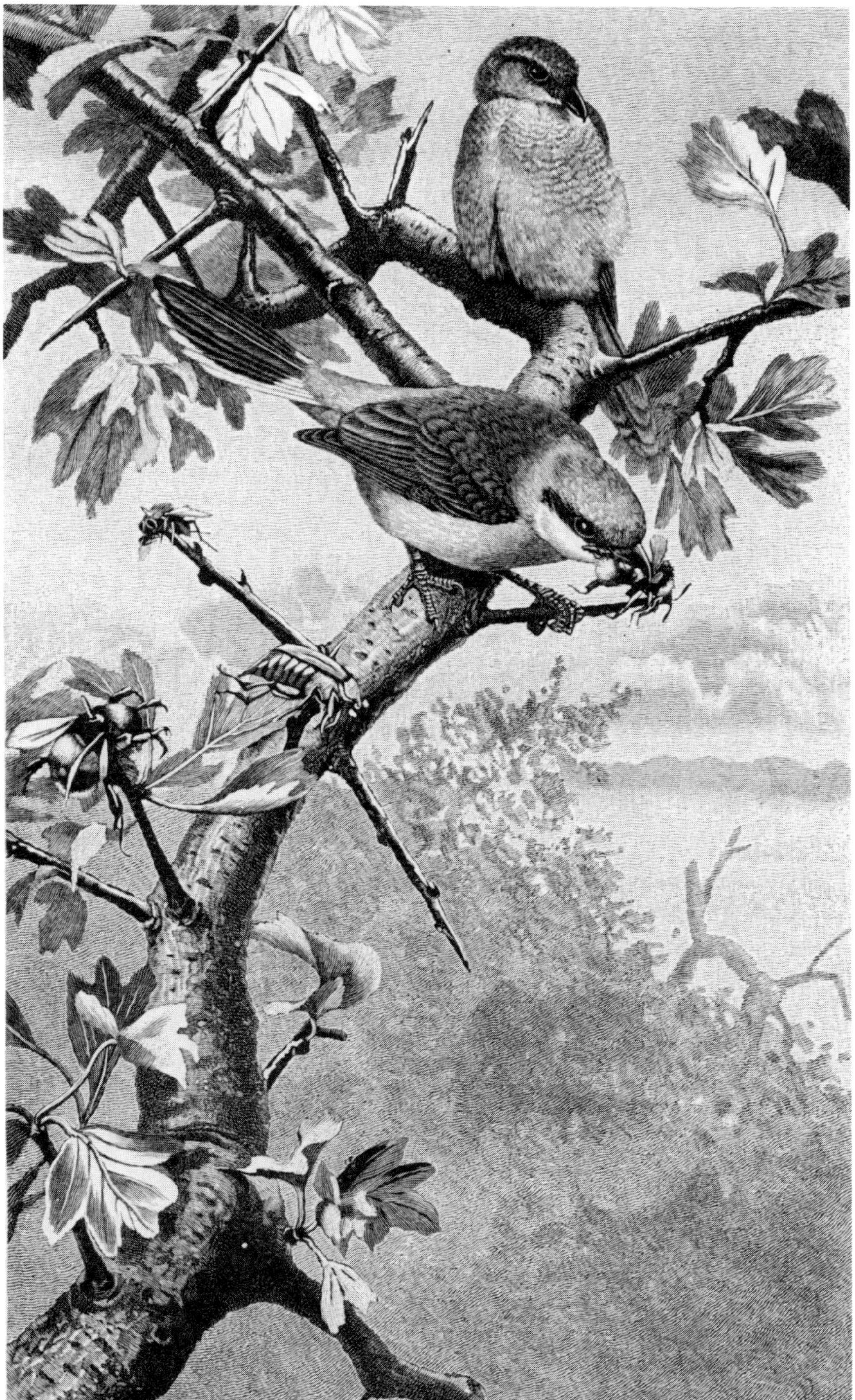

53

make a rapid sketch or two on the spot, and might find the spontaneous result more in tune with the taste of the time than a careful version done after the event. Edward Wilson (of the Antartic), a fine naturalist and versatile artist, was critical of Lodge's drawings of birds in flight when, in 1900, he visited Lodge and Thorburn to ask their opinion of his own work.

Lodge's paintings of mammals, such as deer or hares in landscape surroundings, have been too little seen or appreciated. Some of his landscape paintings, with little or no wildlife interest, were a revelation to me. He quite obviously delighted in the wonderland of mountain plateaux, in storm-swept skies and distant vistas of birch or pinewood, always unpopulated but for the occasional hint of a timbered house among the trees. In one early watercolour, of a Normandy coastal scene, there

54. Waxwings (colour plate 33)

54

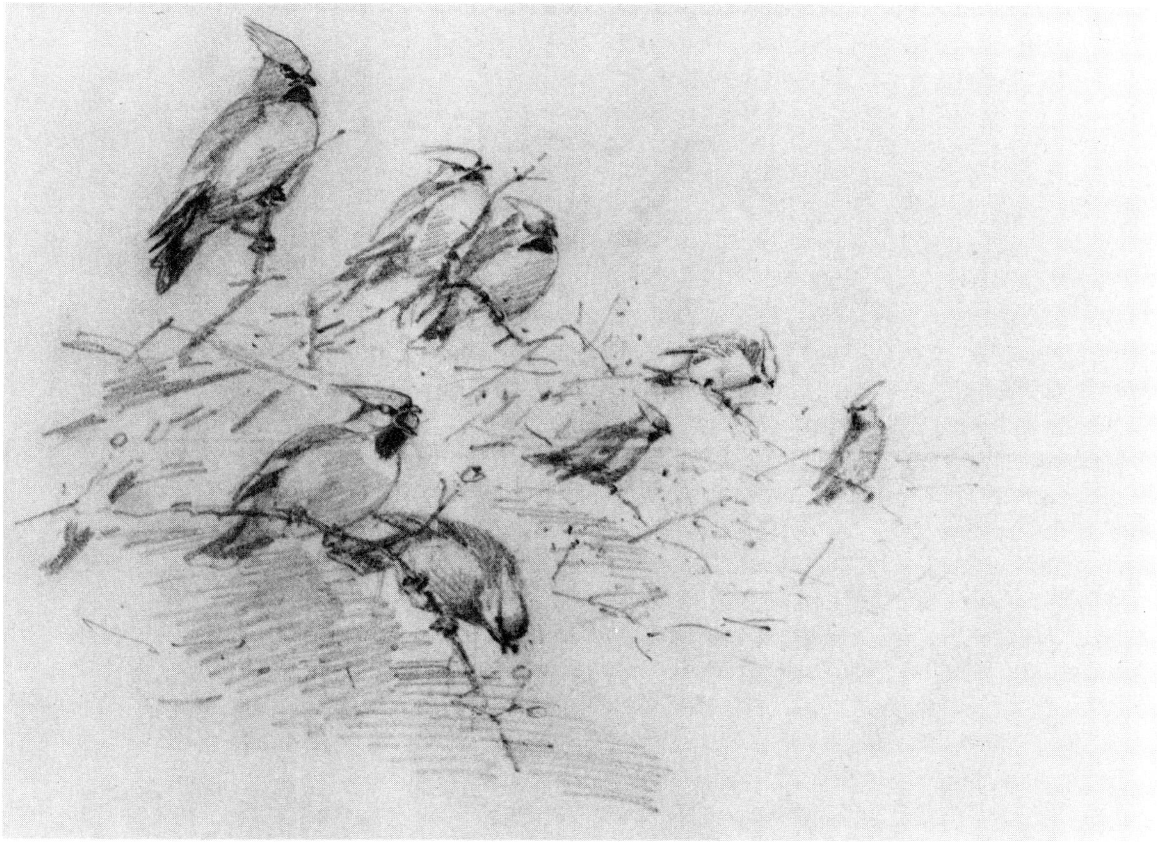

seems to be more than a suggestion of the early Turner or Bonnington. One of his most evocative landscapes, with a lonely gull in the sky (Pl. 48), illustrates how well he could handle a featureless, almost eerie expanse of sea and threatening sky. Not everyone will agree with his opinion that 'there is always a much more beautiful effect in a landscape when viewed from a point facing the sun', but the charming oil painting of a pinewood (Pl. 47) is a good example of why he believed this.

In his best pictures he was extremely successful at giving a broad yet botanically convincing indication of a mass of vegetation among which ptarmigan, grouse or woodcock are skilfully camouflaged. His rocks are always solid and hard and as truly observed as the falcons which so often top them. His great love of painting feather-detailed gyrs or peregrines resulted in some repetition and perhaps too frequent use of the device of the huge slab of rock rising from the base of the picture, but his sure grasp of scale produced effective pictures in which the distant backgrounds were delightfully indicated. Sometimes, especially in some of his book illustrations, conviction seemed to desert him and vegetation became fussy or uninteresting; one can surely spot the paintings which he did with little joy. Perhaps his own complaint that he had to live in London for 39 years and sometimes had to send away to the country 'for some rubbish or other', to help in painting surroundings for his birds, is revealing in this context.

Some comments on particular examples of Lodge's art, among those reproduced in this book, may be of interest. Lodge's studies and paintings of birds of prey are of such a consistently high quality that there is unlikely to be agreement on which were his best. Many of his close-up studies are unbeatable in their genre — for example the two of the falconer's peregrine Vic (Pl. 7) with her blue-grey back seen against a plain brown background, or the eyass tiercel Iceland falcon (Pl. 3). Sylvia, the immature peregrine from Lundy (Pl. 9) is an exciting portrait with its contrast of dark brown above and white below. The strong cast shadow below the wing is unusual in a Lodge painting. Among the paintings with landscape backgrounds I particularly admire the white gyr falcon (Pl. 4), with ruffled flank feathers, leaning intently forward from a great rock slab. The strength of the rock and bird stand out against an enchanting distance with a defiant blue crag. Another powerful painting (p. 10) shows a gyr falcon about to feed its brood. The peregrine lifting off (Pl. 6) from a chalk cliff shows keen observation of a difficult attitude and a fine swirl of sea far below. The characteristic black points of flint in the chalk can be seen in this and another peregrine painting (in black and white on p. 15). In the latter there is great tonal subtlety in the painting of the cliff against the sky. The highly-finished and very accurate hobby (Pl. 13) perched on a foreshortened dead branch is a more conventional Lodge picture and might have been done for a book plate. The female merlin on a skylark kill (Pl. 11) convinces the onlooker that he has just surprised the falcon and the whole painting has an instantaneous quality. The sparrow-hawk on an old larch tree (Pl. 15) may be even better. It is a far finer painting than others he did of sparrow-hawks at the nest; somehow Lodge was never at his best painting nests with eggs. The goshawk in a larch wood (p. 32) is exactly as an exceptionally lucky birdwatcher might see it. His sea eagle pictures (Pl. 18) certainly stem from his Norwegian experience, but in *Memoirs of an Artist Naturalist* he wrote an account of two days in June 1914 when he had brief views of the famous albino sea eagle which survived in Shetland until 1918, having been there for about 30 years. Lodge made on-the-spot sketches of the old eyrie, in wild weather. Did he ever make further use of these? The golden eagle, with very foreshortened wings and carrying a red deer calf (Pl. 17) was evidently painted not from his own observation, but from a detailed description of a sighting in June 1931 by an Inverness-shire crofter (see p. 38, *Memoirs of an Artist Naturalist*).

Among the many fine action sketches of raptors, in charcoal or pencil, everyone will find their own favourites. I especially like the quick sketch of a sparrow-hawk on a branch (p. 23) and the peregrine preening its tail (p. 15). The wood-engravings of owls (pp. 35 and 36) are Lodge at his classical best.

I have already mentioned partridges in a turnip field (Pl. 22), arguably the best oil painting he ever did. The composition is wholly satisfying, the beautifully painted birds bristle with alarm and relate perfectly to their foreground surroundings, which include delightful but not intrusive botanical touches. Most of all his pictures, I think, this carries a hint of a Dutch landscape of the Hague School with its gentle and harmonious patchwork of distant fields, trees and farmstead. The tiny figures of the beaters are integral to the concept of the picture. It is full of a sense of a particular place and season. It was painted in 1896, at the height of his powers, before much of his colour work had been reproduced in books.

There is much to admire in the painting of ptarmigan crouching on a mountain top (Pl. 24), with its beautifully camouflaged birds intensely watchful of a distant peregrine. Like all his mountain pictures it has a great sense of weather. Tone and colour in land, sky and birds are wonderfully true. Ptarmigan alighting on a rock slab (p. 39) has an awesome sense of wild weather on high ground, with difficult drawing of birds in action, bravely tackled. In the watercolour of blackgame on a moor (Pl. 26) the birds stand urgently, ready to go, and the stone dyke is painted with fine assurance. A pair of Mongolian pheasants and their young (1933) (Pl. 20) shows Lodge's mastery at handling foreground, here all quiet ochre and brown, setting off the dark cock pheasant and blending with the others. The sentinel capercaillie (Pl. 27) is one of many pictures in which the bird is seen against a very atmospheric distant landscape. Lodge had a liking for snowy settings but rarely, if ever, painted snow in bright sunlight (Liljefors did so more often). Sometimes I feel that more sacrifice of detail in the birds would have been truer in the 'bleak midwinter' pictures. The question of the amount of detail to be given on birds 'in a landscape' perhaps also arises in the fine group of red grouse among heather and rocks (Pl. 25).

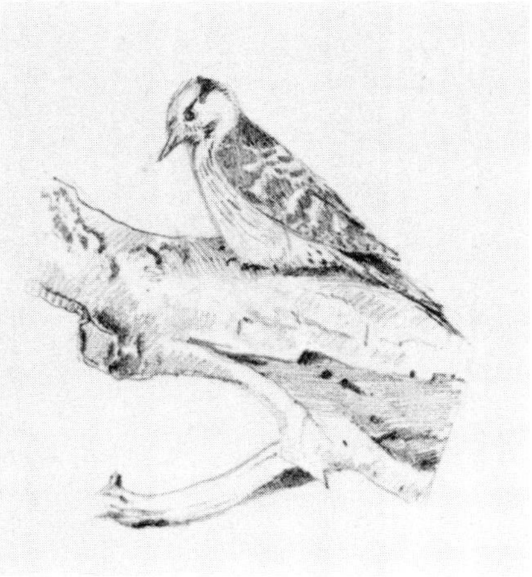

55

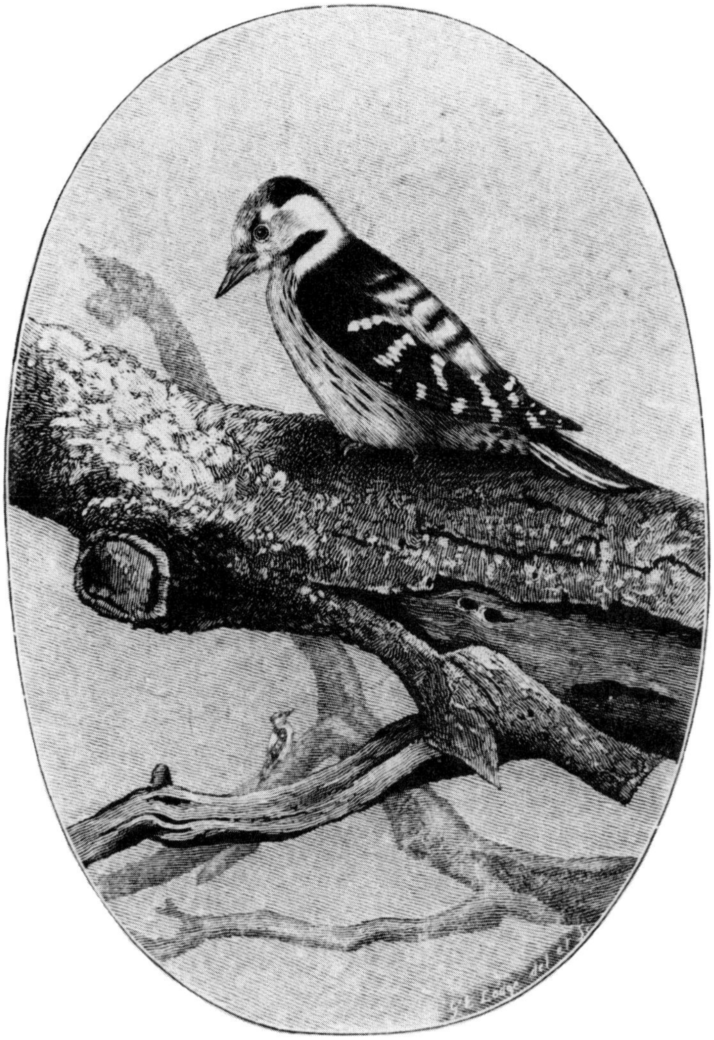

55

55. Lesser spotted woodpeckers

Some may say that the almost miniaturist detail of the birds is inconsistent with the summary treatment of heather and rocks. Yet it is a convincing painting cleverly leading the eye to the craned necks against the sky.

The fine wood-engravings of game-birds speak for themselves. The unusual blackgame variant (p. 43), from a drawing by Millais, is of special documentary interest. Woodcock ready to rise (p. 47) combines first-rate observation with complete mastery of the wood-engraver's technique, while Pallas's sand-grouse (p. 51) shows how richly-detailed work can be done without losing the three-dimensional form of the bird. Among the sketchbook drawings of game-birds one of grouse in flight (p. 40) conveys real speed. On the page of great bustard sketches (p. 50) (perhaps done in charcoal) the half-crouched female at bottom right is a personal favourite.

The examples of Lodge's pictures and engravings of 'other birds' are not so consistently satisfying. The long-tailed ducks riding the waves (Pl. 29) are attractive and evocative, and the pair of crested tits (Pl. 31) and the waxwings (Pl. 33) show that he could be very successful with small birds. The bearded tit (Pl. 32) is a charming study, although its bill may be too dull-coloured. I have always thought the jay (p. 74), reproduced here in monochrome, was one of the very best illustrations in *The Birds of the British Isles.* Two outstanding wood-engravings are the red-backed shrikes (p. 83) and the night heron (p. 56), both showing an impressive variety of textures and tonal richness.

Personally I think that many of the finest examples of Lodge's art are in the parts of this book concerned with mammals and landscapes. It is very difficult to make preferences but he rarely surpassed the haunting picture of roe deer beside a still, wintry loch (Pl. 41). The same can be said of the landscape, with no wildlife in sight, of woodland and snow-streaked mountains (Pl. 45), painted in Norway. The red deer stags on a tawny slope (Pl. 42) are beautifully drawn and have so clearly caught a human scent while the mountain masses have a fine solidity. In the painting of brown hares in the snow (Pl. 40) the low winter sunlight steals across the landscape, just touching the animals with a hint of warmth. There are some fine sketches from life in this section, none of which has been seen widely before. The delightful black woodpeckers (Pl. 43) (notice the distant unmistakable silhouette on the dead tree) has a remarkable history. On the back of the picture is written: 'It will be observed that this painting is in two parts, torn through from top to bottom. This occurred in a London blitz during World War II. The upper portion on the right was

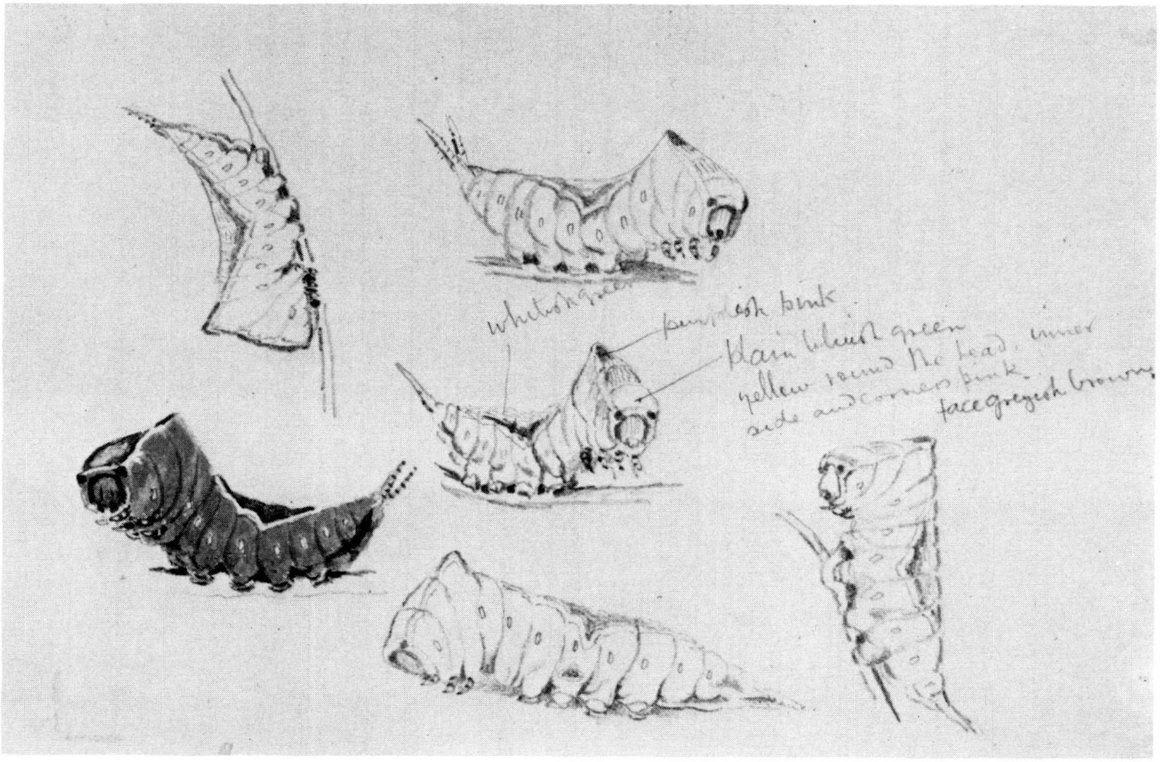

56

56. Puss moth caterpillar sketches

punctured with splintered glass. Lodge had it back to his studio, mounted the two parts together and painted the tree trunk and top branch over the join. He then painted in the black woodpecker (and smaller one on tree) where previously there had been a sparrow-hawk nearer the base of the fallen trunk.'

The selection of Lodge's work in this book is designed to show the width of his range. I have been privileged to see transparencies or prints of far more, many of them in no way inferior to those finally chosen.

Young wildlife artists today seem to have many advantages denied to Lodge's generation. Optical aids are vastly improved, superb wildlife film can be studied, field guides make the likeness of every rare species familiar. Birds and other animals which Lodge could not hope to see in the wild are accessible to those who can afford to travel. Anyone with a little talent has opportunities to exhibit work up and down the country, at galleries or conferences, while there are many publishers looking for book illustrators. Yet to do the best original work remains as great a challenge as ever.

I append a list, with dates, of leading wildlife artists who worked or were born in the nineteenth century.

Some leading wildlife artists of the nineteenth century

Thomas Bewick 1753-1828
Alexander Wilson 1766-1813
John James Audubon (USA) 1785-1851
William Swainson 1789-1855
William Macgillivray 1796-1852
Edwin Landseer 1802-73
John Gould 1804-81
Elizabeth Gould 1804-41
Benjamin Fawcett 1808-93
Edouard Traviés (France) 1809-66
Edward Lear 1812-88
Joseph Wolf 1820-99
Jemima Blackburn 1823-1909
Edward Neale 1833-1904
Joseph Smit (Netherlands) 1836-1929
John Gerrard Keulemans (Netherlands) 1842-1912
L.P. Robert (Switzerland) 1851-1923
Charles Whymper 1853-1941
Richard B.L. Friese (Germany) 1854-1918
Henrik Grönvold (Denmark) 1858-1940
Bruno Liljefors (Sweden) 1860-1939
George Edward Lodge 1860-1954
Archibald Thorburn 1860-1935
William Wallis 1860-1942
Joseph Crawhall 1861-1913
F.W. Frohawk 1861-1946
W. Kuhnert (Germany) 1865-1926
John Guille Millais 1865-1931
Allen W. Seaby 1867-1953
Allan Brooks (Canada) 1869-1946
Carl Rungius (Germany/USA) 1869-1959
Edwin Alexander 1870-1926

A.R. Dugmore 1870-1955
Carl von Dombrowskie (Germany) 1872-1967
Frank Southgate 1872-1916
Edward A. Wilson 1872-1912
Louis Agassiz Fuertes (USA) 1874-1927
Winifred Austen 1876-1964
A.F. Lydon 1883-1915
Otto Murray Dixon 1885-1917
Francis L. Jaques (USA) 1887-1969
H.F.W. Buddenberg (Germany) 1890-1967
George M. Henry 1891-1983
Gerhart Löbenberg (Germany) 1891-1967
Philip Rickman 1891-1982
E. Fitch Dalglish 1892-1966
J.C. Harrison 1893-
A. Schrijnder (Netherlands) 1894-1968
Roland Green 1896-1972
R.B. Talbot Kelly 1896-1971

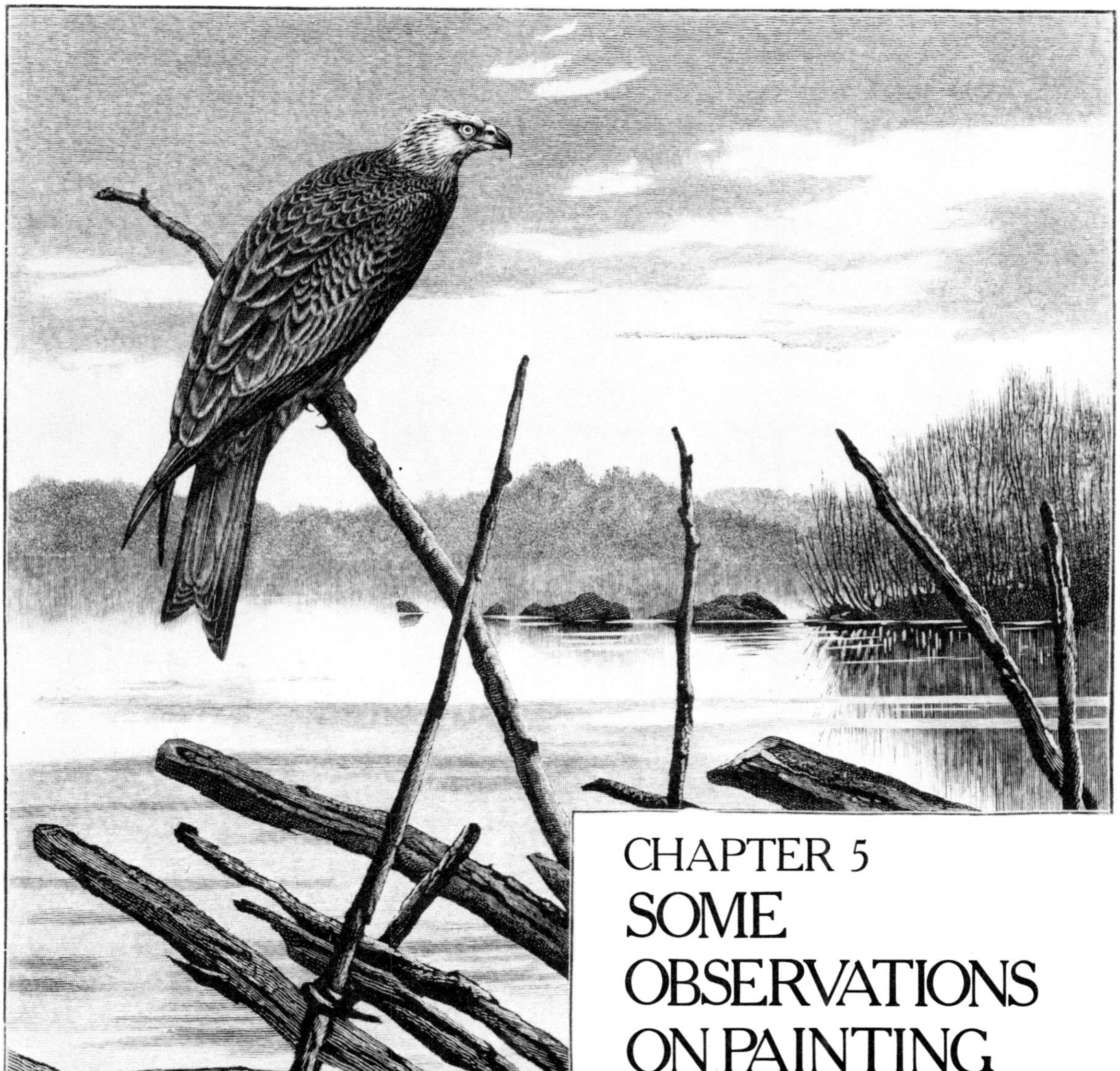

CHAPTER 5

SOME OBSERVATIONS ON PAINTING BIRDS

George Lodge

57

(An abbreviated chapter from *Memoirs of an Artist Naturalist*)

This is not an easy subject to write about and must not be approached with assurance or dogmatism, as every one who studies art has his own ideas and methods and, quite rightly, follows and uses them in order to get the results that appeal to him. Entirely different methods produce good results, and who shall say this or that is the right way? Individualism is necessary in all branches of art — if only to do away with monotony. It is to be supposed that 'modern' artists would say that painting birds is not art at all, only 'copying from nature'. But those who have given their lives to painting pictures of birds will say that few things in nature are more beautiful and full of grace than birds: therefore, why not 'copy' them? Especially so when one has the sense to realise how very difficult it is to copy a living bird.

You cannot requisition a living bird and direct it to sit for you in a certain pose for a long time as you can a human model. You are entirely dependent upon whatever attitude the bird happens momentarily to adopt, and you may never see a bird in just the pose you would like to represent it. Suppose you want to paint a picture of half-a-dozen ravens mobbing a pair of golden eagles. You would have to wait a long time to see such an event at all, though I saw it one day and remember it particularly, because it was while I was stalking my first stag on Ardlussa Forest, Jura, on 22 September 1905. Now, even seeing this incident, there was no possible chance of 'copying' it, for the birds' movements were far too rapid for the eye to register. But if you were clever enough and knew sufficient about the anatomy of the birds and were a good enough draughtsman, you might evolve a satisfactory picture. Knowing your birds well enough you might paint the picture without having seen the event. It is the *drawing* of the subject that is so difficult, especially of birds in violent action.

The drawing of birds in movement demands not only the ability to represent foreshortening of the body, but also of the markings on the plumage. In

57. Red kite
58. African elephant

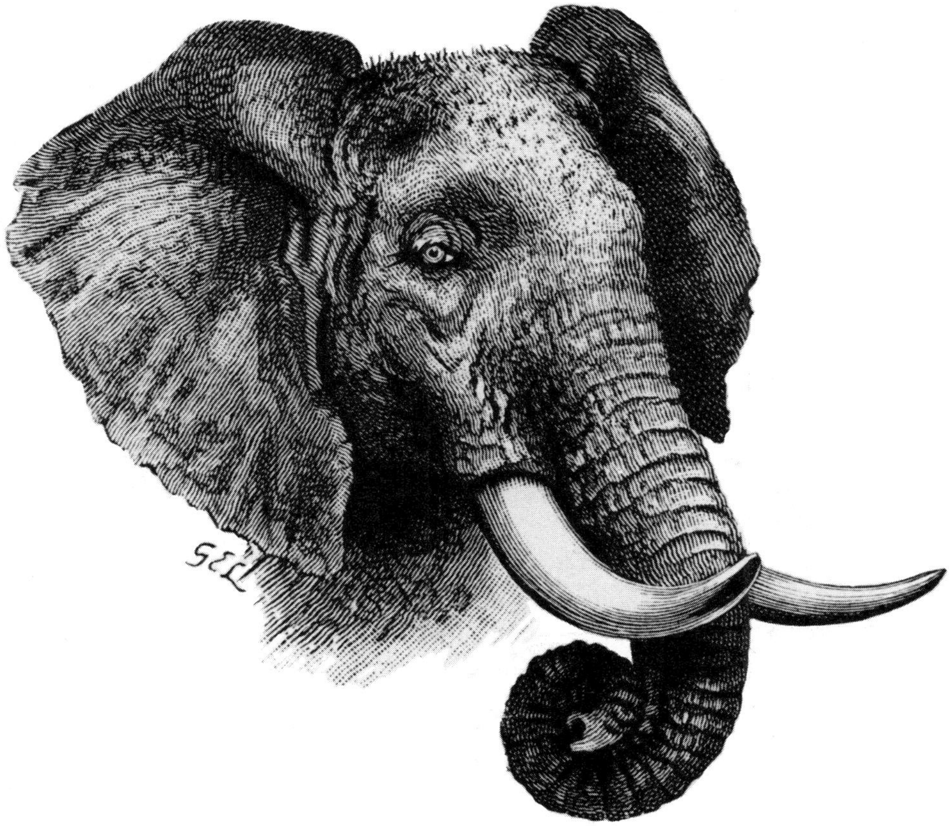

58

such cases a certain amount of impressionism is obviously necessary; in fact, in painting *pictures* a lot more impressionism might be practised. But that is not to say that one should in any way dispense with scientific accuracy. As a matter of fact, preoccupation with scientific book illustration is a handicap — and a big one — to painting pictures: one tends to aim simply at producing nothing but an accurate map of a bird's plumage. I feel my own pictures have suffered by this.

In the old days — by which I mean the early days of my own career — there was a good deal of antagonism between science and art in the minds of the people who wrote scientific books about birds. Apparently the accurate mapping of a bird's plumage was the first and only thing required, except a preposterous mass of landscape intended to show the bird's natural habitat. I was even told by a very eminent ornithologist of those days that the great fault of Wolf's illustrations was that they were too 'artistic' — Joseph Wolf — who was the greatest draughtsman of birds who ever lived, and, as I truly think, ever will live! But I am glad to say that at the present day authors and publishers are much more appreciative of the fact that art and science need not be in antagonism.

An absolutely correct map of the pattern and colour of plumage is a *sine qua non* for a scientific work, especially as some species are so closely allied that the differences of their plumage are very slight. But granted all this, there is no reason why light and shade and reflected lights should be eliminated. Light and shade help to convey an accurate impression of reality. Too much background is to be deprecated for scientific work. Realistic *foreground*, in the immediate vicinity of the bird, yes, but let it fade away into a wash of suitable tone and colour. Let the objects in the foreground be in proper relation to the size of the bird; let it be remembered that a blade of grass may be as tall as a snipe, and that one frond of bracken may be larger than a pheasant. It is extraordinary how easy it is to

59. Tiger charging

59

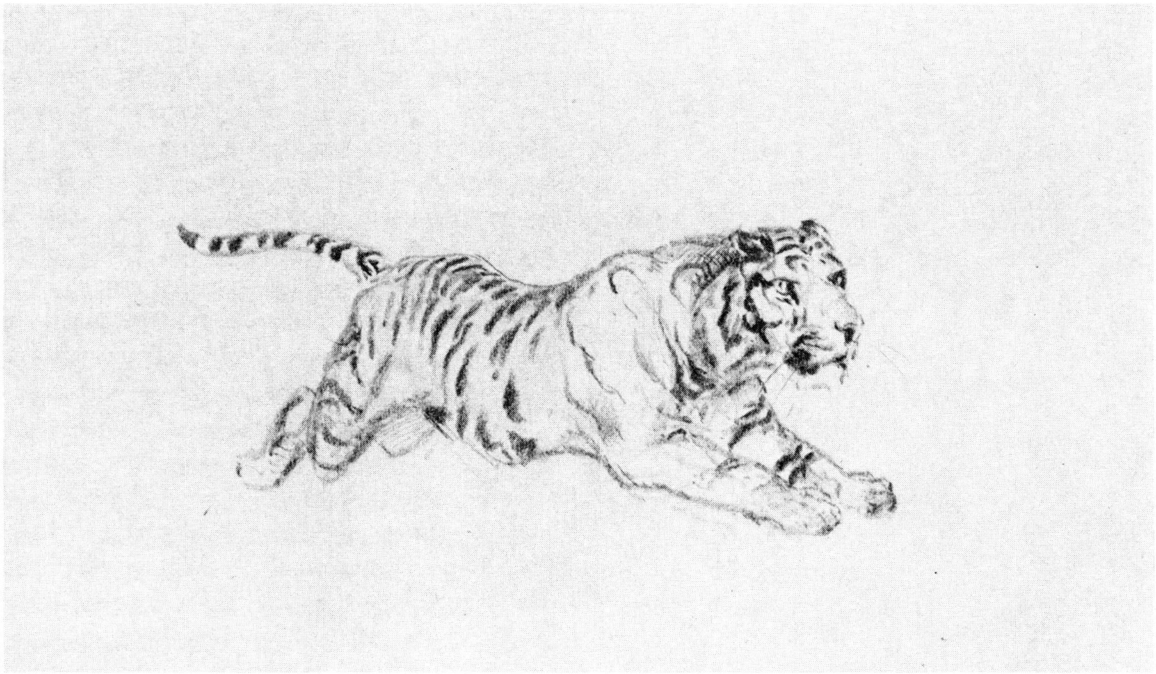

make pictures and illustrations with the birds out of proportion to their surroundings. I have certainly done it many a time myself. If a *landscape with birds in it* is to be the subject for a picture, then paint the landscape first and put the birds in afterwards, taking care to keep them in proportion. But if it is to be a *picture of birds*, paint the birds first and add just sufficient landscape and foreground to give verity to the size of the birds.

Another phenomenon which frequently proves a stumbling block to the illustrator is the position of reflections on the surface of water in relation to the object reflected. The reflection of a bird flying over calm water is exactly below it, and when correctly represented suggests to the spectator the position of the bird in space. In order to find this correct position it is necessary to fix the point on the *surface* of the water above which the bird is situated; the reflection should then be placed exactly the same distance below this line as the bird is above it. The same is true of birds standing or swimming in water, whose reflections should reach exactly the same distance below them as their height above the surface of the water.

I suppose all landscape and animal painters make innumerable sketches direct from nature in order to have material for the surroundings and foundations of the pictures they paint. When I was young and strong I used to do a good deal of work in oils, and I have many sketches done in various parts of the world from the Tropics to the Arctic regions. I never hesitated to take out easel, canvas and painting gear in midwinter. I would work all day with snow deep on the ground, or skate out onto the ice and paint away until I was too cold to work, and so had to stop and take a cruise around on my skates until circulation was good enough to allow me to continue work.

I had a bad habit in those early days of trying to make rather highly finished little pictures of these sketches, and to this end used to go out several times to work on the same thing. This is a great mistake unless you can hit off exactly the same kind of weather at the same time of day as when you started. Otherwise different atmospheric conditions will give totally different effects and, of course, as the sun alters in position as the day wears on, the effect of light and shade is constantly changing. So by degrees I found it much better and safer for getting truth of effect to do as much as I could at one sitting, taking pencil notes if necessary of detail I might need, and using these as material at a later date. But even so, I began to find it wearisome to lug oil-painting kit about for miles, especially in hilly country. I found I could never cope with watercolour, so gave it up years ago in favour of tempera for small pictures and book illustrations, and came to the conclusion that a pencil and a small-sized sketch book were really the best things to carry for sketching purposes.

Landscape sketching direct from nature was especially useful to me at the beginning of my career, as I had to live in London for 39 years of my life. There was some advantage in this in the near proximity of the Zoo and the Natural History Museum, which gave me opportunities for studies I might not have been able to make elsewhere; but London is not a good place to live in when one wants to paint partridges on stubble fields, falcons on rocks and like things. I could get on with the partridges and falcons all right but had to trust to my sketches for stubbles and rocks. I used to go out into the parks at night and surreptitiously lift a few twigs and bits of foliage from which I was able to make suitable drawings of perches for my tom-tits! But this kind of material was restricted in variety and I had sometimes to write to the country for some rubbish or other to be sent to me by post. I never wasted my time, however, when there was a chance to sketch from nature. I filled many sketch books with drawings in pencil of the varied growth of grasses and reeds, the way their leaves grow from the stems, the foreshortening of branches of trees — both towards and receding from the observer — the light and shade which emphasise foreshortening, clods of earth in a ploughed field, formation of clouds in the sky, rocks, stones and dead leaves. All these things drawn from nature are valuable when

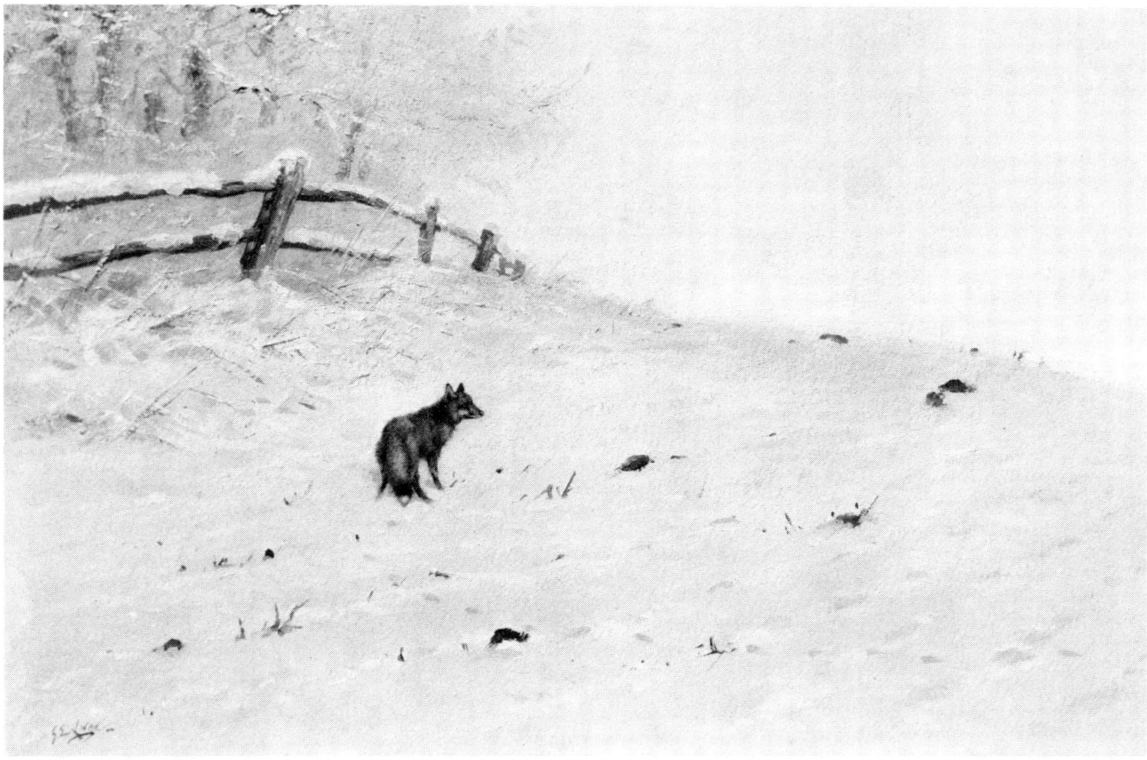

60

60. *Fox in winter landscape*

one comes to spend long spells in the studio, and one useful sketch will provide material for perhaps a dozen pictures.

I was always especially interested in rocks, and have numberless carefully drawn sketches, some in pencil and some in oils. Most of these have been done in Norway, Scotland and Ireland. Rocks near the sea have different kinds and colours of lichens on them and therefore need quite different treatment from rocks on a mountain-side. The vegetation round different types of rock or cliff also needs most careful attention if a picture is to carry conviction. Rocks are not the only things to be studied in this way; trees and branches are equally important. A dead branch, foreshortened towards the spectator is a far more interesting perch for a sparrow-hawk or jay than a straight horizontal branch going across the picture. These details are important.

One of the difficulties of drawing birds is coping

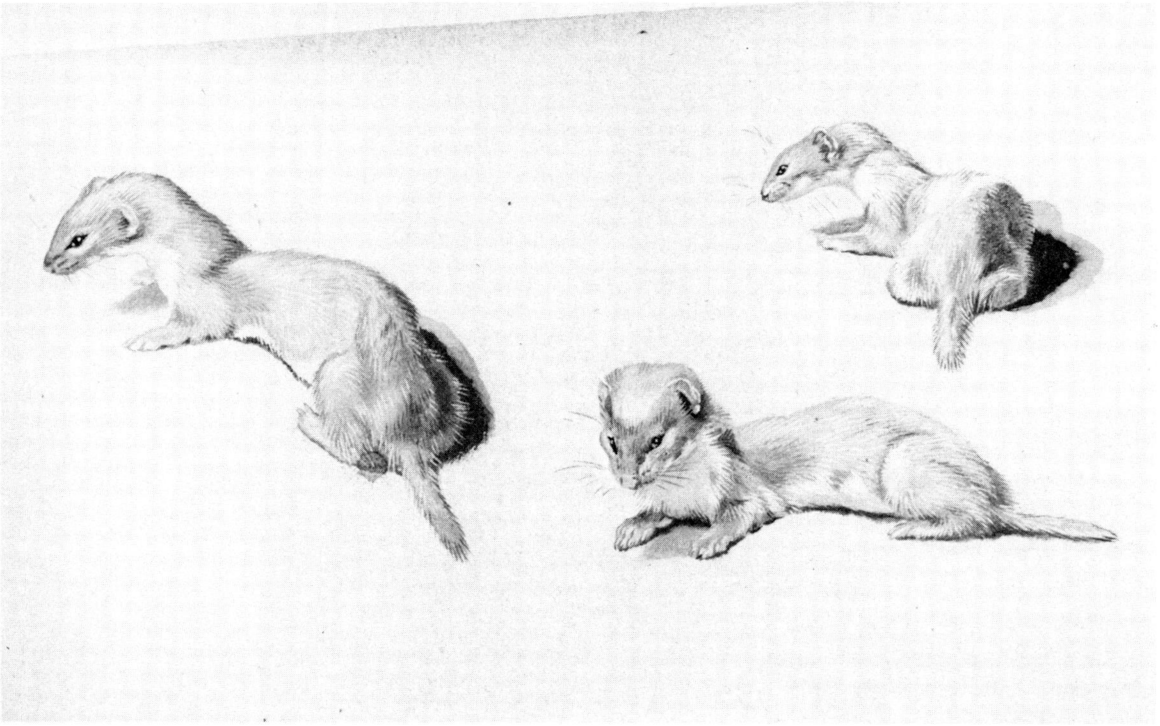

61

61. Weasel sketches
62. Pine martens

satisfactorily with foreshortened postures. The movements of birds, also, are so lively that it takes a very quick eye to see and know what one is looking at, and what a bird is really doing. The only way is to make sketches as rapidly as possible and afterwards make the best one can of a bad sketch. Errors can often be rectified at leisure without spoiling the freshness of the sketch from life. But never let it be said by the bird artist that such and such a thing must be right because it was done from life: I know the fallacy of this all too well. Sometimes a bird painter must make up his drawing in piecemeal fashion, doing a few strokes at a time until the detail of the movement is captured.

No doubt the modern developments of ultra-rapid photography will become increasingly useful in elucidating such matters as these, but in painting pictures of birds, photographs should be used with the greatest caution. I am thinking particularly of birds flying. Personally, I never use photography as a help; I much prefer to do as much as I can with my

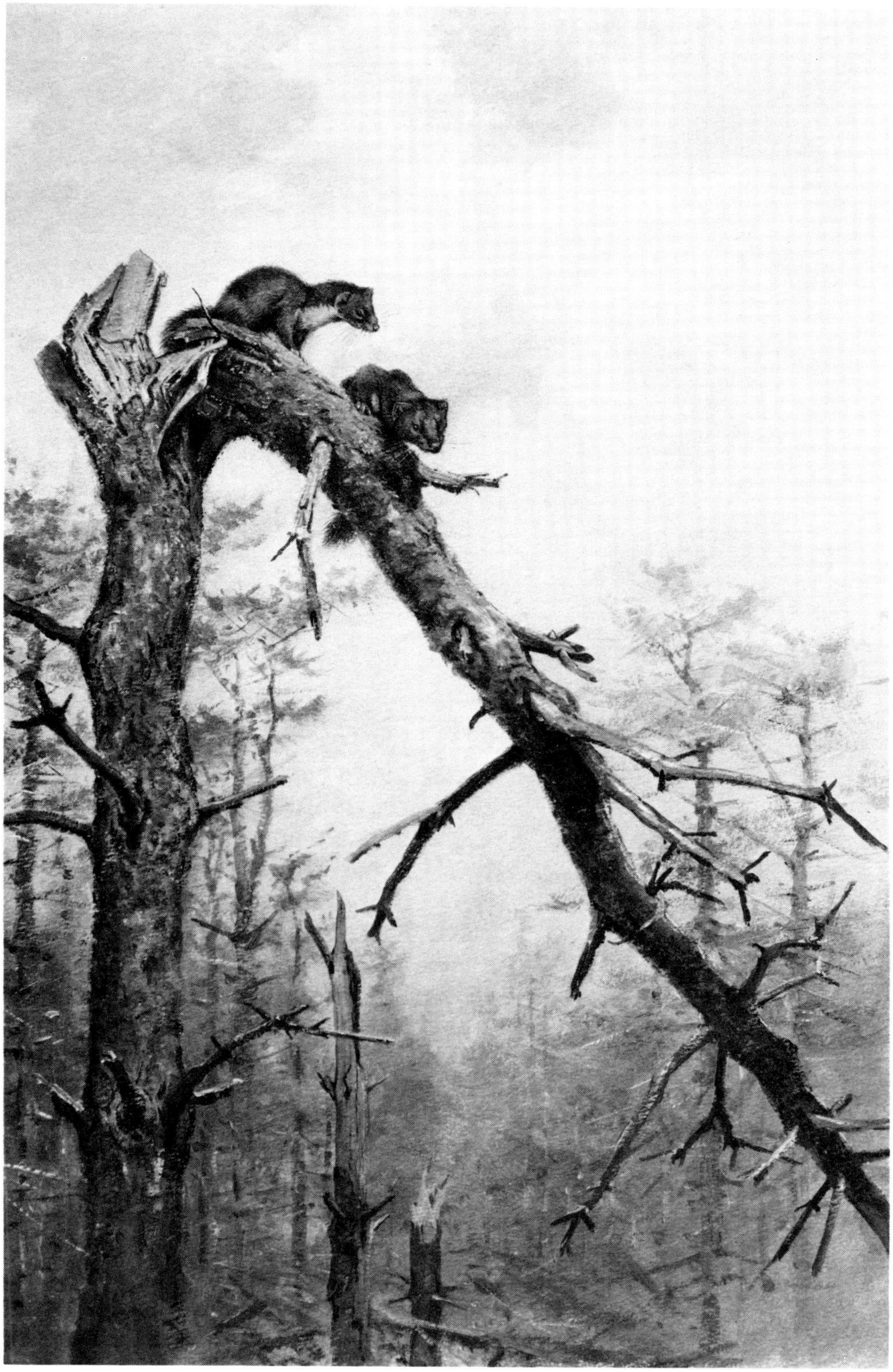

62

own eyes. I have never taken a photograph in my life and, of course, would never dream of using anybody else's photograph. However erroneous one's effort may be, given some natural ability for the job, it is surely better to rely on one's own careful observation.

How, then, are we to paint flying birds? It is more difficult to get the impression of the speed of birds flying in the air than of animals running on the ground, the chief reason being that there is no visible displacement of air in a bird's progress; whereas with animals on the ground there might be violent, visible displacement of solid material such as flying clods and smothers of sand and dust which may obliterate much of the detail of the beasts causing such a disturbance. A bird soaring or skimming with motionless wings is much easier to paint than one in rapid flight, for then only a blur of wings is visible; indeed, in the case of a hummingbird hovering before a flower, we see no evidence of movement at all. We know all about how the feathers clothe the wings, but if we paint in all these feathers with their colours and markings, we petrify the bird. On the other hand, if we paint the wings in a blur the result is a daub. So what is to be done? It is no good giving the counsel of despair by saying don't paint flying birds. Something must be sacrificed and a compromise made; and each individual artist must be a law unto himself and solve the problem in his own way.

I once had a conversation with the late E. Neale on how to get the idea of speed into a picture of flying birds, such as a covey of grouse. I told him that to me a covey of grouse on the wing always conveyed the impression that each bird was doing exactly the same thing at the same time — I meant so far as the position of the wings is concerned, and that I should paint them accordingly. The monotony of this similar attitude would be broken by tilting some of the birds a little and placing some above and some below the eye — all of which would necessitate different methods of representing each bird's wings, although the main idea would be kept in view and all the birds would have their wings on

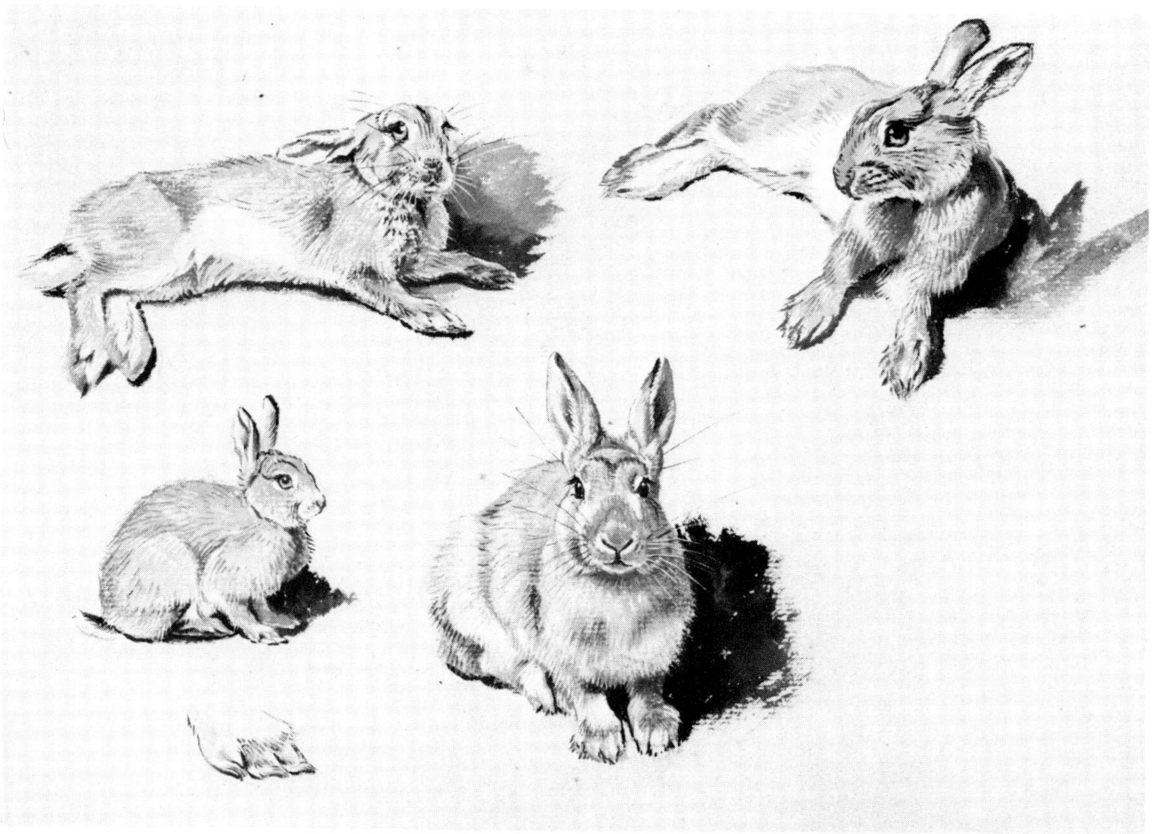

63

63. *Rabbit sketches*

the downward or upward stroke. This I thought helped to convey the idea of speed and movement. But he held an entirely different point of view and said his idea would be to paint the birds in as many different positions of flight as possible. There can be no hard and fast rules.

As a rule, stuffed mounted birds should never be used as models unless, indeed, one knows so much about the subject that the imperfections of the stuffing can be rectified in the drawing. No matter how well a bird may be stuffed — and there are few such — it will always lack the grace of the living bird. But stuffed specimens may come in useful for getting correct ideas of light and shade and reflected lights. They may also help in getting a proper drawing of foreshortening.

Place a grouse in three-quarters profile before you and you will find that drawing the foreshortening of

64. Rocky mountain bighorn ram
65. Elk (or moose) swimming

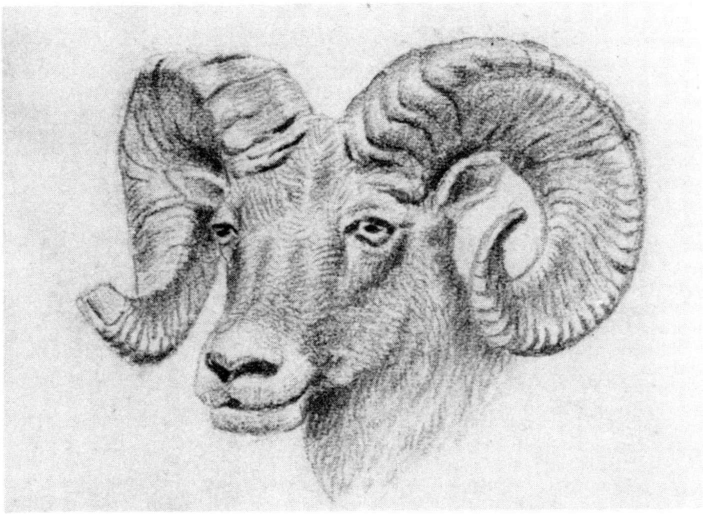

64

the near wing does not merely consist of delineating the principal rows of feathers such as primaries, secondaries, secondary coverts and so on a little shorter than they would be if the bird were entirely in profile; you will find rather that these rows of feathers, or some of them, according to the angle of the bird, have disappeared from view as the natural curve of the bird's contour slopes away from the eye's viewpoint. It will be found also that the markings of the plumage of a bird may be altered in shape entirely when seen obliquely.

It is useful to have some wings of birds preserved in extended positions, as a help in drawing correctly these in foreshortened positions. Drawing a widely spread wing in this position is no simple thing, nor to get the corresponding wing into the right position on the other side. Birds use their wings simultaneously, like a man using a pair of oars in a boat, except when they are turning. I have sometimes found it helpful to make diagrams of a pair of outspread wings, cut out of cardboard. Some of these I have widely spread and others more flexed. I make these by drawing one wing in the position required, then allowing for the distance of half the breadth of back between the two wings, I double the piece of cardboard and cut out the wing with scissors. By this means I have a pair of wings which I can hold to any angle I wish for a drawing and have a rough guide to the relation of the wings to each other. Let me emphasise that being only a flat piece of cardboard this device gives no indication of the thickness of the wing, nor of the convexity of the upper surface and corresponding concavity below.

A general knowledge of pterylosis (the distribution of and growth of feathers on the bird) is indispensable. It is an intricate subject for there is considerable variation in the different Orders of birds throughout the world. The artist must realise that feathers do not grow haphazard all over the body, but are confined to definite tracts with bare spaces of skin in between. A knowledge of the arrangement of these pterylæ is most helpful when doing illustrations for scientific books, especially if one has to work from bad dried skins. Skins made by collectors in the field are often poor, especially if they were obtained in the tropics, where speed in preparation is necessary. The feathers are in disarray and the patterning far from obvious. Anatomy is also a helpful science, and the painter should know without doubt upon which bones of the wing the different lots of feathers lie. My own

65

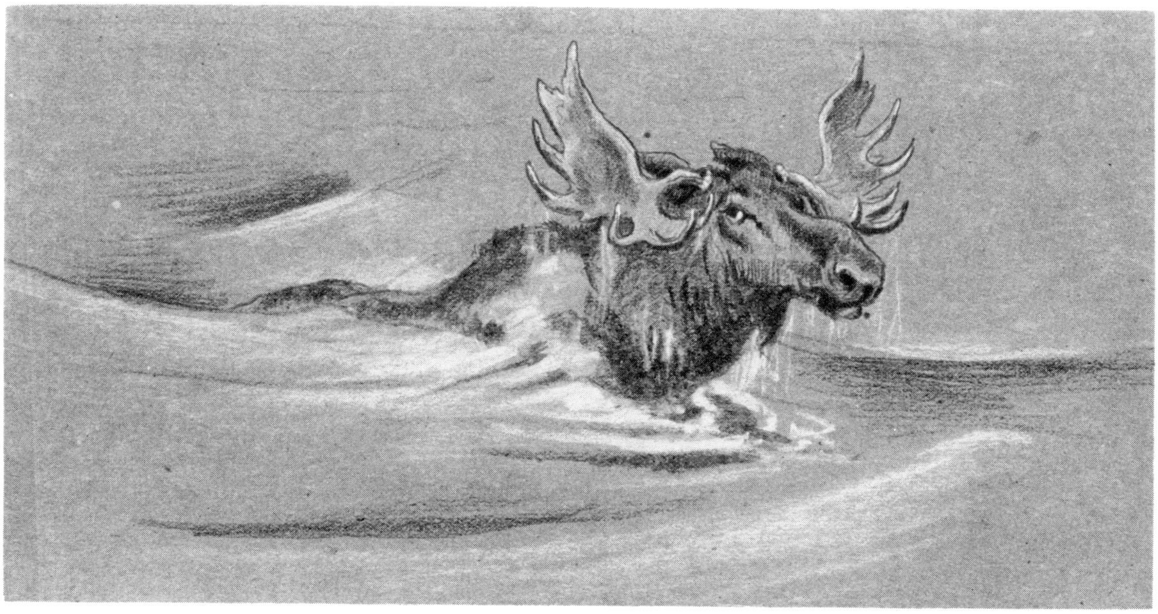

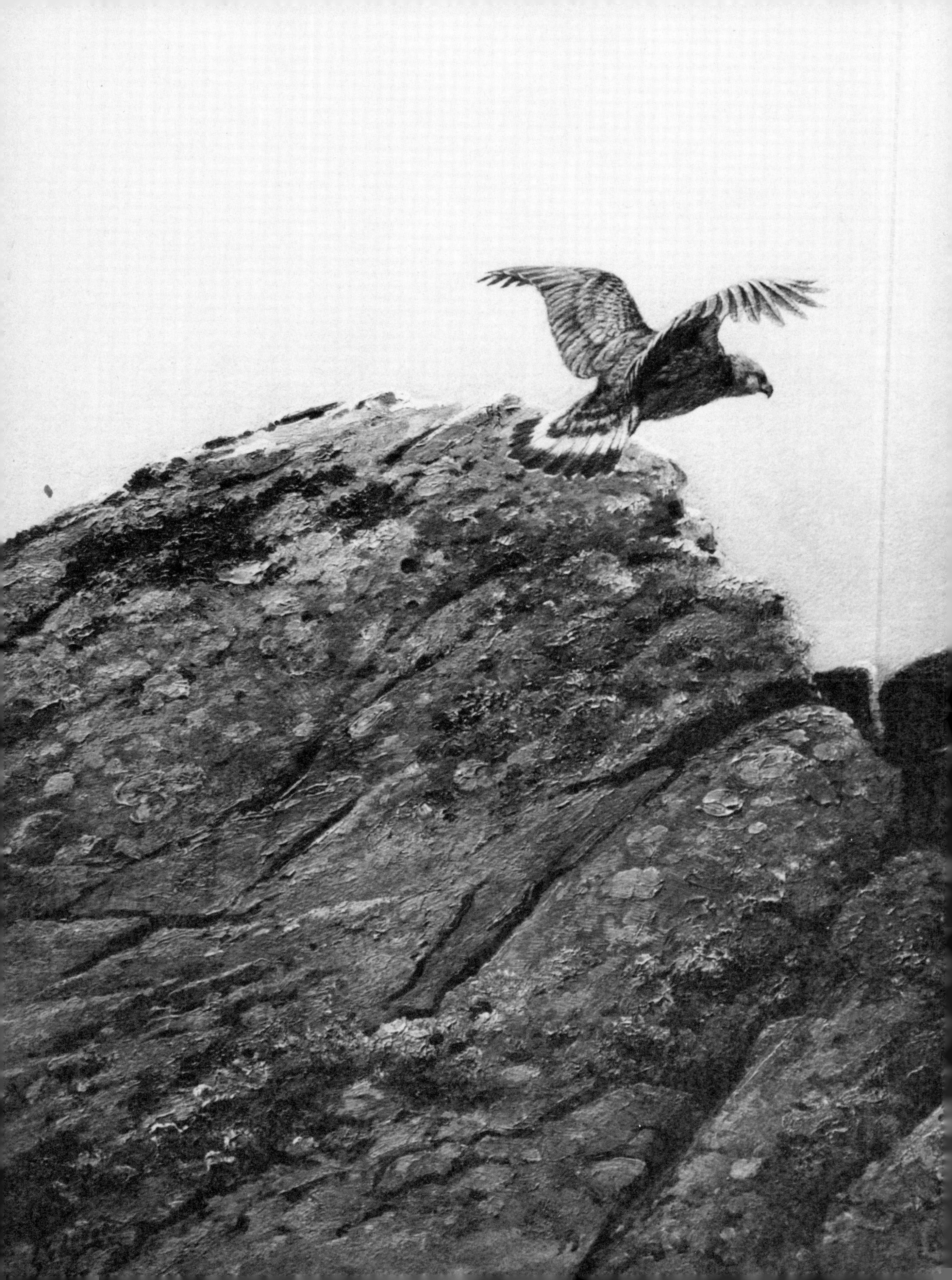

knowledge of anatomy and pterylosis has come entirely from my own investigations in the course of preparing skins.

There are a lot of men who have shot all their lives and are yet quite incapable of intelligently criticising a picture of game-birds — or of any other bird or beast. The silliest remark I ever heard in connection with this matter was that of a shooting man who said he had picked up hundreds of shot partridges but had never yet seen the flank feathers coming up over the wings. It is a pity he had not the inclination, which every sportsman should have, to observe and find pleasure in watching closely in life the birds and beasts of the chase. I have been fortunate in my hosts on grouse moor, partridge manor and deer forest, for they have all had a keen interest in natural history.

There is sometimes a certain amount of antagonism between field naturalists and so-called museum naturalists. This should never be. The bird

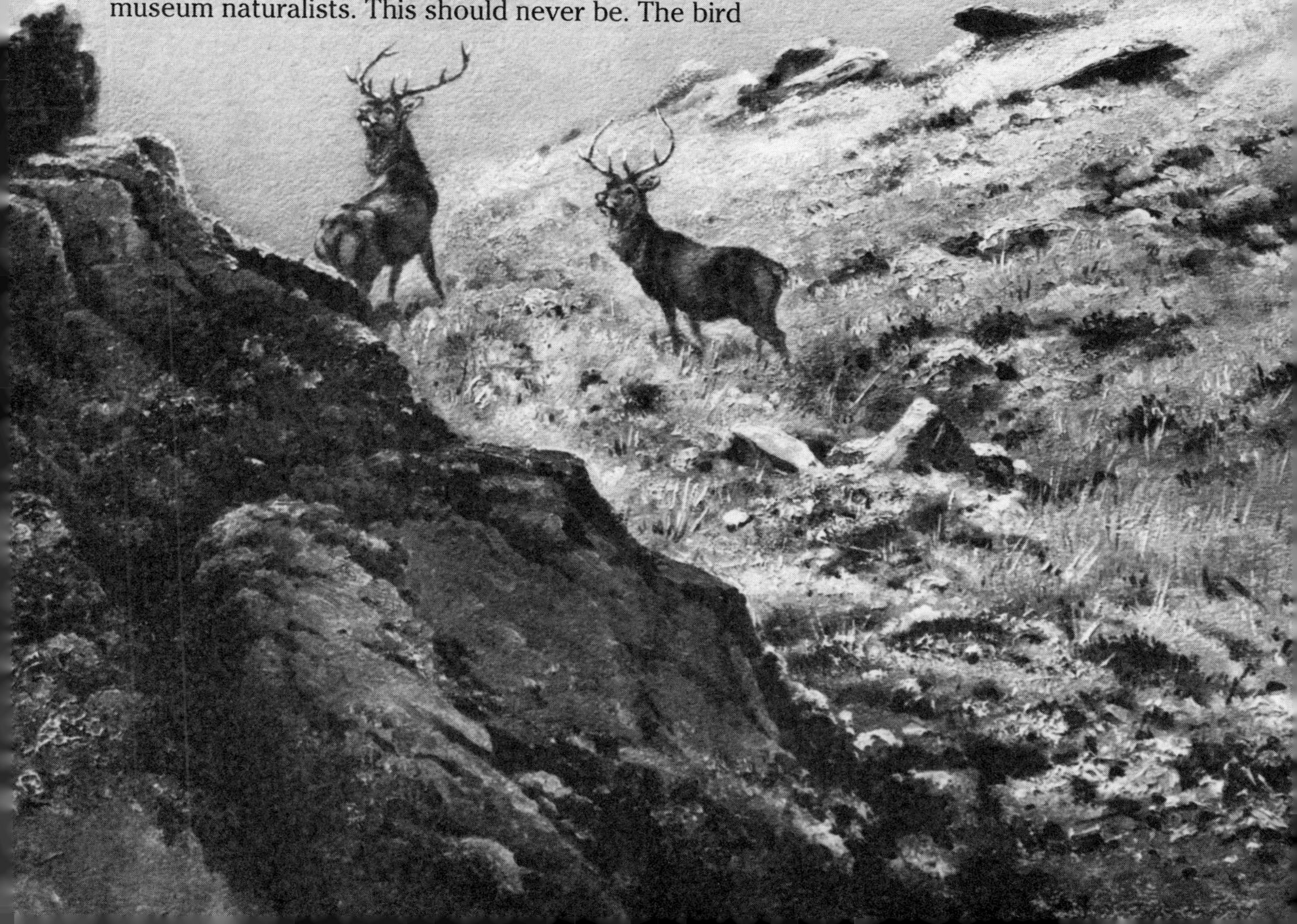

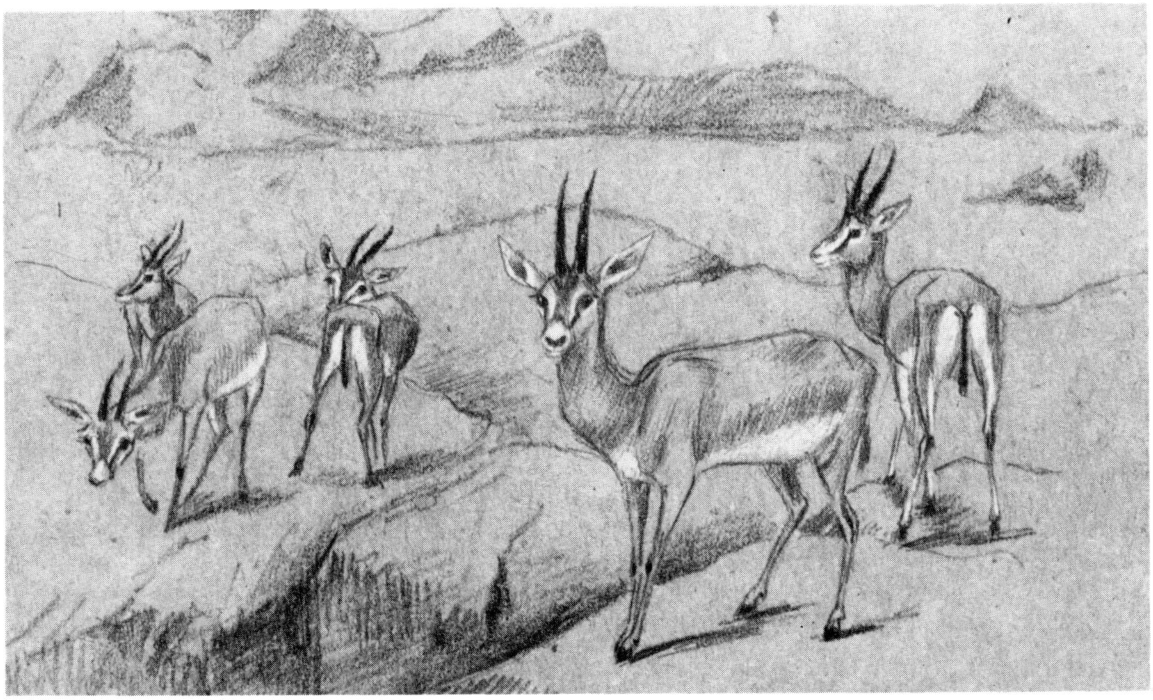

67

66. Rough-legged buzzard and red deer stags

67. Dorcas gazelles

68. Stag's head (probably wapiti)

watcher often claims that a knowledge of the living bird is the important thing. But he is apt to forget that the vast number of birds all over the world cannot be intensively watched in the wild state; and if they could, but few of them would be identified and classified correctly. The results of collecting by field naturalists and classifying by the museum naturalists form the fine body of exact knowledge we have at present and which is available to all who care to read. The observers who decry collecting and yet treasure their illustrated bird books should remember that at least one painter owes his accuracy in part to collections of skins and birds in the hand.

The best medium for painting birds for scientific book purposes is undoubtedly watercolours, but it is quite impossible to get the intricate pattern of many plumages without having recourse to the use of body colour. As I have said, I always use tempera for book illustrations. Tempera is an opaque medium, like oils, and cannot be used for clean transparent washes like watercolour, but has to be used with the

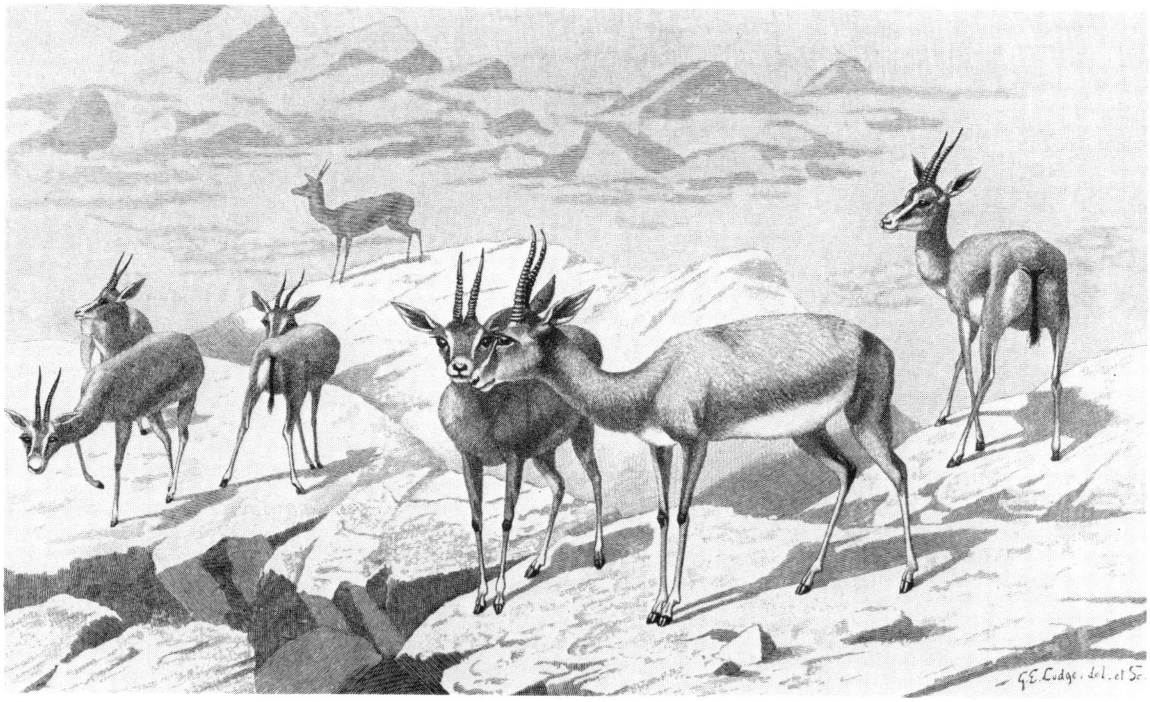

67

help of white and as a rule has to be worked with a very dry brush. The details of a bird's plumage can be got just as well in tempera as in watercolour; the effect is almost that of an oil painting. Tempera has the merit of drying very permanently so that one can paint in details over an already painted groundwork without disturbing the under-colour. To such an extent can this be done that I have painted an entirely different subject over a picture already done. Also, I have left a picture face downwards in a bath of water for an hour, in order to detach it from the mount, without a single particle of the colour being altered by running.

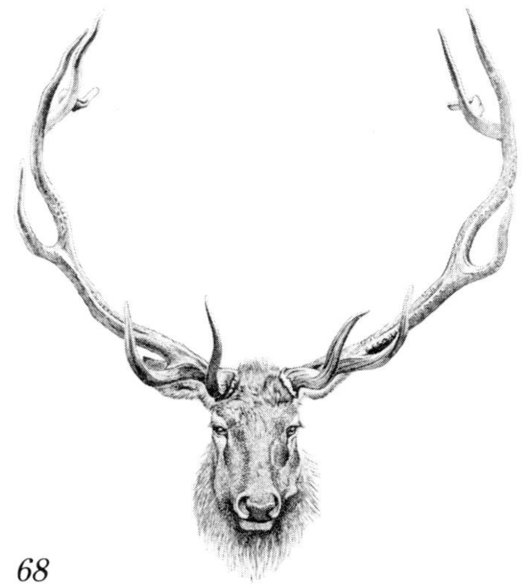
68

Sometimes when painting I have found myself quite unable to draw a bird satisfactorily in the position I wished. After much ineffectual labour I found the best thing was to leave the problem and come back to it in a day or two; then, seeing it with a fresh eye it can often be tackled with success. During the stages of painting a picture I find it useful after a day's work to have the thing under constant observation — so that whatever I happen to be

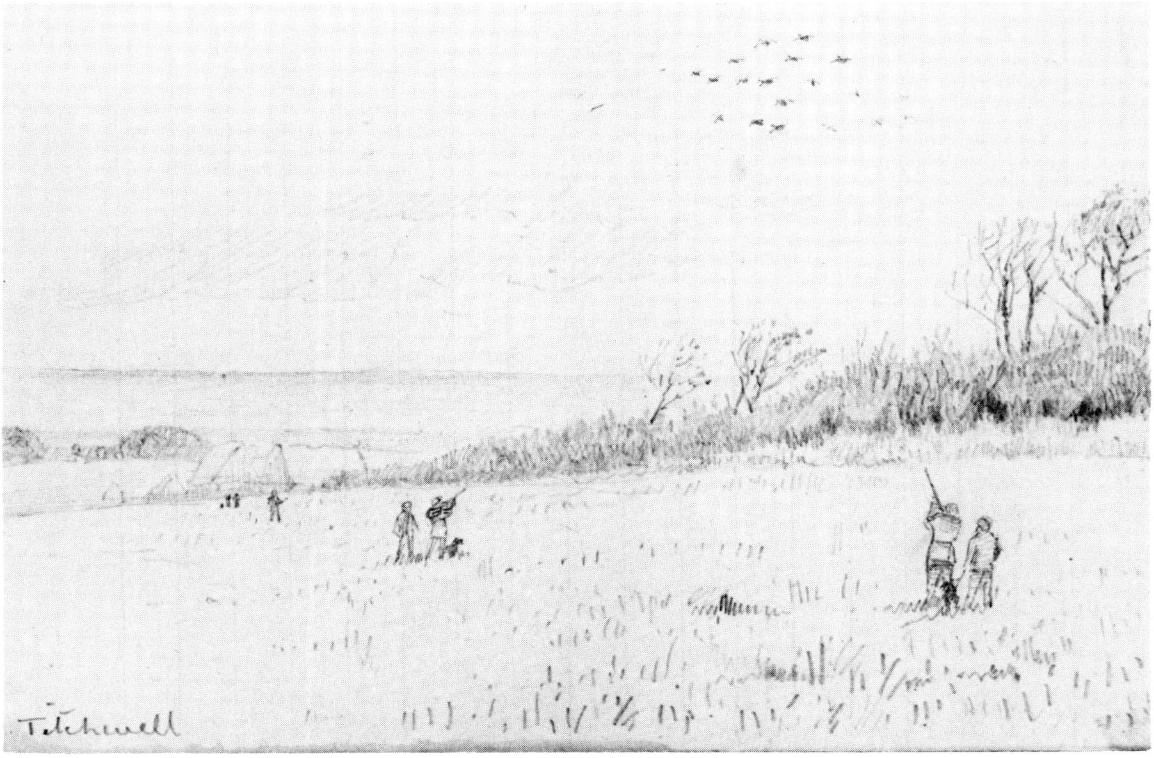

69

69. Duck shooting at Titchwell
70. Annotated sketch of a Norwegian landscape

doing I can take a glance at it, or even just sit in front of it smoking a pipe. All sorts of little improvements then become manifest. A bit of bad drawing can be rectified, the composition improved, relative tones adjusted and so on. When actually painting one is concentrating on a limited part of the picture. This later contemplation gives a breadth of view and helps in 'pulling the thing together'. The main subject of a picture — bird, beast, tree or clump of bushes — no matter what it is, should be so placed as to keep the eye inside the picture, and the arrangement should be asymmetrial rather than symmetrical. That is my idea, at least, of composition, though that is a matter of individual opinion.

There is always a much more beautiful effect in a landscape when viewed from a point facing the sun. It is infinitetly more delicate in colour and much less flat and monotonous in tone than when seen with the sun at your back. But it is often difficult to get or to canvas a correct impression of what one sees. I remember painting — or rather trying to paint — an expanse of heather in full bloom facing a low afternoon sun. It was sparkling and beautiful to see, but was so grey that I could only make it look as if it were covered with hoar frost. When looking at that view, there was the knowledge *in my mind* that I was seeing a mass of lilac-coloured heather and therefore the lack of the colour in this momentary effect of light was not missed. But it was quite otherwise with the attempted painting. Every one knows what a beautiful effect is to be seen when looking at a flock of sheep or a herd of deer from a position facing the sun — each beast in a deep tone of shadow with a brilliant golden halo touching the top of their backs. This effect can also be given to birds in a picture, but not in a book illustration where the subject must be in full light and showing details of plumage.

For me, it is far more interesting to paint pictures than to illustrate scientific books. But as the latter are numerous and necessary, let us have as much

70

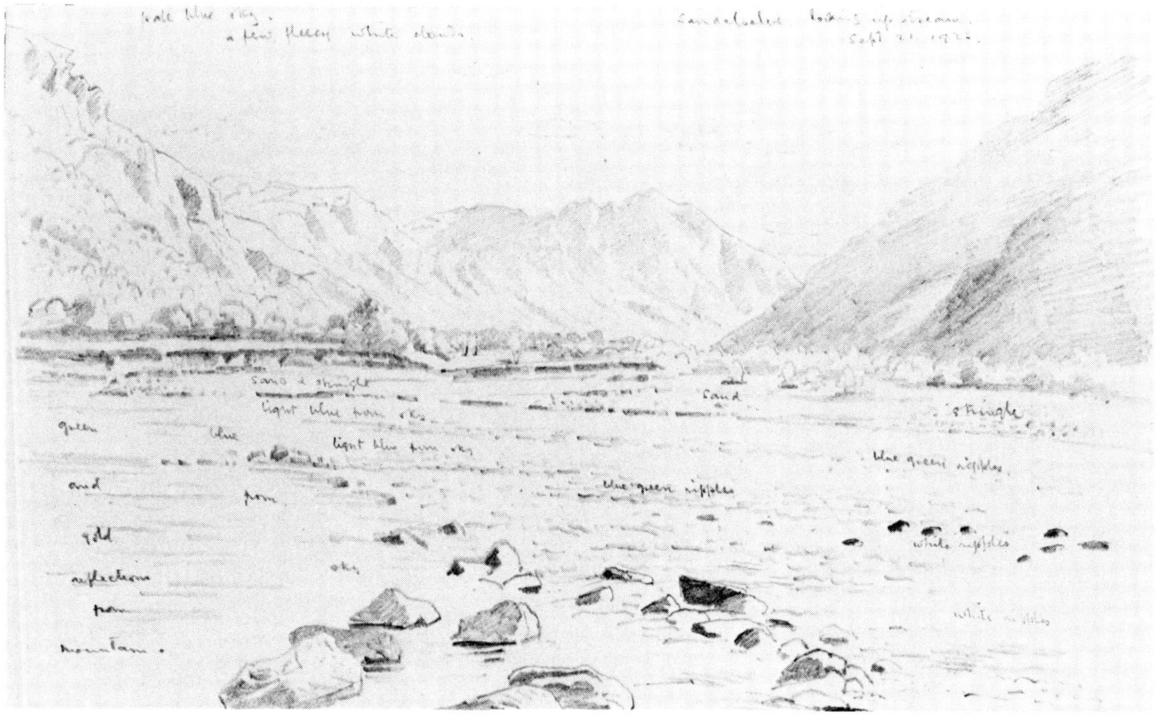

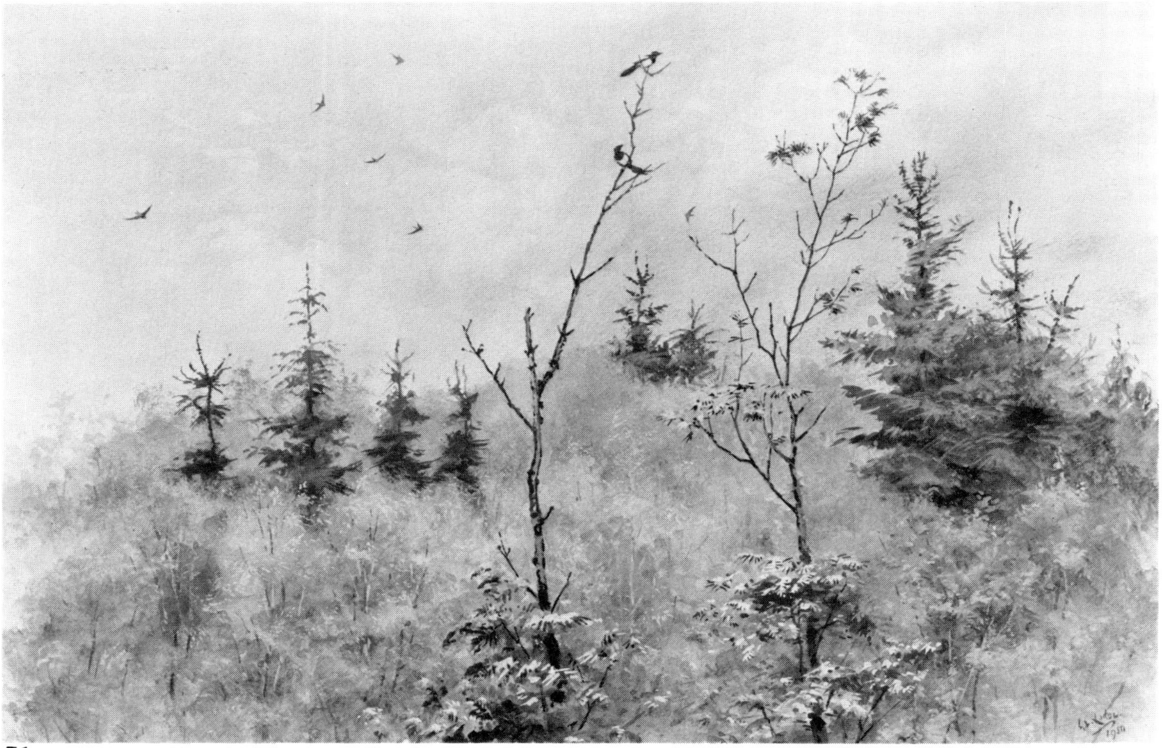

71

71. Magpies and swifts

art in them as possible in order to offset some of the extreme crudities of science. This, at least, is my philosophy.

PICTURES EXHIBITED AT THE ROYAL ACADEMY BY GEORGE LODGE

(As Listed in the Academy's Catalogue)

Date	Exhibition number	Title
		LODGE, George E., Painter
		— 17 Collingham Place (London)
1881	1426	Peregrines
		— 28 Holborn Viaduct
1884	174	Broken Slumbers
1886	169	Roving Wild and Free
		— 5 Verulam Buildings, Gray's Inn
1888	628	Peregrines
1889	1076	Master Stripes
1890	960	Wild Duck
1891	898	Brer Rabbit
1899	492	We Two
1900	596	Freshwater Cliffs, Isle of Wight: herring gulls mobbing a peregrine
		— The Studio, 5 Thurloe Square, S.W.
1905	37	Ptarmigan Ground: Norway
1910	760	Golden Eagle
1917	742	In Arctic Norway

BIBLIOGRAPHY

Books and Journals containing illustrations by George Lodge

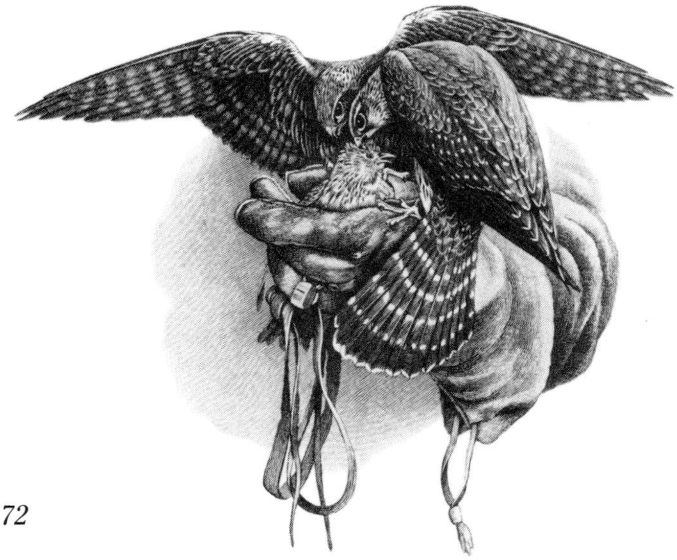

72

Aflalo, F.G. *A Sketch of the Natural History — Vertebrates — of the British Islands*, 1898

Baker, E.C.S. *The Indian Ducks and their Allies*, 1908

____ *Indian Pigeons and Doves*, 1913

____ *The Game-birds of India, Burma and Ceylon*, 1921-30

____ *Fauna of British India, Birds*, 1922-30

Bannerman, D.A. *The Birds of Tropical West Africa*, 1930-51

____ *The Birds of West and Equatorial Africa*, 1953

Bannerman, D.A. and Lodge, G.E. *The Birds of the British Isles*, 1953-63

Bannerman, D.A. and Bannerman, W.M. *Birds of Cyprus*, 1958

____ *Birds of the Atlantic Islands*, 1963-8

Bannerman, D.A. and Vella-Gaffiero, J.A. *Birds of the Maltese Archipelago*, 1976

Baxter, E.V. and Rintoul, L.J. *The Birds of Scotland*, 1953

Beebe, C.W. *A Monograph of the Pheasants*, 1918-22

Bosworth-Smith, R. *Bird Life and Bird Lore*, 1905

Chapin, J.P. *Birds of the Belgian Congo*, 1932-54

72. A cast of merlins with a skylark

Christy, R.M. *The Birds of Essex*, 1890

Coape-Oates, W. *Wild Ducks: How to rear and shoot them*, 1905

Coombes, R.A.H. *Mountain Birds*, 1952

Coward, T.A. *The Birds of the British Isles and their Eggs*, 1920 (new edn, 1950)

Cox, H.E. and Lascelles, Hon. G.W. *Coursing and Falconry* (Badminton Library), 1892

Darling, F.F. *Wild Life of Britain* (Britain in Pictures Series), 1943

Drewitt, Hon. Mrs C.M. *Lord Lilford: A Memoir by his Sister*, 1900

Evans, A.H. *Birds* (Cambridge Natural History Series, Vol. IX), 1899

Fisher, J.M.M. *The Birds of Britain* (Britain in Pictures Series), 1942

Fleming, Sir C.A. *George Edward Lodge: Unpublished Bird Paintings*, 1983

Gathorne-Hardy, Hon. A.E. *My Happy Hunting Grounds*, 1914

Glasier, P.E.B. *Falconry and Hawking*, 1978

Graham, P.A. *Country Pastimes for Boys*, 1908

Greene, W.T. *Birds of the British Empire*, 1898

Harting, J.E. *Hints on the Management of Hawks, and Practical Falconry*, 1898 (new edns, 1970, 1981)

____ *The Rabbit* (Fur and Feather Series, No. 6), 1898

____ *Recreations of a Naturalist*, 1906

Hartley, G.W. *Wild Sport with Gun, Rifle and Salmon Rod*, 1903

____ *Wild Sport and Some Stories*, 1912

Hollom, P.A.D. *The Popular Handbook of British Birds*, 1952

____ *The Popular Handbook of Rarer British Birds*, 1960

Howard, H.E. *Territory in Bird Life*, 1920 (new edn, 1948)

____ *An Introduction to the Study of Bird Behaviour*, 1929

____ *A Waterhen's World*, 1940

Hubbard, E. *Bird Notes by the late Jane Mary Hayward*, 1895

Hudson, W.H. *British Birds*, 1895 (new edn, 1930)

Ibis: Quarterly Journal of the British Ornithologists' Union, illustrated by Lodge 1900-7
Jackson, C.E. *Bird Illustrators: Some Artists in Early Lithography*, 1975
____*Wood Engravings of Birds*, 1978
Jackson, Sir F.J. *The Birds of Kenya Colony and Uganda Protectorate*, 1938
Journal of the Bombay Natural History Society
Journal of the Federated Malay States Museums
Kirkman, F.B.B. *The British Bird Book*, 1910-13
Kirkman, F.B.B. and Hutchinson, H.G. *British Sporting Birds*, 1924
Kirkman, F.B.B. and Jourdain, F.C.R. *British Birds*, 1930 (new edn, 1938)
Lascelles, Hon. G.W. *The Art of Falconry*, 1971 (new edn of part of Cox and Lascelles, 1892)
Lilford, Lord *Coloured Figures of the Birds of the British Islands*, 1885-97
____ *Notes on the Birds of Northamptonshire and Neighbourhood*, 1895
Lodge, G.E. *Memoirs of an Artist Naturalist*, 1946
Lodge, R.B. *The Story of Hedgerow and Pond*, 1906
Mansel-Pleydell, J.C. *The Birds of Dorsetshire*, 1888
Mathews, G.M. *The Birds of Australia*, 1910-27
Mavrogordato, J.G. *A Hawk for the Bush*, 1960
____ *A Falcon in the Field*, 1966
Meinertzhagen, R. *Nicoll's Birds of Egypt*, 1930
____ *Birds of Arabia*, 1954 (new edn, 1981)
____ *Pirates and Predators: The Piratical and Predatory Habits of Birds*, 1959
Michell, E.B. *The Art and Practice of Hawking*, 1900 (new edn, 1960)
Millais, J.G. *Game Birds and Shooting Sketches*, 1892
____ *A Breath from the Veldt*, 1899
____*The Mammals of Great Britain and Ireland*, 1904-6
Millais, J.G. *et al. British Deer and Ground Game, Dogs, Guns and Rifles* (*The Gun at Home and Abroad*, Vol. 2), 1913
Mitchell, F.S. *The Birds of Lancashire*, 1892
Nethersole-Thompson, D. *Pine Crossbills*, 1975
Neumann, A.H. *Elephant Hunting in East Equatorial Africa*, 1898
Ogilvie-Grant, W.R. *et al. British Game Birds and*

Wildfowl (*The Gun at Home and Abroad*, Vol. 1), 1912
Parker, E. *Predatory Birds of Great Britain*, 1939
Pycraft, W.P. *A History of Birds*, 1910
Rothschild, Hon. L.W. *Extinct Birds*, 1907
Saunders, H. *An Illustrated Manual of British Birds*, 1889 (new edn, 1927)
Seebohm, H. *A History of British Birds*, 1883-5
____*The Geographical Distribution of the Family Charadriidae*, 1887
Selous, E. *Bird Life Glimpses*, 1905
Stewart, H.E. *The Birds of our Country*, 1897
Thomas, W.B. and Collett, A.K. *Birds Through the Year*, 1917
Thornton, T. *A Sporting Tour through the Northern Parts of England and Great Part of the Highlands of Scotland*, 1896
Upton, R. *A Bird in the Hand: Celebrated Falconers of the Past*, 1980
Vincent, J. and Lodge, G.E. *A Season of Birds: A Norfolk Diary 1911*, 1980
Walsingham, Lord and Payne-Gallwey, Sir R.W.F. *Shooting: Moor and Marsh* (Badminton Library), 1886 (new edn, 1889)
Walton, I. and Cotton, C. (ed. by J.E. Harting) *The Complete Angler*, 1893
Watkins, W. *The Birds of Tennyson*, 1903
Witherby, H.F. *A Practical Handbook of British Birds*, 1919
Witherby, H.F., Jourdain, F.C.R., Ticehurst, N.F. and Tucker, B.W. *The Handbook of British Birds*, 1938-41
Yeates, G.K. *Bird Haunts in Northern Britain*, 1948
Zoological Society of London: *Proceedings and Transactions*, illustrated by Lodge c. 1900-21

Also illustrated articles in magazines such as *The Badminton Magazine*, *English Illustrated Magazine*, *The Field* and *The Illustrated London News*. A few of Lodge's paintings were used as Christmas cards by societies like the Camberley Natural History Society, the Association of Bird Watchers and Wardens, and the Royal Society for the Protection of Birds.

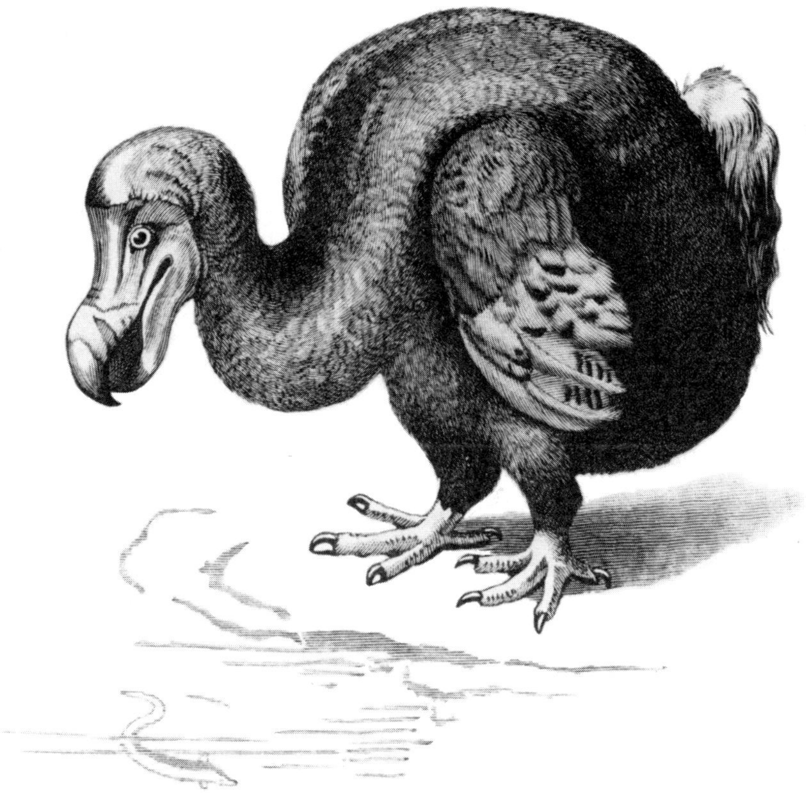

73. Dodo (after Roelandt Savery's painting of 1628)